'I wish you all the joy and happiness that comes with a new baby,' says the greetings card, 'but most of all . . . I wish you sleep.' Fashion has dictated that babies born into American, Australian and northern European homes must be trained to sleep alone. And so, immediately after each birth, parents prepare to do battle with their babies – and to do without sleep themselves.

Nights spent pacing corridors, crying-it-out, feeding at all hours and waking at dawn are all characteristics of a cot-bound society. Sleep training was a regime conceived in the nineteenth century to civilize children who must spend all their days in the nursery. But there is another way. There's a method as old as mankind itself and full of infinite variety. It's known as co-sleeping.

Three in a Bed is the classic childcare manual for parents seeking an alternative to broken nights. This new edition includes exciting new evidence, vividly describing the many ways in which babies and parents can benefit from sharing a bed. It details the invaluable benefits for breastfeeding mothers, reviews the history of babies in the bed and, through interviews with parents, explores current attitudes to the idea. It also contains a new perspective on the tragedy of cot death, as well as practical advice on how to sustain your sex life, hints on safety in the bed and answers to all the common objections. Finally, the author deals with the moment when the baby leaves his parents' bed.

If you are a parent, or a parent-to-be, the approach advocated in this book could change your life. After all, one half of our parenting could be done at night.

Deborah Jackson is a freelance writer who has contributed to many newspapers and magazines including the *Independent,* the *Daily Mail* and *The Guardian.* She writes a regular column for *Natural Parent.* Deborah lives in Bath with her husband, Paul, and their three children, Frances, Alice and Joseph.

Tom Newton, Deborah's father, was born Albert Edward Newton in Birmingham in August 1929. He preferred to use his childhood nickname and was known by his grandchildren as 'Grand Tom'. He was a fine artist and popular cartoonist – his Gordon Fraser greetings-card designs on sporting and family themes were instantly recognizable. He and Deborah had always hoped to work on a book together, and managed it just this once. He died on January 1991, following a stroke.

THREE IN A BED

The benefits of sleeping with your baby

DEBORAH JACKSON

Illustrations by Tom Newton

NORTHFIELD PUBLIC LIBRARY
210 Washington Street
Northfield, MN 55057

BLOOMSBURY

1/10

Copyright © 1989, 1999 by Deborah Jackson

All rights reserved. No part of this book may be used or
reproduced in any manner whatsoever without written
permission except in the case of brief quotations embodied
in critical articles or reviews. For information address
Bloomsbury Publishing, 175 Fifth Avenue, New York, N.Y. 10010.

Published by Bloomsbury Publishing, New York and London.
Distributed to the trade by St. Martin's Press

A CIP catalogue record for this book
is available from the Library of Congress

ISBN 1-58234-051-X

First published 1989

This U.S. paperback edition published 1999
10 9 8 7 6 5 4 3 2 1

Typeset by Hewer Text Ltd, Scotland
Printed in the United States of America by
R.R. Donnelley & Sons Company,
Harrisonburg, Virginia

TO PAUL, FRANCES, ALICE AND JOSEPH
WITH ALL MY LOVE

Acknowledgements

I should like to thank everyone who has helped with and supported me in the preparation of this book. I am indebted to many individuals for their kindness, and to the following organizations for their co-operation:
CRY-SIS
Foundation for the Study of Infant Deaths
Great Ormond Street Children's Hospital, London: Crying Baby Clinic
Guy's Hospital, London: Department of Clinical Psychology
Institute of Child Health, Bristol
John Radcliffe Hospital, Oxford: Community Midwives
The Law Commission
London School of Economics: Department of Anthropology
Loughborough University: Sleep Research Laboratory
Manchester University: Law Department
Marriage Research Centre
Museum of Childhood, Bethnal Green, London
National Childbirth Trust
Nottingham City Hospital
Organization for Parents Under Stress
University Hospital of Wales, Cardiff: Sleep Clinic
And for the 1999 edition:
Bob Wright, for permission to reproduce parts of his article 'Go Ahead – Sleep With Your Kids'
Jeanine Young, The Sebastian Diamond Mother and Baby Sleep Physiology Laboratory, Institute of Child Health, Bristol
Andrew Radford, Baby Friendly Hospital Initiative

Contents

PREFACE TO THE FIRST EDITION

Someone once asked me how I would fill a book on the subject of sleeping with babies. If bedsharing were as simple as allowing our children to scramble between the covers with us at night, there would not be much to say. But it is a long time since families slept together in Western society. Most parents regard the practice with suspicion, and commentators tend to dismiss the idea as – at best – eccentric.[1]

This book attempts to put cots in their context. It begins with the moment my own ideas on mothering were changed. It explores the reasons why mother and baby should not be separated for sleep. It looks at the confusion in mothering today, and the centuries of advice that have made mothers struggle against their instincts.

I have supported my arguments for co-sleeping with evidence from many fields: medicine, anthropology, psychology and common sense. The central themes of the book explore the value of touch, the creating of confidence and the answering of infants' physical needs, as well as the benefits for parents. Scientific studies now reveal the importance of bedsharing in an understanding of cot death, and mothers intending to breastfeed will find an entirely new approach in the chapter on sleep-feeding.

The third section of the book answers practical questions about taking a child into bed. It takes a historical and global look at family sleeping, considers how parents maintain a private life and asks when the baby leaves the nest. It tackles the most common objections to

1

having a baby in the bed. Finally, parents relate their experiences of sleeping with their babies and older children.

The title of the book, *Three in a Bed*, refers to the most typical arrangement in Western society. It is not, however, a prescription. Single parents make happy twosomes with their children at night, while large family groups still sleep together, as in the days before central heating. Every home should find the arrangement to suit its needs.

Throughout the book, I have referred to the infant as 'he' and the primary parent as 'she', for clarity. This is not intended to discriminate against men who look after children, or against baby girls – my own daughters included. I have also used the adjective 'primitive' to describe a variety of cultural groups, including hunter–gatherer tribes, remote rural villages and pre-literate peoples. It is intended to imply an 'ancient' existence which may or may not perpetuate today. It is not intended to be a judgement or a criticism.

PREFACE TO THE 1999 EDITION

When I started to write *Three in a Bed*, my family had just moved to Manchester, England. I had a six-month-old baby, few friends in town and a word processor in the dining room. I could work for only an hour before it was time to collect Frances from the child-minder. Every sentence was written between breastfeeds.

Another city, another two children and now I have the privilege of updating *Three in a Bed*. My work station is a bit grander – a messy home office with hardware, software and walls full of books. I have a circle of friends from Cardiff and Manchester to Bath, where each of my babies was born. I receive letters and e-mails from parents all over the world, with stories of births, unusual sleeping arrangements and instincts battered by other people's cynicism. It's getting harder to reply to them all.

Inevitably, the children are bigger too. Frances, Alice and Joseph know I write, but they are not too interested in the details. At the age of three, Alice told me, 'When I was a baby, I slept in a cot.' The stereotype is obviously stronger than the memory. Our vast queen-sized bed still welcomes the occasional young visitor, but most of our co-sleeping is over. It's been a wonderful ten years.

From time to time I give workshops to interested parents. I remember one event years ago in my home town, when parents arrived eager to meet Frances. Her first year in our bed had made her a minor celebrity. Some were disappointed that I had not brought her along to view.

It's hard to keep bringing your children along – to workshops, or

3

even to the pages of your books. I want to resist the temptation to consider mine as 'products' of certain childrearing methods. There is also their privacy to consider. But they wouldn't mind me saying that I'm so proud of them all – their loving natures, their strength of character, and their amazing independence. And I'd like to take this chance to say thank you to my husband, Paul, who has always been committed to exploring new ways of being a loving parent. Paul never needed persuading. He still loves to wake up with a child on his pillow.

This new edition has been an opportunity to immerse myself in the world of the newborn baby, to review the latest, exciting medical literature and to feel passionate once again about a favourite subject. I have included new evidence about the benefits of the family bed, balanced with reassurance and ideas for parents wishing to wean the child out again.

Yet after all the theory, the only evidence that counts is the relationship between you and your own baby. *Three in a Bed* is not a prescription, it's just a very, very old idea. Whether you take it or leave it, I hope this book will give you a new perspective. And I wish you fun along the way.

Deborah Jackson
Bath, February 1999

INTRODUCTION

It all began in a hospital ward when I was thirty-five weeks pregnant. I had been admitted in something of a panic, when the junior doctor inspecting me thought the baby had stopped growing. They had me in a hospital bed within the hour, muttering things like 'induced labour', and told me not to walk around, other than to answer calls of nature.

This was the first time I had ever been in hospital as a patient. I lay on my back, feeling quite well, and certain that the baby kicking around inside me was not in any danger. Midwives wired me up to a monitor that looked like one of those vibrating machines for reducing flab, and for the first time I could hear the infant heart drumming away.

I lay on my back, excited to hear the rapid 'doof, doof, doof' that accelerated every time the baby jabbed out with a heel or a hand. We were in the antenatal ward, the room heavy with anticlimax, where babies are busy not being born, and everyone is on the look-out for signs of the abnormal. But all around us was evidence of normality. Day and night, the air was filled with the screechings of new lungs. Babies, new-born, crying without end, calling for something they couldn't name and no one seemed able to supply.

At that time it seemed to me that the sound of a baby crying was a happy thing – evidence, at least, that the child was alive. It was just a matter of perspective. A cloud had settled over my own pregnancy, and I would have given anything to be safely on the other side of labour, with a new baby yelling in the cot next to my bed. The screams from the postnatal wards sounded like heavenly wails celebrating birth.

Unable to walk around, and unable to concentrate on work I had smuggled into hospital, I picked up a book someone had lent me a few days before: *The Continuum Concept* by Jean Liedloff – a passionate paperback, telling of the author's travels to the heart of the South American jungle and her life with the remote Yequana tribe.

Her first chapter – 'How My Ideas Were So Radically Changed' – drew me into a strange world. A society where mutual love and respect are the basis for every dealing with others, where work and play are the same thing, where the atmosphere is happy and optimistic. It was a description of a real world, but one that lived up to the expectations of the humans in the group; a world where material greed and wilful destruction were unknown, but where individual expression was encouraged. In this society the children did not throw tantrums, toddlers did not run away from their mothers at the first opportunity, babies did not scream.

I lay in my hospital bed, listening to the contented doof, doof, doof on the foetal heart monitor. Inside the amniotic sac, my baby was in a kind of Utopia. Constantly fed, warmed, nurtured, all her needs were being perfectly met. Birth would be a rude awakening, however gently it was administered, and the rest of her life would be a series of reminders that the womb was a paradise lost. The nine months of nurture could not be regained.

But perhaps there was another way to start out on life. Given the advances of modern technology, many of the babies born in this large teaching hospital in 1987 could reasonably expect to live another eighty-seven years. Some might even see in the twenty-second century. Was that really something to scream about? Why should we all spend our first few months 'testing out our lungs', as the midwives called it? As my hospital stay stretched into two days, those testing infant cries began to sound like torture.

Of course, things always seem worse in the middle of the night. But when you're eight months pregnant and woken up by an unsubtle blend of trips to the loo and other people's children crying, it's hard to tell where your dreams end and the nightmares begin. I started to have visions of a lifetime of pain and struggle for my unborn child, and began to realize why some friends had said, 'it's just not fair to bring a child into this world.'

After all, what was there to look forward to? Who did I know who was really happy? I struggled to think of someone without hang-ups or bitterness, someone whose life had not been torn apart by divorce or disappointment, someone who was content with his lot, even if it did not amount to very much. My nightmare turned into a kind of *Apocalypse Now*, ten episodes of *EastEnders* rolled into one, a tragedy of personal torment and atomic horror. I was relieved when the ward clock struck six, and the tea trolley came rattling into view.

Like the man who read that smoking was bad for your health, I suppose at this point I could have given up reading. But I felt much better the next day, especially when the ultrasound scan showed that my baby was doing very nicely. Her apparent refusal to grow was, according to my consultant, because her head had engaged in the pelvis. Labour was not to be induced, and I could go home that afternoon. I finished Liedloff's book, and left hospital with a new outlook.

The altered approach was quite simple. I explore the reasons for it in the following chapters. It did not take long to persuade my husband Paul that we weren't going to need the beautiful second-hand cot we had just bought. Not for a while, anyway. Our new baby, when it arrived, was going to be sleeping in bed with us.

I suppose, at the time, we thought that would be that. A simple, personal decision that affected no one else, and pleased the two of us. A perfectly 'natural' arrangement, in so far as we understood the word. It fitted in with our views of how we wanted to bring up the baby, and we really did not envisage any problems. We certainly had no idea about the depth of feeling our sleeping arrangements would arouse in others. But it would not have stopped us if we had known.

Three weeks later (10.9.87 – countdown day), Frances Rose was born in a Cardiff hospital. She travelled through the night to be with

us, as did her father, who was working in Manchester. She arrived
two hours before he did, just in time for breakfast, and two weeks
early according to the charts.

That night, I was once again in a hospital bed, worn out but
ecstatic. All the visitors had gone, leaving showers of pink carnations,
and as the lights went out on the ward, midwives came round
volunteering to look after the babies for each weary mother. 'Are you
sure you don't want her to go to a nursery?' they asked me. 'You'll
need all the strength you can get. We'll wake you up to feed her.'
However exhausted I was, I could not see that a night's sleep for me
was more important than my little girl's first night in the world.
Anyway, I was still running on adrenalin.

The lights went out and I drew the curtains around our bed and
plastic cot. I had held Frances all day – she seemed to want to feed at
twenty-minute intervals – and snuggled into bed with her now. In
the darkness of the room she opened her eyes wide for the first time,
and held out her hand to me. She stuck her tongue out at me, and
stared wide-eyed as I stuck my tongue out at her. I could not believe
how much beauty and intelligence was wrapped up in this tiny
person, only six pounds heavy and ten hours old. I'd had no idea a
new baby could be as controlled and calm as this.

I did not sleep much that night, mostly as a result of keeping alert
for the night nurses who patrolled every few hours. They would stop
at my curtains, peep in and say 'You won't fall asleep with the baby in
the bed will you, Mrs Jackson?' 'Oh no,' I promised. Frances slept,
fed and quietly played her way through the night – and on and off, I
slept, too. It was, without doubt, the happiest night of my life.

1 | CRISIS – WHAT CRISIS?

Sticker on the rear windscreen of a car: 'I can handle any crisis. I have children.'

A child is born. No sooner do parents begin to appreciate this miracle, than the problems begin. Babies cry, they're unsettled, they won't sleep. Mother finds it difficult to carry on with her old life, her career or her relationships. She becomes resentful. Father finds it hard to know what his role should be. His nights are disturbed, his partner distracted and he may feel resentful, too.

'The expectation is that the birth of the first baby will be an event of joy and happiness,' says marriage counsellor Marian Jackson. 'In fact, this time can be the start of a major rift between many couples.

'The baby has to be attended to because he cries loudest. The mother is often tired – she needs tremendous support. In the nuclear family, she can only look to her partner for this. He, meanwhile, may be feeling jealous and resentful of the baby, who is taking all her attention.

'Because of society's expectations that all should be lovely when the first child comes along, the couple are unlikely to admit these problems. The pressures of the nuclear family are very intense.'

With its emphasis on romantic love and the search for the perfect partner, Western society sets great store by the couple. In countries where strict purdah is practised, women live together in separate quarters, caring for and supporting each other. Living in a large family unit bring its own problems of course – the pressure to conform, for

9

instance, lack of personal space and privacy. But if we compare the communal life of a Pakistani mother in Pakistan with that of a modern British mother, it is clear who has the better support network.

In her family village, the Pakistani woman can count on the support of her in-laws and cousins when bringing up her children. Following the birth of a baby, she is exempted from all household duties – other than feeding and caring for her child – for forty days. When her children have children, she will in turn take her part in rearing them and caring for the new parents. (The forty-day 'honeymoon' period for mothers and babies is also a traditional practice in Japanese and other societies.)

In urban society, where many people live alone, drive to work alone and eat alone, people have to fend for themselves. Yet a selection of headlines from any problem page in a women's weekly magazine reveals how dissatisfied we are with this arrangement. In relationships and out of them, we complain:

'My marriage was a disaster, but I can't bear a future alone.'
'I've lost all confidence in myself as a mother and can't seem to please anyone in the family.'
'Why don't my friends need friendship the way I do?'
'Our relationship's changed, but I feel mean leaving now.'
'Even though I'm only 19 and in love, my life seems to be full of so many worries.'
'The man I love can't bear the thought of being the cause of a marriage break-up.'
'People just don't understand that men can feel hurt and devastated by divorce, too.'

(*Best*, 8 July 1988)

The emphasis is on our capacity to cope as individuals. Women, who have fought for – and won – the rights to vote, work and equal pay, are often expected to rear their children single-handed. While extended families lend all their support to the childbearing woman, the nuclear system means some must survive on their own. The result is that in many 'civilized' countries, the family is in a state of crisis. Modern marriages and relationships often consist of the smallest of family units: a man and a woman. This may be a stable arrangement, but any change – the loss of a partner, or the arrival of a third party – is bound to bring immense complications and adjustments.

Parents today are aware of the changes babies bring. The Marriage Research Council's survey of sixty-five young wedded couples in the 1980s revealed that people thought it was important to 'be ready' to have children:

> The definition of readiness to have children is highly subjective yet founded upon a common image of parenthood which stresses the disadvantages of becoming parents. Descriptions of the impact of children included, 'like having a bomb dropped', 'an extra burden' and 'a strain on the marriage'. Good parenting requires accepting a severely limited social life, constant financial worries, the intrusion of a third person and so on. Above all it demands tolerance, resignation and selflessness.
>
> (Penny Mansfield, *Journal of Sociology and Social Policy*, 1982)

These were the expectations of newly-weds without children. Our society teaches us that, far from enhancing a marriage, children may ruin it. Although one husband in the survey said a child would be 'the cream on the wedding cake', most couples weren't prepared to share the cake with anyone:

> . . . for the majority, their chief concern was the preservation of closeness against the intrusion of a third party – the child.

For all its problems, the extended family can take the pressure off a young couple and make mothering less intense. Having plenty of close, practical help enables parents to have time alone within a supportive emotional unit. Parents on their own rarely get time off.

11

Grandparents and other useful relatives may not even live in the same town. Studies suggest that the absence of grandparents (or neighbourly equivalents) may have a negative effect on a child's upbringing. Lynn Fairbanks of the University of California has shown that proper development of the African vervet monkey is dependent upon older relatives being around:

> Youngsters with grandmothers were brought up in a much more relaxed fashion. They encountered fewer restrictions on their movements, spent less time in the maternal embrace and wandered off on their own more frequently.
> By contrast, babies without a grandmother came in for an excess of maternal devotion. Their mothers clung to them, thwarting their attempts to strike out on their own. Maternal caresses were more likely to take the form of a stifling hug than a casual reassuring contact. As a result, they gained their independence at a slower pace.
> (Stephen Young, *Independent*, 16 May 1988)

Even the most casual observer will acknowledge the connection between this behaviour and modern mothering. Whether we are smothering our children with kisses, or screaming at them to 'stop it!' we are undeniably baby-centred. Women with children worry inordinately about their offspring, and when they gather together, tend to talk about nothing else.

After intense mothering, many Western children find it impossible to live alongside their parents. If grandma was excessively protective in her day, she may find that her daughter is still struggling for independence, and shuts her out of life with the new baby. Grandparents are then unable to enjoy the more relaxed role of extended parenting.

Just as modern parents may shun help from older generations, so they in turn are themselves shunned by their peers. A person with a baby may find herself unwelcome in the child-free zones she used to inhabit. As Brigid McConville outlines in her book, *Mad to be a*

Mother, our find-your-own-feet society can be a cruel place for mothers and babies:

> Most venues of the adult world are alien and hostile to her if she is in the company of children. Of course, there are places – like offices – where the majority of people would agree children simply shouldn't be. That consensus is itself rather a sad reflection on the extent to which we have divided the life of home from that of 'work' . . .
>
> Most mothers, in the depths of their humility, don't really expect to be welcomed into the places where people without children go. It's probably just as well.

While attempting to bond with her baby, a mother may find herself rejecting, or being rejected by, the adults around her. Small wonder, then, that postnatal illness (depression) affects up to fifty per cent of mothers with young children. Doctors tell suffering mothers that baby blues are a normal reaction after the birth. A potent mixture of hormones, shattered expectations and lack of support might have something to do with it. And as we shall see later, relatively few mothers in 'civilized' countries have the chance to satisfy, or even explore their deep maternal needs. They are encouraged to put the baby down as often as possible, when their instinct tells them to hold him close.

Great and valuable efforts are spent preparing the pregnant woman for the actual Birth Day. For months, women go through their paces, learning the exercises, the breathing, the positions for labour. Some then enjoy giving birth; but few urban women are prepared – emotionally, physically or practically – for the arrival of the babies themselves.

When Frances was small, we attended a weekly mother-and-baby group. Watched by health visitors, the young mothers would sit in a circle and swap horror stories about the traumas of twenty-four-hour parenting. We may all have been capable, independent, sociable beings before our babies were born, but many had since regressed into fearful, overprotective mothers. The lack of confidence in the group was striking – and these were the ones who were bold enough to turn up. One shudders to think of those struggling alone at home.

We all desperately wanted to be good at this new role, but we didn't know how. For some, every attempt was thwarted by an infant who cried and cried and cried. 'I'm sure he does it on purpose,' complained one young mother of her four-month-old son. 'She's got my temper,' said another, talking about a child only ten weeks old. The babies would lie on changing mats in a circle, while their mothers drank coffee and complained. It reminded me of teenage days, dancing round a circle of handbags at a disco. People stared at me because I kept Frances on my knee.

Much as we love them, our children cause us a lot of trouble, and their behaviour doesn't seem to improve with age. To quote one mother who wrote in a family magazine under the headline 'Avoiding GBH':

> There should be some strong warning issued about how the sweetest babies can turn into 18-month-old hooligans: wailing, nattering, disobedient little horrors who know exactly how, where and when to humiliate you. There should be warnings given about the overpowering urge which can overtake one to do something unimaginable – bang their heads together, swing them round the room, heave them through the nearest window . . .
>
> The only thing to do is tip the offending offspring into pram, pushchair or wheelbarrow and get them out of the house at once. Pushing them at least keeps your hands off their throats!
>
> (Mrs S.M. of Bridlington, *Family Circle*, 28 November 1984)

This melodramatic, half-humorous style is very common among mothers exchanging baby stories and only thinly disguises the real fears and frustrations going on in most homes. Another newspaper report told how a desperate mother did throw her two young children out of the window of their high-rise apartment.

Social worker and mother Pam Laurance was surprised by a feeling of anger towards her demanding baby boy. She conducted her own survey of postnatal emotions. 'Most mothers,' she concluded, 'experience chronic feelings of aggression, and harbour aggressive fantasies to do with their very small babies. These are frightening and guilt-inducing.'

Pam's study was entitled 'Excuse Me, I Must Just Go and Strangle The Baby', a sentence once uttered by a friend on the telephone. It elicited this response from one new mother called Claire:

> I felt desperate rather than angry. I felt I was a slave to this tiny demanding human being – as though he was absorbing my whole identity.

Prospects like these result in more and more couples choosing to remain childless. Whether because of friends' disastrous experiences, personal preference or fears for our children's future in the nuclear age, it is fashionable to deny all instincts to reproduce. And with a scenario like the one from Bridlington, it is easy to see why. Childcare expert Penelope Leach recalls:

> I had a friend to tea when my daughter was two and she left saying, 'Thank you for letting me come; now I *know* I don't want children.' It had been a good afternoon by toddler standards, too!
>
> Having children is one of many adult-life options. It is neither a romantic obligation nor a hobby and anybody who can be put off the idea altogether ought to be.
>
> (*Family Circle*, 28 November 1984)

Yet there are still many pressures to procreate. Biological instinct urges us to conceive, parents long to become grandparents, and the child-centred family remains the advertisers' ideal on television and cereal packets. In the media world, it's mum, dad and the kids – preferably one girl and one boy – who will go on to meet their ideal partners and have more children . . .

Many of us are keen – some desperate – to have babies. Others see it as a duty. There is even the recent phenomenon of parents planning their quota of kids as close together as possible, 'to get it over with'. In a world that prefers images of perfection to genuine support, babies can be one big interruption to real life.

If mothers used to suffer in silence, they can now turn to many organizations and outlets when baby plays up. Choose between OPUS (Organization for Parents Under Stress), M.A.M.A. (Meet A Mum Association), The Family Network, CRY–SIS, and Parents Anonymous. And that's just a shortlist of British charities. In America, Australia and New Zealand, a wide variety of helplines is open to match your specific brand of parenting problem. Grass-roots support networks do an invaluable job in keeping harassed parents from harming their own children, but their work is indicative of the scale of the crisis of modern parenting.

The British public in the 1980s was scandalized by a series of fatal child batterings – apparently preventable incidents in 'at risk' homes which went undetected by social workers. At the same time, hospitals in Cleveland and Manchester reported a rush of suspected sex abuse cases, as a result of which some children were removed unnecessarily from their parents.

In 1987, reports of child abuse rose by twenty per cent in Britain. The NSPCC (National Society for the Prevention of Cruelty to Children) concluded from this that either children were more at risk than ever before, or that the public was only just beginning to admit the extent of the problem.

Society's attempts to care for its children are badly out of line. We reel precariously from abuse to overprotection. In 1988, while British families suffered in the Cleveland crisis, an epidemic of child sex abuse claims was reported in America – this time brought by the parents themselves. The implication was that here was a new bandwagon for unhappy spouses, a sure way of securing divorce.

Lost in all this mess are the children. We are producing babies, toddlers and teenagers who learn to communicate through violence, survive via competition, rebel without a real cause. Depression, destruction and suicide are the legacies of a society that is programmed for negative living. And it all starts, in the smallest of ways, with the patter of tiny feet.

One psychologist has said that family anxieties may be reflected in a baby's sleep problems.[1] Society has a childcare crisis, and so do many families, when parents confront their children over the issue of sleep. It is widely acknowledged that sleep is a problem for babies. One of the first questions visitors ask about your infant is whether or not he sleeps through the night yet. Where there are problems, people believe it is the child who causes the trouble. It is the child who wakes crying, the child who disturbs parents and neighbours in the night. It is the child who must adjust, and learn to sleep soundly like grown-ups. But children are not the only ones with sleep problems. Insomnia – the inability to get to sleep or to sleep as long as society expects[2] – is one of the commonest complaints brought to the family doctor. In 1983, the National Health Service in Britain spent thirty million pounds on sixteen million prescriptions for hypnotic drugs to aid sleep.[3]

Many people suffer bad nights as a matter of course and wake up unrefreshed every morning. Others require laboratory-style conditions for sleep: dim lighting, complete quiet, firm mattress, pillows just so. And few can doze at will in the daytime.

Irritations like these are common in industrialized countries. One is considered lucky to be able to sleep at will – but in some cultures luck does not come into it. Here is a description of men from the Tauripan tribe, travelling through the South American jungle, with enough wild noises and real animal dangers around them to keep an urbanite awake for a week:

> . . . [they had the habit of] telling a joke in the middle of the night, when everyone was asleep. Though some were snoring loudly, all would awaken instantly, laugh and in seconds

resume sleep, snoring and all. They did not feel that being
awake was more unpleasant than being asleep, and they awoke
fully alert, as when a distant pack of dangerous peccary [wild
pigs] was heard by all the Indians simultaneously, though they
had been asleep, while I, awake and listening to the sound of
the surrounding jungle, had noticed nothing.

(Jean Liedloff, *The Continuum Concept*)

Compare this with British surveys which report that less than a third
of young-to-middle-aged adults say they wake up in the morning
feeling rested and refreshed. Around thirty per cent admit they find it
hard to get up in the mornings.[4] We tend to treat sleep like a
protected species, a rare creature to be sought out and preserved
before we lose it altogether. It serves as an escape from real life. We
lay great stress on the standard eight-hours-a-night prescription,
complete with a DO NOT DISTURB notice on the door.

It is true that many Westerners, once interrupted from a night's
sleep, find it difficult to get back to sleep again, which is why babies
can wreak such havoc at unholy hours. Deprived even slightly of our
regular due, we cannot function properly in the day. By the time we
are adults, the art of effortless sleep has often slipped us by. We are no
longer in control of sleep – it controls us.

We are all born with the ability to sleep easily and well, yet by the
time we are able to speak, our dreams have turned to nightmares, and
we are frightened of sleep's natural element – the dark. The average
three-year-old with a talent for telling stories will invent a dozen
reasons why he shouldn't go to bed. Parents, at their wits' end, supply
twelve equally incredible excuses why he should. It is a war both sides
are losing.

The toddler is an old hand at the sleeping game. He has been
playing it with his mother since the day he was born. Remember the
first few weeks, when he cried for six feeds a night? And that sticky
patch at seven months old when you thought he was teething? No
teeth appeared, but he always wanted cuddling at five in the
morning.

And again after his first birthday, just when you thought he had settled into a nice routine, there he was, rattling his cot at all hours. In fact, when you think about it, there have been as many disturbed nights as peaceful ones since he was born. But all his little friends are exactly the same, so surely there's nothing you can do about it. You've read enough books on the subject to form a library, and none of the experts seem to agree, so what do they know?

Professionals recognize two main problem areas in infant sleeping patterns: a difficulty in settling at bedtime, and regular wakenings throughout the night. Some consider these struggles to be normal phases of development:

> Common sleep problems, such as bedtime struggles and night waking, occur regularly in at least 20% to 30% of children in the first four years of life . . . Among some developmental authorities such as Gesell, they are considered nearly universal and transient developmental phenomena in the first two years of life.
>
> (Lozoff, Wolf and Davis, *Pediatrics*, March 1985)

The diagnosis and remedy will vary according to the discipline of the doctor or adviser concerned, but one thing the experts do agree on is the urgency of the sleep crisis in our society. No one disputes the drastic effect of non-sleeping children on a household. Infant sleep problems can tear families apart.

The Sleep Clinic in the University Hospital of Wales in Cardiff was one of the first of its kind in Britain. Sleep clinics, where teams of psychologists and child development advisers deal with many thousands of cases every year, are now commonplace on both sides of the Atlantic. The number of complainants is rising rapidly, as parents realize that their problem is a common one, and there is someone who will listen.

The extent of the infant-sleep problem is now fully appreciated, as clinics and helplines are set up to advise frantic families. Principal clinical psychologist Reetta Bidder, who founded the Cardiff clinic in the early 1980s, says twenty per cent of children suffer from major sleeping problems – and about one half of British families have regular difficulties getting their children to sleep. Dr David Haslam, author of *Sleepless Children*, says around a quarter of all pre-school children wake during the night. This is a persistent and highly common experience in our society.

While even new-born babies sometimes refuse to sleep, the largest age group seen by the Cardiff Sleep Clinic is in the range of seven months to one year. 'Children should be sleeping through the night by then, and on their own as well,' says Reetta Bidder. 'Lots of families say the child is getting up once or twice a night – for some that is intolerable. Different families have different expectations.

'We see people in dreadful situations. For instance, in one family the mother had moved to sleep in the child's bedroom, and the parents were ready to split up. The father said, "We've come to you just in time." '

Advisers at the Cardiff clinic give each family a chart on which to keep a record of current sleeping problems, and then discuss their lifestyle before looking for solutions to get the child to sleep. Recommendations include moving the older baby to a single bed – his cot may be too small – creating a calming bedtime routine, or offering a late-night supper. The aim, of course, is to get the child to sleep through the night on his own, but on his own, a child may be refreshed by much less than eight hours' sleep. Waking in the early hours, he is ready to play again. As Dr Haslam points out:

> Some children sleep happily through the night, with additional naps of an hour or so during the day, while others only sleep solidly at night for a couple of hours at a time, and rarely seem to need a daytime nap. Despite the differences both types of children will grow up equally healthy, happy and bright. If children could be left to their own devices and did not need the attention of adults, then no one would really be the least concerned about whether they sleep or not.
>
> (*Sleepless Children*)

Left to his own devices, a baby will drift easily in and out of sleep as his body requires it. But scarcely any child in the West is left to his own devices. The most likely cause of conflict will be the adult's attempts to manage a child's sleeping routine. 'Food and sleep are the big battlegrounds,' says child development adviser Maria Tucker, 'because children know that the parents desperately want them to do these things. They know that by seven o'clock the mother is desperate to get them off to bed.'

The usual complaint is that the mother feels her baby is not sleeping enough. It is rare for a mother to moan about a drowsy child:

> It has always struck me as rather odd that in our society we
> call a baby who doesn't cause any problems a 'good' baby. If
> he sleeps all night, never throws his food, never hits the cat,
> never sticks his fingers in the electricity sockets, and never spills
> his milk all over you, then he is a perfect child . . . The rather
> slow, uninspiring, quiet and apathetic baby is looked at as 'ever
> so good', and 'not a bit of trouble' . . . I always feel very sad
> when I hear mothers answer the question 'Is he a good baby?',
> with 'Yes, he's wonderful. I hardly know I've got him.'
>
> (Haslam, *Sleepless Children*)

The trouble is, we expect our babies to be responsive and loving when we want to play with them, but inert and undemanding when we decide it's time for bed.

The 'perfect' child goes directly to sleep when his parents tuck him in. He does not scream in the darkness as soon as you creep out of the nursery. He does not wake again an hour later for a suckle or cereal or – as in the case of my four-year-old friend – to be allowed to sleep on the floor. He sleeps serenely until the morning, when he is woken by neither the dawn chorus, nor the first rays of sunshine filtering on to his cot. He rises just before his parents are due to get up, and plays quietly with the bright plastic amusement arcade they have placed at the foot of his bed. He does not rattle his bars, or yell, or run full pelt

21

into the parents' room calling 'Geronimo!' He smiles sweetly when his mother puts her head round the door, and the day begins with a big hug and a kiss.

We do not expect to have perfect children, but we do tend to treat them as if they were born from the folds of a textbook. We forget that doctors who describe 'normal' infant sleeping patterns use data taken from artificial tests.[5] We only know what is normal for a baby sleeping in a cot in a science laboratory, or alone in his middle-class American nursery. It is forgotten that for millions of years babies slept alongside their parents.

In order to coax a child off to sleep, many parents recreate the conditions of that sleep laboratory: large cot, firm mattress, own room, lights out, door – if necessary – shut. As they grow up, people depend on these conditions for sleep.

One mother told me how a friend of hers locked her two-year-old in her bedroom every night, ignoring her screams, which would go on for up to an hour. When the child did finally submit, exhausted, to sleep, her body would be pressed against the closed bedroom door on which she had been hammering. Her mother would then go and pick her up, and put her back into bed.

'I feel awful listening to it,' said the friend. 'The mother says, "Oh, she'll learn that I won't go up to her and it's useless making that noise." But it's been going on for weeks now, and it doesn't seem to be getting any better.'

This is the kind of child abuse our society tolerates, because it is in the name of socially educating our children. Medical anthropologist James McKenna does not hesitate to question the practice:

> It is ironic that the human primate infant – which is born the most immature neurologically, develops the most slowly, and is thus more, rather than less, dependent physiologically on its care giver – is the only primate that, in urban settings, is expected to sleep alone and at a much younger age. Monkey and ape parents would no doubt regard this as a form of child abuse, as do peoples living in preindustrialised societies

when told of parent–infant sleeping arrangements in urban settings.

(Medical Anthropology, 1986)

Catherine, a French friend, said her four-year-old daughter had asked her: 'Mummy, why do I have to sleep on my own when you sleep with Daddy?' and she could not think of an answer. 'What can I say to her? Why should she have to sleep alone?' Other mothers told her this was an imponderable question, like 'Why has teddy got a yellow nose?' Sleeping separately was just another of life's quirks, not something to be reasoned out, and certainly not to be challenged.

I asked Catherine why she did not allow Stephanie into her bed. 'You know I would love to,' she said, 'but I would never sleep at night. I find it difficult sharing a double bed with my husband as it is. I am a terrible sleeper.'

Catherine's story turned out to be an extreme example of the sleep crisis passing on its effects down the generations. As a small baby, Catherine was brought up by her grandparents, and slept in a cot in their bedroom. At the age of two, she went to live with her father, who put her into a separate room, with the lights off and the door shut. The young girl screamed for nights on end, but no one answered her calls. She was taken to see many specialists for her 'sleep problem', and a doctor finally prescribed tranquilizers. Catherine still remembers the trauma of those years vividly. Any small disturbance – including sometimes the tactile presence of her own husband next to her – is enough to stop her sleeping.

In her clinical work as a child psychotherapist, Dilys Daws deals with many family crises that enter the domain of 'sleep problems'. These vary from the child's nightmares and sleep walking, to violence – or the threat of it – from the parent:

It can be very confusing for parents to deal with a baby's anger in the night and also to face the anger in themselves at their

23

own need for rest and sleep not being met. Many parents are justifiably afraid of battering their baby in the night.

(Journal of Child Psychotherapy, 1986)

If a parent should actually hurt a baby, then the problem becomes a matter for public concern – for neighbours, social workers, the NSPCC and newspapers. Few parents are pushed this far, of course, but the thin line between fury and physical violence can seem as nothing in the torment of yet another sleepless night.

Jacquie, a mother from South Wales, recalled the horror of one particularly bad night when her son had cried ceaselessly and she felt she just couldn't take any more: 'The desire to hurt him was overpowering, and I just had to keep telling myself that I couldn't. Eventually we both collapsed on a chair, and I woke up to find us still clasped in each other's arms.'

Advisers at Cardiff's Sleep Clinic recognize that one bad night can obliterate the memory of three good ones for a family. A child who loses sleep is clearly being deprived of his bodily needs – growth hormones are secreted during sleep – while the effects on parents can be shattering in the short and in the long term.

'If you lose a lot of sleep your memory starts faltering,' says Reetta Bidder, 'and that's no fun. With young children you are always on call. I suspect that more accidents happen where the parents have a sleepless child, because human error creeps in. I wouldn't be surprised if there were more accidents on the road.'

Sleep problems can be at the root of many family crises, according to nurse Kathryn Conder:

Almost every survey of child behaviour pinpoints sleeping problems as being of great concern to parents. Families are under stress as yet another sleepless night passes and a vicious circle results with increasing tension. Negative results are all too easy to visualise, with battered children and marriages strained to breaking point.

(Midwife, HV and Community Nurse, April 1988)

Dr Haslam also catalogues the dire effects on adults when babies cannot, or will not, sleep:

> Happy families need parents who get their sleep. A mother from Manchester made her feelings very clear. 'By the time Thomas was a year old we were obsessed with the idea of sleep. Even our own families found us unbearably dull as we could talk or think of little else. We decided that if this was parenting you could keep it! My husband had a vasectomy before Thomas was two.'
>
> *(Sleepless Children)*

This brings us back to the desire not to procreate. Parenting in the Western world is in a mess, and sleep – essential to our well-being – has turned into a nightmare. In this state of crisis, parents and guardians cling to any passing theory to drag them out of the mire. Reetta Bidder uncovers some incredible stories of parents attempting to put old-school advice into practice: 'I can clearly remember one 2½-year-old who refused to go to bed,' she told me. 'Every night the mother would be holding the nursery door on one side, and the child would be hanging on to the other side, screaming "The monsters are coming to get me!" '

What makes us bar the door to our children? Let us start at the very beginning: the hospital birthing room.

2 | ALL NIGHT, EVERY NIGHT

'I wake up with two women by my side: my wife on the one
and my daughter on the other.'

(Actor Richard E. Grant)

It has been a hard day's night. All that pain and yelling and space.
Where once there was a warm, enclosing womb, it's gone cold.
Nothing to hold you in, no limits to your new world. Perhaps you
were drugged, perhaps you struggled fully conscious through the
dark passage and out, slippery, into a pair of hands in rubber gloves.
Maybe you found the nipple straight away – or did they weigh you
first, naked on cold plastic, while you screamed? Were you wrapped
in linen and placed in a cot to sleep? Did anyone think of turning off
the lights?

I'm not talking about someone else's baby. I'm not talking about
your baby, or my baby. This is about you – and me. We all went
through it, and like it or not, the experience is still etched somewhere
in our subconscious.

Birth may be the moment of greatest vulnerability in our lives,
and it comes directly after nine months of trouble-free motoring
inside the womb. We are born into a bewildering realm of space,
cold and light. The muffled sounds and familiar tastes of the
amniotic sac are ripped away. Someone has turned the volume
up, and the treble knob, too. Human contact is no longer a
constant, but an intermittent delight.

Dr Frédérick Leboyer was one of the first Western doctors to consider the feelings of the baby during birth. As Chef de Clinique at the Faculty of Medicine in Paris, he observed Eastern birthing practices, and concluded that intervention was rarely necessary for a successful delivery.

In 1966, Leboyer wrote 'Birth Without Violence', an obstetrician's plea for mercy on behalf of the new-born child, presented in the form of a long poem. Not surprisingly, this emotional approach brought controversy to the labour room. Leboyer's portrait of the modern baby born in anguish implied that much of the infant's suffering could be avoided, but that the adults around him were refusing to respond to his tortured body language:

The evidence is there before us.

The tragic expression, those tight-shut eyes, those puzzled eyebrows . . .
That howling mouth, that burrowing desperate head.
Those outstretched hands beseeching; then withdrawn, raised to the head in the classic gesture of despair.
Those furiously kicking feet, those knees drawn up to protect the tender bulging stomach.
The whole creature is one jumping, twitching mass.
Far from not speaking, every inch of its body is crying out: 'Don't touch me!'
And at the same time pleading: 'Don't leave me! Help me!'
Has there ever been a more heart-rending appeal?
And yet this appeal – as old as birth itself – has been misunderstood, ignored, indeed unheard.
How can this have been? How can this still be?
So can we say that a new-born baby doesn't speak?
No. It is we who do not listen.

The Victorians thought that when a baby cried, he was exercising his lungs. But now we know babies do not have to cry, either at birth or afterwards. One explanation for their screaming puts it like this:

27

Early in infancy, the baby comes fully awake only at times
of crisis, such as hunger. At these times, he is on the
verge of what the adult would call panic; the baby has no
time perspective, for him the crisis drags on interminably,
and he is helpless to do anything about it. If relief is
delayed, he becomes even more upset or exhausts himself
with crying; already a tiny seed of distrust has been
planted, and next time the panic is a little closer, the crisis
more exigent.

(Stone and Church, *Childhood and Adolescence*)

When we admire a baby for having a lovely pair of lungs, could it be
that we are ignoring nature's most obvious distress call? It is, of
course, the signal to which all humans and many other mammals are
programmed to respond.

The principle of separating mother and baby at birth is still
common in hospitals around the world. British writer Harriet
Sergeant records the treatment she received during her pregnancy
in Tokyo, where autocratic antenatal consultations were followed by
regimented postnatal separation:

Mothers are permitted to hold their new-born children only
in the corridor at feeding time. Otherwise babies were
confined to a nursery with a glass wall in front of it. A
mother would ask for her child, a nurse would wheel up the
cot and everybody would exclaim and video-tape through the
glass.

In the breast-feeding corridor nurses walked up and down
massaging engorged naked breasts. Women closed their eyes
and submitted with only the occasional grimace of pain. At my
turn I screamed, begged for aspirin and burst into tears.

'Is it so different in the West then?' demanded the
exasperated nurse.

('The Japanese Way', *AIMS Journal*, Autumn 1993)

The answer is yes – well, it ought to be. Westerners were first with the idea that it is preferable for new babies to be viewed at a distance, rather than comforted in their parents' arms. But while many British – and some American – hospitals are waking up to the importance of neo-natal contact, some of the most 'modern' Eastern clinics still keep mother and baby apart except at allotted feeding times.

There are innumerable reasons why baby is better off with mother than alone in a postnatal nursery. They range from the potential for mix-up (which still occurs regularly in hospitals everywhere),[1] to the physical and psychological cocktail of needs expressed both by infants and parents. We shall examine these in the following chapters. Meanwhile, there seems little reason why mother and baby should *not* be allowed continued close contact after birth, as midwife Sally Inch describes:

> Unless the baby is in need of the care of a paediatrician and intensive-care nurses, there is no need to remove him from his mother . . . Researchers have shown repeatedly that the normal baby is especially alert and receptive after birth, ready to interact with his mother; any rest he needs he will take later, and unless he is in need of specialist observation, or the mother has been given narcotic drugs, there is no one who will 'observe' her baby better or more keenly than she. Moreover, all these necessary procedures can be and are carried out perfectly satisfactorily at home when that is the place of delivery.
>
> (*Birthrights*)

Practices are changing in the West, where a mother is likely to be allowed to keep her baby near her during her stay in hospital. In 1991, UNICEF and the World Health Organisation launched a global campaign called The Baby-Friendly Hospital Initiative. In order to be granted the Baby-Friendly award, hospitals must meet specific targets: Ten Steps to Successful

Breastfeeding. One of these states that mothers and babies should be allowed to be together twenty-four hours a day and encourages hospitals to practise 'rooming-in' which means babies must be kept with or next to their mothers, not whisked away to a nursery at night.[2]

In February 1998, Andrew Radford, director of the UK's Baby-Friendly Initiative, said around three quarters of British hospitals were known to be working towards the award – at that time only four had actually achieved it. 'In most hospitals here, mothers are allowed to keep babies near them,' he said, 'but we are going further and encouraging professionals to make sure this happens.'

With US soap operas like *ER* still depicting babies on the wrong side of a glass panel, the American Baby-Friendly Initiative was already working to reverse the damage of years of separationist policies. By 1998, sixty hospitals held a certificate of intent to implement the Ten Steps – including 'rooming-in'. Australia, too, had a Baby-Friendly programme under way.

Even in the most enlightened establishments, a baby is taken away for weighing and the swift Apgar test, which rates the health of the new-born for heartbeat, breathing attempts, muscle tone and so on. Later, he is placed near his mother for convenience.

Yet for a new-born baby, nearness may not be enough. An infant lying in his cot does not understand that his mother is just across the room. He also has no sense of time. He cannot know that she was with him two minutes ago, or that she will pick him up again in two minutes' time. Writer Jean Liedloff puts the new-born baby's perceptions into perspective:

Even years later, at the age of five, the promise of a bicycle 'next Christmas' is, in August, approximately as satisfying as no promise at all. At ten, time has pulled itself together in the light of experience to the extent that the child can wait a day more or less comfortably for some things, a week for others and a month for special items; but a year is still quite meaningless when it comes to mitigating want . . .

Only at the age of forty or fifty do most people have any sort of perspective of a day or a month in the context of a lifetime, while only a few gurus and octogenarians are able to appreciate the relationships of moments or lifetimes to eternity (by fully realizing the irrelevance of the arbitrary concept of time).

(The Continuum Concept)

A new-born child has only immediate desire, yet hospital policy often dictates that he spend most of his hours tucked up in a plastic cot. Premature babies are even more likely to find themselves mothered by an incubator for their first weeks of life. In most British hospitals, mothers are not even allowed to carry their own babies, for fear of insurance claims should there be an accident.

Hospitals create barriers between mothers and their children, as women wheel their new-born babies around the ward, allow them to cry in the cot at the bottom of the bed, or send them to the nursery. If you sit cuddling your baby all day long, a midwife is likely to advise you to get your rest. As one mother put it:

I have been told off by a midwife for cuddling my one-day-old baby when he couldn't sleep ('You'll have him spoilt rotten before you even get him home.')

(Joy Henderson, Dumfries, *Independent*, 2 August 1988)

However, times are changing, and many doctors and midwives now suggest that cuddling up close to another human being may have a rejuvenating effect. Some even recommend continuous body contact as essential for the optimum health of your new child.

The Jessop Hospital for Women in Sheffield, where up to 4,000 babies are born every year, was one of the first to achieve UK Baby-Friendly status. However, this involved a drastic change of policy and the reintroduction of a practice which was then discouraged by

31

health visitors all over the country: allowing babies into their mothers' beds.

One of the Ten Steps to Successful Breastfeeding demands that babies should be given 'no food or drink other than breast milk unless medically indicated'. But an initial audit revealed that the Jessop, like most other British hospitals, fed formula supplements to nearly half its babies. It was found that this was most commonly done at night, to help the new-borns settle to sleep. Infant Feeding Adviser Susan Ashmore reports on a drastic change in hospital procedures:

> To help tackle this problem, the previous strict policy of not allowing babies in bed with their mothers was re-examined . . . a new 'Babies in Bed' policy was devised in an attempt to encourage mothers to feed their babies as often as required, whilst still allowing them to rest.
>
> Following the introduction of the new policy, supplementation rates were reduced by half . . .
>
> The hospital has not had nurseries for many years. However, as previously mentioned, it was quite common to find babies in the ward offices, to allow mothers to rest, often for considerable lengths of time. A greater understanding of how rooming-in influences breast feeding success was required and therefore incorporated into the staff education programme.
>
> (*Modern Midwife*, June 1997)

So, we move from 'rooming-in' to 'bedding-in', a concept which was given full consideration and measured approval as long ago as 1988 in the official Royal College of Midwives' own handbook *Successful Breastfeeding*.[3]

However, the most forward-thinking institutions in the Western world are no match for a century of indoctrination on the dangers of 'giving in' to the new-born child. In many postnatal wards, a mother is encouraged to believe that her baby's needs and will are set against her own. When it comes to lights-out, she listens to the nurses who tell her she'll be better after a good night's sleep, and baby should go to the nursery. In the old days, there would be no choice in the matter. Now they promise to wake you up when he cries. Neither solution is satisfactory, either for mother or for baby.

A new-born child lives in a world of sharp contrasts; either his needs are being met, and all is well – or his needs are not being met – and he will quickly let you know which is which. If you hear a baby who is screaming with all his power, it might be that he lacks only one or two small details to make his world right again, details which may range from digestive difficulties ('more milk now' or 'I've got wind') to separation problems ('I want to be held', 'I want to be held by that person over there', and 'don't put me down'.)

Sleep clinicians would have us train children from the earliest possible age to overcome their fear of being alone. But while babies can be trained into nocturnal obedience, many also learn to fear. Unable to cope with unreasonable adult expectations, they pin their fear on the elements surrounding sleep: the dark, the nursery, the bed itself. Australian paediatrician Dr Christopher Green describes the panic of a toddler who is left alone to 'cry it out':

> Many health workers tell parents that when their child cries at night they should not go near him, but leave him to cry himself to sleep. This can often take three or four hours; I think it is not only cruel but also an ineffective method of treatment. After ten minutes, most children become hysterical and have no idea why they are crying. They get themselves into a lather, sweat profusely, their hearts pound and they become very frightened. Fear is not a good way of teaching any child good behaviour.
>
> (*Toddler Taming*)

Trying to teach a person something at this stage is akin to torture, because a child cannot comprehend anything but his own panic, or his sense of well-being. The new-born is even more vulnerable. He expects warmth and movement, food and comfort, all of which are supplied at once by his mother's presence, and access to her breasts. Any experience that denies him these things may be understandably horrific to him. If his mother (or an equivalent care-giver) is not there, instinct tells him she might as well be dead. If his mother is dead, then he is likely to die, too. These are the meanings of an isolated baby's cries.

Some parents follow advice that says a baby should never be allowed to cry, but at the same time try to educate their babies into sleeping alone at a young age. The net result is that when the babies scream, a parent comes running. This is the beginning of a pattern that may haunt them for the rest of their days.

Many parents have been led to believe that letting the baby cry is the only way to control him – by ignoring his calls for help, they attempt to suppress his will and curb his infant temper. Then a different pattern may emerge. The baby displays a syndrome known as 'learned helplessness', a term taken from scientific experiments with animals in the 1960s:

They divided some dogs into two groups. The first group was given electric shocks from which they could do absolutely nothing to escape. The second group of dogs was placed in identical cages, but given no shocks at all. The same two groups of dogs were then tested in a special box which had two compartments divided by a barrier. In one compartment, the dogs received an electric shock. But by jumping over the barrier, they could escape the shocks. The second group of dogs, which had never had any electric shocks before, very quickly discovered the escape route and jumped over the barrier. But the astounding thing was that the first group of dogs – those which had previously been shocked – did not make any attempt to escape. They just crouched helplessly in the electric shock compartment. Even when the dogs were lifted over the barrier to the safe side, it still made no difference. They had learned from their first experience that nothing they did made any difference, and they were unable to control events.

(Michael Odent, *Primal Health*)

Dr Benjamin Spock, leading American childcare expert since the 1940s, tells mothers to leave their babies to cry. He describes the state of learned helplessness perfectly, though without believing it does any damage: 'The second night the crying is apt to last only 10 minutes,' he writes, describing the effects of his 'let-them-cry' programme. 'The third night there usually isn't any at all.'[4]

The Spock-trained baby has resigned himself to the hopelessness of his situation. He has learnt a cruel lesson: there isn't any point in trying to improve things. Is it possible that babies who are raised by the popular technique of 'controlled crying' are learning an unnecessarily cruel lesson – that suffering is the human condition and you can't do anything about it? There certainly seem to be plenty of adults willing to endure their lives that way. In her book *Feel the Fear and Do It Anyway*, Susan Jeffers describes the everyday fears which beset us and keep us in 'a place of pain, paralysis and depression'.[5] She identifies the common fears of rejection, failure, being vulnerable and helplessness. These would also seem to be the unnamed fears of the baby who finds himself in an unhappy place and without the power to put himself where he needs and wants to be.

Whether we leave our babies to cry, or use their tears as an alarm to bring us running, we are missing out on the potential for small, subtle, positive communications between parent and child. If only we knew how not to battle. We need to rediscover what families throughout history have known instinctively – how to offer children complete security, so that they can grow and develop in confidence.

The prevailing theory runs contrary to this line of thinking. Society presumes that children are anti-social, and that 'pandering' to their needs will 'spoil' them. Christianity, the major religion of the West, tells us that even new-born infants need to be cleansed of their sins. Doctors, agony aunts and psychologists insist that babies are trouble. Children are wilful, manipulative, and they'll never let you have a moment's peace. We are conditioned to expect the worst.

But let us start from a more positive perspective. Perhaps the infant human being is a sociable creature. Let's imagine he is equipped with all the faculties he needs for survival. Operating mostly on instincts and reflexes, he does not cry without reason. His communications are urgent, and they relate to his immediate needs.

All the evidence shows us that a baby needs to copy, to follow, to behave as we expect him to. This is the key to his survival. If a child's instinct were programmed to upset the social order, manipulate his parents and be generally obnoxious, the human race would have died out aeons ago. If babies were meant to scream all day and keep us awake at night, our ancestors would simply have chucked the little brats into the river.

A new-born child, motivated by the instinctive will to survive, needs to integrate for his own good. So why do they cry as babies, and manipulate us when they're old enough? Those cries and moans are designed to irritate us as much as possible, so that we change our response. They are certain indications that something is wrong.

The parents who say their baby is a monster are describing the behaviour of a human being looking for comfort. He cries because his needs are not being fully met. A baby who screams is talking to you. At least he feels there is something worth crying for. Pity the child who has withdrawn into a resigned silence.

Babies are not naughty – just needy and utterly helpless. For a long time it puzzled me why a human infant was *so* vulnerable and dependent, when new-born deer can struggle to their feet within hours of birth, when ewes do not have to carry their lambs around everywhere, and kittens can be toilet trained within weeks; why a baby is completely lost without its mother or guardian.

Human babies are born with relatively small brains, although the cranium grows rapidly in the first months after birth. Scientists

"He put her down at night and we never hear a thing"

believe this is because the infant head has to force its way through the narrow maternal birth canal, and a larger brain would risk damage on the way. The new-born baby, operating on a primitive level with a brain that has yet to undergo many complex changes, is completely dependent on his mother for his existence.

Animal-watcher Desmond Morris describes how physical immaturity hinders the human infant, while his ancient cousin, the monkey, is swinging from the trees with its parents soon after birth:

> During its waking periods the newborn infant moves comparatively little. Unlike other primate species its musculature is poorly developed. A young monkey can cling tightly to its mother from the moment of birth onwards. It may even clasp on to her fur with its hands while it is still in the process of being born. In our own species, by contrast, the newborn is helpless and can only make trivial movements of its arms and legs.
>
> (*The Naked Ape*)

This seems a massive drawback for human babies who, like monkeys, expect to be carried everywhere by their parents. In the (at least) three to four million years of the evolution of man, the human foetus grew inside the mother's womb while she foraged for food. At birth, the baby was held or bound to the parent's body, while he or she continued the daily struggle to survive.

Humans, like monkeys, are a 'carrying' species. Other creatures – birds, for instance – work on the 'cache' principle. Their young are kept in nests while the parents look for food. In evolutionary terms, at least, human babies are not designed to be kept in cots while both parents are away.

To feed her baby, the human mother has to guide him to her breast and hold him while he suckles. If she wants to carry on with her daily duties, she must learn to do without one arm, or contrive a sling to hold him in place – or put him down. The quality of a human baby's nurturing is completely her responsibility, and the only clues a baby offers are his cries and smiles.

How did Neanderthal baby, curled up in the foetal position and unable to wipe his own nose, ever reach adulthood? The answer is, that his parents did not leave him alone. Day and night, he was held next to the skin of his parents and other care-givers. He was not expected to fend for himself. The plight of the new baby is even more puzzling when we consider his potential in contrast with that of other animals. Small-brained or not, surely our superior intelligence ought to aid us to stand, walk, feed and hold things faster than our four-footed friends? We ought to be able to cope with the physical niceties in minutes, leaving us free to talk, invent, explore and create.

Why should man have this massive handicap, when he has to compete with lions and gazelles and snakes?

Within months the human baby makes up for lost time, learning more than a monkey could assimilate in twenty years. By his first birthday, a child may not be able to walk, but he has mastered the necessary vocalizations for language, a skill no monkey can ever match. And something else is going on during the first year of life. A human infant is developing his ego . . .

> . . . the 'baby' is a very sensitive and knowing human being. He is going through various experiences that are laying down some of the basic, automatic emotional patterns of the personality. He is learning that other human beings can or cannot be trusted. He is learning that they can be kind, reasonable, gentle, dependable and consistent, or that they can be evasive, cruel, loud, capricious and unreasonable. And we know from thousands of observations that what he learns in the first year is not easy to unlearn.
>
> (English and Pearson, *Emotional Problems of Living*)

Helplessness is the vital condition of the human baby, because he requires the company of those who are teaching him what it is to be

39

human. His frailty is our cue to pick him up and hold him. A baby has to sort out his own ego from the muddle he sees around him, and he does that by first identifying with his mother. He does not initially see a distinction between himself and the breast that feeds him. What he has to learn is not merely how to take control of his legs, his hands and his bowels, but a sense of himself. This is what makes him different from every other animal on earth.

At the beginning, the mother and infant are as one – the rest is a slow struggle towards independence. There is nothing in the struggle that a child cannot cope with, but why should we make it more painful or more abrupt than necessary?

Child psychotherapist Dilys Daws makes the connection between infant sleep difficulties and the development of the infant personality:

> Looking at sleeping problems makes us aware of the complexity of the emotions involved in being a parent. We see how subtle is the process by which mothers and babies move from their early closeness to seeing themselves as two separate beings.
>
> (*Journal of Child Psychotherapy*, 1985)

When you put a newborn baby down to sleep in his cradle and tiptoe out of the room, he thinks a part of himself has gone – the part that sustains life and gives him comfort. He does not have many resources to cope with this separation. Whether he protests or not, he needs you. It is such an obvious explanation for infant misery that medical handbooks tend to overlook it. Experts keep telling us to put the baby down, because (apparently) it is easier, and mothers should not be subject to the whims of their children. They are missing the point altogether.

Until quite recently, all that childcare experts seemed to offer was a series of schemes to increase the gap between mother and child. This intervention disturbs the child's development, and reduces either parent's ability to meet a child's needs. The baby suffers and cries. It is not surprising that in modern Western society, where one of the primary aims of parenting is to put the baby down, childrearing is commonly regarded as a chore.

Luckily, scientific research is now on the trail of babies' real needs and is rediscovering wisdoms which our foremothers and forefathers knew instinctively. For instance, the more you hold a baby, the more you want to hold him.

> A great deal of the work done on very early separation has been carried out by the paediatricians Marshall Klaus and John Kennell. In one interesting study of theirs, a group of nine Guatemalan mothers were given their naked babies immediately after they had left the delivery room. A second group of nine mothers and babies were separated according to the usual hospital routine.
>
> The babies in both groups were then sent to the newborn nursery for the next twelve hours and returned to their mothers for their first feed. Observations during this feed of maternal fondling, kissing, gazing into the baby's face, and holding him close showed that the mothers who did much more of all of them were those who had had early contact with their infants.
>
> (Aidan Macfarlane, *The Psychology of Childbirth*)

This is the phenomenon known as 'bonding', which troubles so many parents today, to judge from the welter of newspaper articles on the subject. 'Mothers who don't love their babies' was the postnatal topic of the 1980s, followed by the 'Mad to be a mother' articles and novels scripted by angry young parents of the 1990s. Bonding and the benefits of babycare no longer seem to compensate for the dreary job of looking after a new, helpless life (when you could be going out to work and hanging on to your prenatal figure).

If mothers are not allowed to follow their instincts when it comes to feeding and nurturing their babies, they will hardly satisfy their

41

own emotional and bodily needs. It seems incredible that parents, in the privacy of their own homes, are afraid to respond to their babies' night-time requirements by taking them into bed.

Critics say that parents who sleep with their babies are succumbing to the infant's whim. Yet nature has designed mother and baby so that their needs are complementary. She to cuddle and feed and nurture her child, he to be cuddled and fed and nurtured.

Many laboratory experiments have been done since the 1960s to discover the effects on animals who are separated from their mothers for extended periods. Monkeys, for instance, display a range of critical physical responses to the lack of maternal contact:

Studies using telemetry [radiophonic instruments] on a variety of macaque monkey species (bonnet, pigtail and rhesus) indicate that when separated from their mothers, primates as old as four to six months of life . . . lose body temperature and can experience disturbances in sleep, with decreased REM [Rapid Eye Movement] sleep periods, changes in EEG [brain] activity, alterations in cellular immune responses, and increases in cardiac arrhythmias [irregular heartbeat]. It has been demonstrated in squirrel monkeys that separation increases their adrenal (stress) secretions and plasma cortisol levels and decreases their ability to combat pathogens [diseases] because of decreases in immunoglobulins . . .

(James McKenna, *Medical Anthropology*, 1986)

Human babies deprived of physical affection likewise have a greatly reduced chance of survival. Studies of infants in institutions in the 1950s identified the 'failure to thrive' syndrome, where babies deprived of mother-love lost weight and often died, though they were fed enough to live on.

There are many dimensions to maternal separation for human infants. Psychological and spiritual factors cannot be separated from the physical. Even if he survives the long-term absence of his mother or crucial other, the child is likely to become depressed – listless, unresponsive, sad – and if placed in an institution and deprived of a genuine mother figure, his overall development may lag in comparison with a child reared at home:

> . . . two groups of two-year-olds living in the same institution were studied. One group was given very little tenderness, although adequately cared for in every other respect, while in the other a nurse was assigned to each child and there was no lack of tenderness and affection. At the end of half a year the first group was mentally and physically retarded in comparison with the second . . . The dramatic and tragic changes in behaviour and feeling which follow separation of a young child from his mother and the beneficient results of restoring him to her are in fact available for all to see, and it is astonishing that so little attention has been given to them hitherto.
>
> (John Bowlby, *Child Care and the Growth of Love*)

Gill Cox and Sheila Dainow, authors of *Making the Most of Loving*, describe the long-lasting psychological effects of separating a baby from its mother:

> Being left completely alone is one of the greatest terrors for human beings. The fear goes back to when, as babies, we realised we were actually separate from our mothers. That realisation created a panic about who would care for us. Each time a baby wakes up and finds itself alone, it cannot know someone is there until it has had enough experiences to provide it with the evidence. By then, the awful fear that aloneness brings is implanted in our experience and can be triggered off at different times in our adult life . . .[6]

Psychologists and counsellors take all this as basic theory for the problems their patients suffer every day – but few believe anything can be done about it. Separation anxiety is the root of many common neuroses. Putting baby in a nursery at night is so usual now, that many mothers and doctors cannot envisage any other way of dealing with bedtime. But there *are* ways of changing our parenting practices, so that fewer people end up in the psychiatrist's chair.

Childcare researchers of the 1970s asking the question, 'Are Mothers Really Necessary?'[7] found that we do have our uses, but still they doubted that the mother's presence was crucial to her baby's well-being. The source of their doubt sprang from medical theories of the last century. Victorian doctors believed that the poor classes were inherently weaker of mind and body than the gentry. Experimenters hung on to the notion that depressed, sickly, retarded babies were products of their parents' genes. They argued that since most of the abandoned babies in the studies were offspring of the working class, their slow progress could be explained by hereditary factors.

The only way to eliminate the genetic factor was to study twins. It is difficult to separate and study human twins, without causing a detrimental effect to one of the pair. Instead, one psychologist compared the behaviour of twin goat kids, separating one from its mother for a short spell each day. Leading psychiatrist John Bowlby described the test:

> Except for the daily experimental period of forty minutes, both kids live and feed with their mother. During the experimental period the lights are periodically extinguished, which is known to create anxiety in goats, and this produces very different behaviour in the twins. The one which is with its mother is at ease and moves about freely; the isolated one is 'psychologically frozen' and remains cowed in one corner. In one of the first experiments the isolated kid discontinued suckling from its mother and, the experimenters being unaware of this and so unable to help, it died after a few days. This is ample demonstration of the adverse effects of maternal deprivation on the young of mammals, and disposes finally of the argument that all the observed effects are due to heredity.
>
> (*Child Care and the Growth of Love*)

Scientists were beginning to admit that maternal separation, even if only for regular short spells, could have detrimental effects on infants. The implications for human babies were even more shattering than for other animals, because of the speed of growth of the brain, the formation of the ego, and the breathing changes a baby has to undergo in order to achieve speech.

But it took a long time before the connection was made between infant behaviour and night-time separation. In 1986, when an American, Dr James McKenna, questioned the use of the cot, he had to cross the fields of paediatrics and anthropology to do so. It was controversial ground:

> For other mammal infants, but especially primate infants, short-term separation leads to physiological consequences. This conclusion forces us to consider the possible effects of nocturnal separation on human infants who, in Western and urban societies, regularly sleep apart from their parents in separate rooms.
>
> (*Medical Anthropology*, 1986)

What happens to a human baby who is left alone in the dark? Sometimes he sleeps, of course, to the pride of his parents and admiration of their peers. A baby who sleeps all night, every night, by himself in his own cot is as desirable a trophy as any Western parent could wish for. A twelve-hour-a-night baby is the stuff of paediatric legend.

Sometimes, however, he does not sleep. He cries, or he has nightmares, or he hits his head against the bars of his purpose-built cage. According to the experts, 'Nightmares occur almost universally in children from three to six years of age.'[8] Head-banging is also common, and is usually explained by the child's desire for comfort:

> When we see a baby pushing his head against the bars of his cot or the top of the bed, we tend to pull him down again, thinking that he will be better. It is a waste of time, because

this position is voluntary, the baby is looking for a point of contact, he wants to find himself once more enclosed as he was in his mother's womb.

(Laurance Pernoud, *J'élève mon Enfant* – my translation)

Thanks to scientific research, we are now beginning to realize why our babies suffer so. Even when separated from their mothers for a short time, infants undergo a series of physical changes, affecting their temperature, breathing patterns, stress levels and many other factors. Dr James McKenna wrote:

In order to understand the form and consequences of separation (primarily mother from infant) for the infant, we must know how the infant's body changes physiologically after separation and, thus, how through contact the mother physiologically regulates her infant's temperature, metabolic rate, hormone levels, enzyme production, antibody titer [the strength of antibodies in the infant's system and thus his ability to fight disease], sleep cycle, heart rate, and respiration so as to promote her infant's health and survival. Together, these data disclose the overall impact of immediate separation and remind us that when human (urban) infants are regularly separated, for example, for nocturnal sleep – which can be regarded as an evolutionarily novel situation – there is no reason to think that their physiological systems are not also affected.

(*Medical Anthropology*, 1986)

Scientific research is still attempting to discover exactly how a baby manages to survive all night without human contact. Do these measurable, physical reactions make an important difference to his overall health? SIDS researchers are beginning to suggest that they do.

Some parents – including many members of the international breastfeeding support network La Leche League in America – choose to sleep with their children because they are convinced of the advantages of this arrangement by alternative books and magazines. Few people, however, have access to the academic discussions that exist mainly in medical journals. Many parents sleep with their children for purely practical reasons, and despite the warnings they receive from health professionals, relatives and contemporaries.

Breastfeeding mothers often take their babies to bed for convenience. Some families sleep with their children because of lack of space. Poverty may mean parents cannot afford a cot (although safe co-sleeping does depend on a proper bed and a firm mattress – see chapters 5 and 10). Other parents simply follow their instincts in responding to their children's complaints at night. For most parents, the decision to comfort the child in bed is made according to the immediate needs of the infant. Many respond to ill babies by taking them into bed as family doctor David Haslam reports:

> From the moment I entered general practice I could not fail to notice how many children are nursed in their parents' bed when they are sick, not in their own. Both parents and children realise the comfort and security that comes from such an arrangement.
>
> (*Sleepless Children*)

Others relent to toddlers who will not let them sleep any other way. Sharing a bed with a baby is extremely common in our society, even though prevailing theories warn us against the practice. Ironically, the Western pattern is to share the family bed with older babies and small children, having failed to sleep-train our infants. Easterners prefer to begin with new-borns in the big bed, weaning them out after a year or two.

Science and common sense are slowly converging to reach the same conclusion: there are many advantages in sleeping with your baby. I shall examine the most compelling reasons in this book, but perhaps all we need to know is that putting an infant in a cot is against the law of evolved human nature.

We go to strenuous efforts to separate mother and baby at night, without fully understanding the dangers involved. So from where, exactly, did we get the idea that babies should sleep on their own?

3 | THEY'RE ONLY TRYING TO HELP

I love waking up next to him on the pillow. All the textbooks say you shouldn't have them in bed with you but I think they are all completely cracked.

> (Actor Pierce Brosnan on his newborn son,
> Dylan, *Hello!* magazine)

Childcare is a multi-million-pound industry, with salesmen, specialists, professionals, authors and journalists to inform us of the latest and best ways of mothering. As many parents in the West have only one or two children – and little other experience of looking after babies – they are keen to seek advice.

Some follow one authority, as, for instance, millions of American and British mothers did with Dr Spock in the 1950s. But today parents are more likely to sample a range of babycare books before choosing the method that suits them. This is the pattern that emerged from a major Marriage Research Council study of British marriage in the 1980s: 'People were aware of all the books written on babycare,' said researcher Penny Mansfield, 'and they wanted to get it right.'

Other parents avoid written matter altogether, but no one in Western society is immune from current trends and ways of thinking. One only has to visit the local shops to see that the done thing is to dress baby up warmly, push him around in a zany coloured pushchair and stop up his mouth with a dummy.

Best-selling books, magazines and television programmes all influence the way we bring up our children. To attempt methods beyond the vision of these fairly conservative authorities is to risk attack. Once a mother takes her baby out into the street she is open to critical comment from anyone passing by. You cannot bring up your child completely on your own.

As a new parent, it is almost impossible to sift useful advice from the dross, especially if the adviser is wearing a uniform. One health visitor told me that Frances, at three weeks old, should no longer be feeding at random. She should be offered the breast every four hours, and I should introduce a dummy. 'Princess Diana,' I was told, 'comforted Prince William by giving him a finger to suck. Dummy is a nasty word, I prefer pacifier. Every baby needs one.'

Not all health visitors are as eager to offer unwanted advice. But when they are, the effect on a young mother can be devastating. I had made no complaint about my feeding arrangements. Frances was gaining weight steadily, and I had had no milk leakage, no cracked or sore nipples, no engorgement – in fact, none of the problems everybody had told me I would encounter in this attempt to nurture my baby. Yet the words of the professional put me off my stride for weeks. It was a long time before I had the confidence to dispel the doubts she had placed in my mind.

It is not uncommon for mothers to read a magazine article saying one thing and a book suggesting the opposite. Relatives offer conflicting advice. Doctors make upsetting comments. A friend does things embarrassingly differently. In today's well-informed society, the new mother is more likely to be over-advised than lacking in help. This can have disastrous effects on her confidence.

Mother and health visitor Jessica Markwell summed up the maternal emotion in her article entitled 'Does Mother Know Best?' She felt full of shame when her baby daughter cried constantly from the moment she was born:

This sort of thing happened to 'clients' not professionals – didn't it? I turned to family, friends, childcare books – anywhere – for help. The euphoric glow of motherhood faded as I was told I was overfeeding her, underfeeding her, not

winding her enough and trying to wind her too hard.
Dutifully I fed her less, fed her more, patted her back, didn't
pat her back. We both finished each day utterly exhausted and
confused . . .

Things can't always have been so. When Neolithic Man first
put his loving hairy arm around Neolithic Woman and they
both gazed enraptured at their little hairy bundle of joy, it
must have been something called Instinct which made Mrs
Neolith pick up the bundle, and put him to her breast . . .

(*Practical Parenting*, June 1988)

Giving and accepting childcare advice is the currency of modern
mothering. New parents searching out the best way to bring up their
children are unlikely to rely on their own experience or to call upon
instinct. With so many professionals around, we have simply lost trust
in ourselves. But a mother in a primitive tribe would be equally
puzzled at the idea of consulting *The Complete Mothercare Manual*.

Women of the remote Yequana tribe in Venezuela, for instance,
are in tune with their instinct. They do not need Dr Spock or any
other professional to tell them how to behave. As Jean Liedloff said,
on her visit to their mountain home:

I would be ashamed to admit to the Indians that where I
come from the women do not feel themselves capable of
raising children until they read the instructions written by a
strange man.

(*The Continuum Concept*)

Women in urban societies have been reading instructions for many
years. In her review of mothering trends through the centuries,
Christina Hardyment traces the origins of baby books to the eighteenth century:

Earlier manuals survive, usually in Latin, and intended for
doctors rather than mothers to refer to. The significance of the

eighteenth century was that books began to be addressed to 'intelligent Parents as well as the medical World' . . . and to be written in English.

(*Dream Babies*)

There was a time when men did not involve themselves at all in matters of birth. This is still so in many primitive cultures, where women are confined to their quarters during labour and sometimes for a set period afterwards.

Ancient peoples considered birth as a process which occurred naturally and spontaneously, unprompted by man's intervention. Women used to be the guardians of dark secrets surrounding the nurturing of children. Even in the highly civilized lives of the Romans and Greeks, medical men kept clear of the traditional 'female' subjects:

> Doctors, who were throughout antiquity with very few exceptions male, concerned themselves only with *diseases*. The normal female functions of menstruation, childbirth, nursing, menopause, were dealt with by women – midwives and wet-nurses. Hence few records exist of normal procedures and reactions.
>
> (Lefkowitz and Fant, *Women's Life in Greece and Rome*)

When doctors first entered the domain of childrearing, it was mainly to describe events, rather than to provide a set of rules. Dr John Ticker Conquest, writing in 1848, observed that 'the bosom of the mother is the natural pillow of her offspring.'[1] The baby slept in his mother's bed.

But observation soon turned to recommendation. Doctors began to take an authoritative stance on breastfeeding and bedtimes. At first they suggested the baby should sleep with the mother for nine months, amending that figure to a few months, then reducing it to six or eight weeks.[2]

Mrs Isabella Beeton, author of the famous cook book, believed that artificial milk was more nutritious for a baby than breast milk.[3] She also recommended that mothers educate their babies to sleep alone:

> No-one of experience will hold the opinion that the mother's arms are not the natural shelter for her child, and therefore at first sight it might be supposed that it would be better for the baby to go to sleep there; and if only early infancy was to be considered no-one could object to it. But if allowed at that age, there is a great difficulty in breaking through the habit, and therefore it is better to begin early, at a time when no habits are formed, and when the child really is quite as comfortable in his soft little bed as on his mother or nurse's lap. It is astonishing how soon some children find out the way to obtain what they want, and as all infants instinctively crave for their mother's presence, so they will certainly prefer her lap, and will cry for it at first, in almost all cases. But if, very early after birth, that is, by the second week, they are left to go to sleep in their cots, and allowed to find out that they do not get their way by crying, they become at once reconciled, and after a short time will go to bed even more readily in the cot than on the lap.
>
> (*Manual of Domestic Economy*, 1861)

As Christina Hardyment remarks, 'bedtime was now an opportunity to show who was boss.' There was a new hierarchy: the childcare professional telling the mother what was best for her, and the mother telling the child what was best for him. Oxford community midwife Chloe Fisher, who has researched the origins of her trade, says that the role of the professional kept pace with the expansion of the British Empire:

> At the turn of the century there was much concern about the high infant mortality rate, which was around 160 per thousand live births. This concern arose more from anxiety about the

preservation of the race and the need to populate the nearly empty Empire than from consideration for the mothers. Artificial feeding had been recognised as a major cause of mortality and this led to the emergence of many feeding 'experts' who were extremely knowledgeable about cow's milk and how to administer it to babies. These 'experts' then proceeded to have a major influence on breastfeeding management.

(*Oxford Medical School Gazette*, Trinity Term 1982)

Those who controlled the country wanted to control the home, too. And the ordinary person was in need of advice more than ever. As people moved into towns they became isolated. The middle classes built suburbs, valuing the privacy of their new family villas. Mothers no longer nursed together. They had nowhere to meet. They employed nannies to do the job 'properly'.

The poor lived in dark and dirty terraced houses, easy prey to vermin and other carriers of disease. Large families might be crammed into one or two rooms. Poverty often forced the mother to go out to work and fathers laboured long hours. Many who could not find work became thieves and beggars, sometimes the only way to make a living.

Artificial milk for infants was often only a weak mixture of flour and water, or merely watered-down cow's milk. Advertising of bottle milk was as likely to influence a mother as advice from a doctor. There was great ignorance about diet and disease. Under-nourished and unclean, the children of Britain were ill and dying, and no product to fight for the Great British Empire.

Professionals believed that mothers had to be taught how to feed and manage their babies. If women could only be educated to be more efficient, cleaner and more disciplined, the high mortality rate might be reduced. No welfare system existed to ease their poverty, no schemes to clean the streets or to provide proper toilet facilities. The responsibility for the future of the nation's children lay entirely with the mother. Her job was to train the child.

New-born infants, who had no self-control and no language other than that piercing cry, must be educated to become little British men (and women) as early as possible. Infant training could begin as early as one liked, and most experts recommended starting from birth, by leaving the baby to cry in his own cot. *Baby*, one of the first mothercare magazines to appear in Britain, recommended just this in 1887:

> Education may, and should, begin from birth, and not only can the senses be trained from the very first, but inherited evils of temper, etc. should be watched for and checked as they rise.

Baby magazine, edited by Ada Ballin, was a vehicle for the expression of the highest authorities on medicine, hygiene and education to

"But the health visitor says she's safer in her own room"

reach mothers and 'those who have the care of children'. It carried regular articles on 'Maternal Ignorance', 'Rational Clothing' and 'Infant Feeding, Debility and Mortality'. The general feeling was that if children could only be educated early enough, a new race of strong, valiant men and gracious, happy mothers could be created.

Mabel Liddiard, writing in her *Mothercraft Manual* which went into twelve editions in the 1920s, illustrates the reasoning behind this early discipline. British babies were neither animals nor uncivilized savages, but budding socialites:

> A baby differs from the suckling animal or from the baby of the uncivilised savage in that, as he grows up, his meal time, sleep-time, play-time and work-time will be determined by social circumstances.

A scientific approach was favoured, calling for many analyses of what was good for baby. Stratagems were devised, and methods of surprising the infant enemy. This was war. Mothers were on a crusade to tame the wild, uncivilized natures of their babies:

> Break their wills betimes; begin this great work before they can run alone, before they can speak plain, or perhaps speak at all. Whatever pain it costs, conquer their stubborness; break the will if you would not damn the child . . . let him have nothing he cries for; absolutely nothing, great or small; else you undo your own work.

This was the advice given to Methodist minister John Wesley by his mother Susanna in 1872. Queen Victoria herself had little time for her children or anyone else's, and by the end of her reign, many mothers felt the same about their own offspring.

Two or three generations of women, including the entire sisterhood of nurses, midwives and health visitors, were raised on the idea that babies should be civilized as early as possible. Fashions may have changed in baby management, but a belief in infant training remains the bedrock of modern mothering.

The dos and don'ts of bedtime etiquette certainly come into this domain. But consult an old advice manual for mothers and you will find no section on sleep problems. The Victorian writer did not allow for any difficulties with his method. He assumed that the whims of the wailing child would always be curbed if the parent was strong enough:

> It is extremely improper to consider every noise of an infant as a claim upon our assistance, and to intrude either food or drink, with a view to satisfy its supposed wants. By such injudicious conduct, children readily acquire the habit of demanding nutriment at improper times, and without necessity; their digestion becomes impaired; and consequently at this early age, the whole mass of the fluids is gradually corrupted . . .
>
> We learn from Daily Experience, that children who have been the least indulged, thrive much better, unfold all their faculties quicker, and acquire more muscular strength and vigour of mind, than those who have been constantly favoured, and treated by their parents with the most solicitous attention: bodily weakness and mental imbecility are the usual attributes of the latter.
>
> (*Enquire Within Upon Everything*, 1882)

Abstinence, even for new-born babies, was believed to be character-building. The idea that crying was beneficial to a baby goes back to these early textbooks, in which physiologists concluded that as babies screamed so much, there must be something useful in it:

> Instead of being feared, the practice of crying in children in want of muscular exercise is most beneficial in its effects. Sickly and weak children cry a good deal, and but for this, it is almost certain that they could not live long. The very first act

which an infant performs at birth is to cry, and many of them continue to do so at an average rate of four to five hours a day during the first years of their existence. It cannot for a moment be imagined that all their cries arise from a feeling of pain. It would be an anomaly in the benevolent working plan of creation and an unmerited infliction of pain on the little innocents, were this the case. Not at all. They cry in default of exercise, or rather, for exercise.

(Samuel Smiles, *Physical Education*, 1838)

Before this, eighteenth-century parents 'had been able to put down the infant's bawls to original sin'.[4] Now crying was considered to be natural and good for the infant, babies could expect to be doing a lot of it, as part of their infant training programme.

The idea that a crying baby is exercising his lungs may belong to the nineteenth century, but it lingers today. The screams of the new-born are still met with admiration from mother, doctor and midwife. 'What a lovely pair of lungs!' they say, as he communicates his terror.

Baby, pioneer of mothercare magazines, offered its own formula for untroubled infant sleep:

Sleep for the child is even more of a vital need than for an adult, and its sleep will be more natural and healthier if it is not rocked. If accustomed from the first to be laid away in a quiet, darkened, but well-ventilated room, at a certain hour, the baby will form the habit of falling asleep, and will never know any other. A light should not be left burning at night; it vitiates the atmosphere, and sleep is not as sound as in the dark.

Routine, clean air and as little handling as possible was the prescription for the late Victorian baby. It sounds a little old-fashioned, but not absurd, as current professional advice runs along similar lines. What is entirely unexpected in the magazine's description of baby bedtime etiquette is the following remark:

For the first few weeks animal heat is usually maintained by sleeping with the mother . . .

Here are the last vestiges of co-sleeping. The writer acknowledges that the parental bed is the proper and usual place for a new-born baby. But the practice must stop there:

. . . on no account should a child of any later age sleep between two persons, as by so doing it must of necessity breathe the emanations from their bodies.

In the 1880s, the fear that the baby would be smothered or spoilt was topped by the belief that bedsharing was unhygienic. Doctors knew that diseases spread through bodily contact, and while they were doing nothing to improve inner-city sanitation, they were keen to prevent intimacy within the home.

A fascinating study of London's poor – though not its poorest – was made between 1909 and 1913 by the Fabian Women's Group. Their aim was to answer the question 'How does a working man's wife bring up a family on twenty shillings a week?' Sleeping accommodation was of particular concern to the well-meaning volunteers who crossed the thresholds of more than sixty tiny Lambeth terraced houses. They were horrified to see babies sleeping in the parents' bed. And in the days before health visitors, the women were there to influence as well as to observe:

. . . some sort of cot was always provided for the little baby. Unfortunately, this is not a universal rule. It appears here because the investigation insisted on the new baby having a cot to itself. Otherwise it would have taken its chance in the family bed.

(Maud Pember Reeves, *Round About a Pound a Week*, 1913)

The poorer classes were urged, despite their lack of furniture and shortage of space, to bed their babies in banana crates and orange boxes. 'In winter,' wrote Maud Pember Reeves, author of the report, 'the mothers find it very difficult to believe that a new-born baby can be warm enough in a cot of its own. And when one looks at the cotton cot blankets, about 30 inches long, which are all their wildest dreams aspire to, one understands their disbelief.'

Scientists now confirm the fear of the poor London women – a baby alone in a cot cannot be kept as warm as if he were in bed with his parents.[5] But the mothers in the four-year study took the advice gratefully, along with hints on diet and sanitation. Soon the whole nation, rich and poor, was putting its babies into cots.

Between 1915 and 1935, behavioural psychologists added their weight to the argument. They claimed that children should be reared along scientific lines, that a baby – even a new-born – could be trained into sociability. Parents handed over their initiative to a grand circle of child experts, such as leading American behaviourist John B. Watson. He wrote in 1928:

> There is a sensible way of treating children. Treat them as though they were young adults. Dress them, bathe them with care and circumspection. Let your behaviour always be objective and kindly firm. Never hug and kiss them, never let them sit in your lap.
>
> If you must, kiss them once on the forehead when they say good night. Shake hands with them in the morning. Give them a pat on the head if they have made an extraordinarily good job of a difficult task. Try it out. In a week's time you will find how easy it is to be perfectly objective with your child and at the same time kindly. You will be utterly ashamed of the mawkish, sentimental way you have been handling it.
>
> (*Psychological Care of Infant and Child*)

It is easy to see why frantic parents, operating against their own feelings and fighting the natural capacities of their children, were unable to sustain this regime. Behaviourism went out of fashion quite rapidly, but its bitter taste continued to sour standard childcare books.

In 1935, *The Motherhood Book* advised against carrying a baby from room to room:

> Babies should be trained from their earliest days to sleep regularly and should never be awoken in the night for feeding . . . Baby should be given his own quiet bedroom from the very beginning. He should never be brought into the living room at night.

The bedtime routine was an essential part of a mother's day. The more rigid and more regular the pattern, the better she was doing her job. By the 1930s, *The Concise Household Encyclopaedia* had waved goodbye to bedsharing, even for the newest baby. The cot was the in-thing:

> After the bath, the baby has a feed and is put to sleep. He should sleep in his own cot from the beginning as it is both unsafe and unhygienic to sleep with mother or nurse. He should lie on a firm hair mattress.

Officious and unemotional, childcare manuals were still not read by the masses. No doubt many mothers resented their dogmatic style and unsympathetic accounts of how the perfect baby should behave. However, in 1946 childcare advice became as fashionable as nylon stockings when Dr Benjamin Spock published his *Baby and Child Care* book in America.

Spock, unlike most commentators, was prepared to inject some emotion into his advice, and allow that mothers and babies were having problems with the infant training routines. His friendly, understanding style made earlier books sound as dry and unreal as the rules for cricket.

I have a copy of the 1985 edition, which justifiably claims to be 'The Century's Greatest Bestseller'. By the time of his death in 1998, more than fifty million copies had been sold worldwide.

Dr Spock was popular with the public because he allowed parents to listen to their children – to some extent – and to supply many of their needs. Nevertheless, his views were attacked by politicians, and critics labelled him 'permissive'. Spock was outraged:

> I don't consider myself permissive and almost all the people who've used this book feel the same way. The people who call me permissive say indignantly that they haven't read it, wouldn't use it. The accusation came for the first time in 1968 – 22 years after the book came out – from several prominent individuals who objected strongly to my opposition to the war in Vietnam.
>
> They said my advice to parents to give 'instant gratification' to their babies and children was what made so many young men who opposed the war 'irresponsible, undisciplined and unpatriotic.' There is no instant gratification in this book.
>
> (Spock and Rothenberg, *Dr Spock's Baby and Child Care*)

Although he famously urged parents 'Trust yourself', Dr Spock certainly did not believe in instant gratification. He referred to babies as tyrants, and, like the old behaviourists, told parents to let the baby cry himself to sleep. He advised that a child should never be allowed in the parents' bed.

But it was proper that his advice should be scrutinized in the political arena. When fifty million and more mothers abandon their instincts to follow one man's advice, then there will be an effect on generations of children.

It is ironic that the politicians thought Spock was being too liberal in his guidance to young parents. When I first read this passage on 'Chronic resistance to sleep in infancy', it made *me* want to cry:

> A baby shouldn't be able to put adults through a performance like this every night. They know it but don't know what to do about it. Even a baby senses, I think, that she shouldn't be able to get away with such tyranny.
>
> The habit is usually easy to break once the parents realize that it is as bad for the baby as it is for them. The cure is

simple: Put the baby to bed at a reasonable hour, say good night affectionately but firmly, walk out of the room, and don't go back.

Most babies who have developed this pattern cry furiously for 20 or 30 minutes the first night, and then when they see that nothing happens, they suddenly fall asleep! The second night the crying is apt to last only 10 minutes. The third night there isn't usually any at all.

(*Dr Spock's Baby and Child Care*)

Nothing at all. Not even a spark of hope. Mission accomplished, as that other Spock, with the long ears and the Starship Enterprise, might have said.

Dr Spock advises setting the kitchen timer to comfort harassed parents who feel as though their child has been crying for hours. He also suggests muffling the dreadful sound with a rug on the nursery floor and a blanket over the window. Oh, and a final suggestion: don't forget to apologize in advance to 'touchy neighbours'.

But neighbours today aren't likely to be that touchy. All children cry at night, don't they? It's 'normal' behaviour, and friends are bound to understand if you say you are following the advice of Dr Benjamin Spock.

Childcare advisers no longer scold mothers or scatter pompous pearls of wisdom before us. Since Spock, their books are often informal and informed, and best-sellers. In France, the popular paediatrician is Laurance Pernoud, who revises her book *J'élève mon Enfant* (I Raise My Child) every year. She says one French family in two knows the nightly drama of the child who refuses to go to bed, and offers this solution:

Should you lock the nursery door if your child gets up and wants to come and join you? No . . . better to prop open the door with a piece of furniture, so that it is slightly ajar, but the child cannot open it further.

(My translation)

The Victorian barriers are still standing, even if we do not actually send our children to bed with bread and water and turn the key. The aim is to put babies to sleep out of sight, and if possible out of earshot too. This is what *Good Housekeeping's Baby Book* – popular from the 1940s to the 1970s – recommends:

> Some of these small-hour wakers are content to lie and gurgle to themselves, and there is no need to go to them. Indeed, it is foolish from your own point of view to encourage them to expect you. If you are worried about the baby being cold, put him in a sleeping-bag, and if he is a cot-rocker, pad the cot to deaden the sound, then accept the rhythmic thuds as a crude sort of lullaby.
>
> (Jane Vosper)

It is reminiscent of a patient in a lunatic asylum. Bound in his padded cell, so as not to bother the warders when he punishes himself against the walls, the inmate is left to protest unheard. 'You have to know your own child,' says Matron, 'and decide for yourself when good-humoured neglect is the best policy.' You wonder who will be in the better humour at the end of the night: mother, trying to stifle her 'foolish' feelings in the marital bed, or her child, alone in his own nursery.

Jane Vosper, *Good Housekeeping's* 'Matron', echoed the views of many doctors of the 1960s and 1970s, when she finally suggested giving the baby a sedative to make him sleep. Offering drugs to non-sleeping babies was a common practice in Europe:

> I often wish I could prescribe a night nurse under the National Health Service, someone to take charge in the early hours while this awkward phase lasts. Some parents take it in turns for night duty . . . But if a weary mother always has to cope on her own, a suitable sedative can be given to the baby for her sake, say for a week at a time.

The idea has filtered through to parents that it is reasonable to administer drugs to babies. The advice on the medicine bottle doesn't tell you that sedating your baby will deprive him of essential Rapid Eye Movement sleep, which he needs for growth, memory and learning:

> . . . of parents asked in a survey published in 1980, 45 per cent found consultation about their sleepless children with doctors and health visitors unhelpful. Significantly, another study published in 1977 showed a group of first-born children as having been given night sedation by the time they were 18 months old. Unofficially, desperate mothers administer cough medicines deliberately to sedate their children.
> (Conder, *Midwife, HV and Community Nurse*, April 1988)

No one knows how many parents are prepared to feed their children medicine in an attempt to induce sleep. Inappropriate, habitual use of the mild analgesic Calpol swiftly earned it the tag of 'mother's little helper' in Britain. Launched in the late 1960s, more than 200 million bottles were sold in thirty years. Used sparingly as directed, it ought not to cause problems, but children put to bed nightly with a spoon of pink paracetamol run the risk of induced headaches and – if given large enough doses – damage to the liver and kidneys.[6]

Western families are not the only ones prepared to use drugs to knock their babies out. Anthropologist Leigh Minturn, observing Rajput mothers of Khalapur, India, commented: 'All babies sleep with their mothers for several years' and said most mothers attended to their infants without letting them cry. However, some were prepared to use opium to induce daytime sleep:

> If the mother is very busy and has no-one to help carry the baby, she may resort to the use of opium to put the baby to sleep. The women agreed that this was not good for babies and should be used only as a last resort. One busy mother

administered two grams of opium a day to a baby that was a few months old. When under the influence of the drug, it was impossible to awaken the baby even by vigorous shaking.

(Leigh Minturn, *Six Cultures: Studies of Childrearing*)

If medicines to sedate the wakeful baby, then why not alcohol? Not so long ago, mothers could legally opt for gripe water – a five per cent alcohol concoction. Since the alcohol content was withdrawn, alarming newspaper headlines have suggested that one third of infants under the age of two are deliberately fed alcohol by their parents – sometimes for amusement, sometimes to get them off to sleep: Many young children are fed small doses of alcohol by their parents because of their reaction or to help them sleep.

According to Elizabeth Murphy, a senior lecturer in sociology at Nottingham University, one mother she had interviewed exclaimed: 'You ought to have seen his face!' after her child had been given a sip of whisky. 'He wouldn't move,' she said. 'He wouldn't breathe. He was in shock.' . . .

Another had used wine to help her child to sleep, but said that it was 'not even half a glass full.'

Donald Naismith, a professor of nutrition at King's College London, said that even a little alcohol goes a long way for a toddler: 'A sip of whisky for a baby is the equivalent probably of four double whiskies for an adult.'

(*Guardian*, 23 April 1998)

Although childcare experts used to sanction the use of sedatives in the first half of the twentieth century, these days their methods of sleep control tend to be more mechanical than chemical.

Bluff and burlesque are often the styles of writers who do not want to harm their children physically, but joke about feeling like it. Paediatricians admit that they do not have all the answers.

Dr Christopher Green, a consultant paediatrician from Australia, advocates tying the handle of the child's bedroom door, so that (and I quote, otherwise you may not believe me) 'the aperture is just one inch less than the diameter of the offending child's head.'[7]

Dr Green's is the ultimate no-nonsense childcare book, brusquely entitled *Toddler Taming*. It includes a long chapter entitled 'Sleep Problems – At Last, The Cure'. In the final analysis, Dr Green's 'controlled crying technique' is no cure at all. He admits as much himself, when he says that parents 'rapidly getting nowhere' should tame their toddlers with rope across the door . . .

> For those who cannot bring themselves to smack their child, but are rapidly getting nowhere, I strongly recommend the 'patent rope trick'. This is one of my better inventions, which came from the drawing-board when I was trying to curb the escape-artist antics of my own children.

Childcare books may be a relatively new invention, but babies have always been brought up according to one set of rules or another. I asked childcare historian Diana Dick whether people were more dogmatic today. 'No,' she said, 'you find people standing on their hind legs in every century, saying "*this* is what you should be doing." '

Of course there will always be people who refuse to accept the given theory, and who speak out against the trend. One such authority was Margaret Ribble, author of the volume *Rights of Infants* published in 1943. Although relatively unknown today, she had a reasonable following then, for her book was reprinted six times in two years. Christina Hardyment summarizes the views of this astounding woman:

> Ribble put forward ideas which were remarkably ahead of her time, although her viewpoint was occasionally idiosyncratic . . . Ideally, she felt, babies should not be taken from their mothers and sent to the hospital nursery at birth, under the pretext of giving mothers a chance to rest. She reasoned from the known fact that lack of oxygen at birth could damage the brain of the newborn child. She extended this principle to the first few

months of life, claiming that the baby needed physical stimulus from the presence of its mother's body to keep it inspiring air as fast as it expired it . . . Ribble's babies were kept in their mother's beds to boost their oxygen intake. She derided 'the ancient belief, still current, that babies who sleep with their mother are in danger of suffocation.' The reverse was effectively true. 'Since the contacts and warmth afforded by the human body are a protection rather than a peril to the infant, he sleeps more safely at his mother's side than in the stimulus-free seclusion of the nursery.'

(*Dream Babies*)

The idea of keeping mother and baby together to promote the infant's well-being has been usefully applied to premature babies around the world. Kangaroo Mother Care was a method first devised at a hospital in Bogotá, Colombia, where expensive incubation techniques were found to be inferior to skin-to-skin contact for promoting the health of premature babies. A study at London's Hammersmith Hospital in 1998 found that these 'skin contact' mothers produced breast milk for longer than controls, while a randomized study in Ecuador showed babies were less likely to be seriously ill in the six months after birth.[8]

But with the tide of medical thinking against her, Margaret Ribble's call for prolonged breastfeeding, increased rocking and nightly bed-sharing went largely unheard. Most advice columns continued to advocate putting the child down in a cot on his own, and weaning him early from night feeds.

Modern textbooks still recommend a battle between mother and baby in the attempt to train him to be sociable. Here, for instance, a health visitor and a paediatrician writing in a free magazine sponsored by a manufacturer of disposable nappies, say that a baby should be left alone to cry at night:

The baby may cry longer and louder than previously, but this apparent worsening of the problem prior to improvement is the last hurdle to overcome before the battle for silent nights is won.

(Dick and Pritchard, *Pampers First Years of Life*, 1987)

Letting the baby Cry It Out is the main weapon in the modern sleep-training armoury, although it may be enforced with greater or lesser gentleness. There's the Quick Check Method, advocated by Schaefer and Petronko, who say 'Twenty minutes seems to be the optimal length of time to let infant night wakers cry.'[9] Or there's the 'cold turkey' approach, as proposed by (for instance) Hackney's Sleep Clinic in East London: 'On the first night, recalls Jo Jackson, the baby "screamed for ten minutes, then wailed for two hours". The next night was similar, but less prolonged. Shortly after that Rosa began to sleep through the night, for eleven hours at a time.'[10]

A couple of distressing nights seems such a small price to pay for complete success, that one may ask why more people don't follow this swift route. Clearly it works for some, but not all – and many parents lack enthusiasm for letting their babies cry. Perhaps they do not share the convictions of Angela Henderson, author of *The Good Sleep Guide for You and Your Baby*, who believes babies' solitary crying is therapeutic – 'In any case,' she says, 'you will probably be far more upset by their crying than they will be.' Henderson's sleep-training method has a helpful appendix to support parents who cannot steel themselves to leave their babies to cry. 'The real proof that it is not cruel,' she says, 'is to talk to the parents of infants who have been through sleep training whose children wake up the next morning, after considerable crying the night before, smiling up at them from the cot, happy and full of beans the next day.'

The infinite optimism of the small child is, indeed, a wonder, especially when it resurfaces *despite*, rather than *because of* a night of 'considerable crying'. Children's tears are, of course, valuable and should never be suppressed. It does not therefore follow that it is safe or advisable to create situations which will make our children need to cry, or that they should be left to cry alone. As Aletha Jauch Solter points out in her astonishing book, *The Aware Baby*, there is a world of difference between a baby who cries by himself and one who cries in the arms of someone who can physically embrace his woes:

> The approach recommended in this book for handling crying should not be confused with the school of thought that claims it is good to 'let babies cry it out,' because the use of that expression usually implies that babies are not to be paid attention during crying spells.
>
> There are three reasons why it is best *never* to leave babies alone to cry. The first reason is that they have a great need for being held and touched . . . That may be the reason they are crying in the first place . . . The second reason [is that] the presence of another human being seems to be necessary for the effective release of tensions. The communication aspect is an integral part of the discharge process. The third reason . . . is that [babies] may grow up to believe that they are lovable only when they are happy. Babies need to know that they are cherished and accepted at *all* times, no matter how they are feeling or what they are doing.

One of the most influential modern sleep-training advisers is Dr Richard Ferber, author of *Solve Your Child's Sleep Problems* and, according to his own blurb, 'widely recognised as America's leading authority in the field of children's sleep problems'. His methods involve strict sleep schedules, elimination of 'bad habits' and fifteen-minute crying episodes. Together, they are popularly known as 'Ferberization'.

Ferber, who is vehemently against the 'bad habit' of the family bed, has a selection of chapter headings which give the reader the general idea of his philosophy and scope: 'Feedings during the night – another major cause of trouble'; 'Sleeptalking, sleepwalking, thrashing and terrors – a spectrum of sudden partial wakings'; 'Night time fears'; 'Nightmares'. This kaleidoscope of nocturnal horror is regarded as entirely normal in American and other Western societies. Ferber's focus is to eliminate the Problem (ie. the waking child) and thus he does not acknowledge that his premise may be creating some of the trauma.

Societies where co-sleeping is usual might find Ferber's chapter headings bewildering, since they are not troubled by any of the alarming disorders he describes. One wonders what they would make of the chapter entitled 'Headbanging, body rocking and head rolling':

> . . . you may be comforted to know that headbanging, body rocking and head rolling are very common in early childhood and, at least at this age, are usually normal. There is little need for concern about emotional difficulties or neurological illness . . . On the *average*, body rocking starts at six months of age, headbanging and head rolling at nine months . . .
>
> If your child bangs his head he probably gets up on all fours and rocks back and forth, hitting his forehead or the top of his head into the headboard of the cot. Or he may sit in bed and bang backwards into the headboard. Some children will lie face down and lift their heads, or head and chest, then bang or drop back into the pillow or mattress again and again. Occasionally a child may stand in his cot, hold on to the side rail and hit his head there. Now and then a child will assume a very awkward posture to allow himself to rock, bang his head, suck his thumb and hold on to a stuffed animal at the same time.
>
> (*Solve Your Child's Sleep Problems*)

In another cultural context, this book might be titled *Create Your Child's Sleep Problems*. When we decide to sleep-train our babies and they protest, we then need whole books reassuring us about the normality of their self-harming behaviours.

More enlightened research now indicates an awareness that sleep-training is not the only way to go and that it can create problems as well as solve them. Scientists reporting in the *Infant Mental Health Journal* compared bedsharing with solitary sleeping and noted: 'Solitary Sleepers engaged in more complex bedtime routines, and had more long-standing and stronger attachment to security objects and sleep aids, than did Co-sleepers.'[11]

Assumptions such as those made by Dr Richard Ferber seem to be made in ignorance of the millions of children throughout the world who do not rock themselves violently, suck their thumbs or grip transitional comfort objects in order to induce sleep or mitigate the pain of being alone. The doctors who describe these behaviours as normal are, perhaps understandably, overwhelmed by their own clinical experience and the side effects of their own advice.

From the perspective of the professional, the mother and child are at war. The sign of victory is silence. Agony aunts reinforce the imagery with their portraits of 'King Baby', who 'sits firmly in control of his adults' lives . . . Suppose,' says one issue of *Woman's Own*, 'you've got a little dictator who won't sleep . . .'

The vision of baby as tyrant, king or dictator is designed to spur a mother into attack. Her advisers tell her to engage in combat with this powerful individual before he ruins her life. No one suggests that mother and baby are on the same side.

In a reaction to this strictness, some authorities advocated letting the child have his own way entirely. But so-called 'permissive' advice, the sort which puts the baby's needs before the mother's, can be as divisive as battle talk. Parents fail to anticipate their child's every desire, as his whims become their commands.

Like behaviourism in the 1920s, the permissive approach was unpopular with parents. Mothers felt guilty, an emotion which was no use to anyone. Parents did not want to be at the beck and call of their children all day and they resented the baby-centred world of some theorists. Authors like Libby Purves were quick to redress the balance and restore confidence:

> This book is about the way real, fallible mothers *really* get through the day. There are plenty of technical baby manuals on the market: some are excellent, some manage to make bathing a baby sound as complicated as stripping down a MIG

fighter engine; nearly all of them are perfectionist in tone. This is an *imperfectionist* book, about the cheerful cutting of corners, without guilt.

(*How Not to be a Perfect Mother*)

Parents could once again feel in charge, if they agreed with Miriam Stoppard:

Having read so many baby books which emphasize looking after the baby's needs, I still feel guilty if I occasionally put my own wishes on par with those of my children. I hope no parent reading this book will suffer any such shame . . . If, by taking a few short cuts and putting yourself a little higher on your list of priorities, life with your baby is more fun and you are happier, go ahead and do so.

(*Baby Care Book*)

But parents still feel torn between their own desires and those of their children. As marriage researcher Penny Mansfield says, 'there is this dilemma between what we put into our parenting, and what priority we give ourselves and our partners. There has been a swing away from putting the children first.'

While a mother is trying to sort her way through all the theories, there is a powerful new influence which adds to her confusion. Newspapers, magazines and television feed her images and try to sell her things. The sales pitch is often disguised as professional advice. Advertisers know that a sound way to sell a babycare product is to bolster its message with a doctor's approval.

The new mother, vulnerable to suggestions which smack of experience, is persuaded to believe an advert that tells her that a certain brand of soap will help her care for her children, or that if she buys a particular cot she is doing the best for her baby. She is more likely to trust a product if it carries a British Standard kite-mark, or if a scientist recommends it.

Childcare and consumerism are thus a happy team. The shops that offer us designer prams and matching bootees now also market advice on bringing up babies. In the book title *The Complete Mothercare Manual*, the word 'Mothercare' is no ordinary adjective, but a brand name. We may overlook this, or the fact that our favourite parenting support charity is reduced to endorsing a particular brand of nappy.[12]

It is understandable that many people prefer solid advice, whatever its source. One woman told me: 'I just keep feeling as if I'm doing something wrong, and I don't know what it is.' Another friend – a midwife – became so bewildered by advice after the birth of her baby, that she became unable to care for the child.

Instinct tells us that something is not well with modern mothering, but we are out of touch with its message. Many mothers are grateful for a firm hand to guide them. Child psychotherapist Dilys Daws recalls playing the part of a stern adviser to a young mother who felt lost:

> One very caring mother of a slightly underweight baby felt she must pick him up every time he cried, which was sometimes hourly through the night. She was sure he needed something, though she was not sure whether this need was emotional, or for more food.
>
> I said sharply that what he needed was a good night's sleep; and so did she. This mother appreciated the matter-of-factness of my comments . . .
>
> (*Journal of Child Psychotherapy*, 1985)

My health visitor remarked that most mothers – inexperienced and unable to cope with an apparently troublesome baby – would rather hear one piece of strong advice than read five books on the subject and be left to choose. The irony is that today's parents have more choices than ever before. Not only must they make fundamental decisions such as whether to breast or bottle feed, but they are also offered hundreds of consumer choices. Should they buy a cradle or a baby nest? Which make of pushchair should they get? What colour curtains for the nursery?

Few mothers run to the health visitor because they cannot decide between the *Boots* or *Mothercare* brand. These are the kinds of decisions we are educated to make, and we cope well when faced with a dilemma on disposable nappies. Even so, there are books devoted to helping mothers select the best in baby equipment. Prams and pushchairs, car seats, high-chairs, toys, playpens and bouncers are all scrutinized.

'Planning for a new baby does not necessarily mean rushing out and buying everything you see in the baby shops,' says Daphne Metland, author of *Getting Ready for Baby*. Implicit in books of this type, however, is the suggestion that the good mother does her best to afford as much baby gear as she can. The list of bare essentials and useful extras would make an Edwardian mother shrink: 'cot, crib or carrycot, pram or buggy, Moses Basket, baby nest, sheepskin, cot mattress, sheets, blankets, baby alarm . . .' A new mother today could cure her insomnia by counting sheepskin rugs.

When we don't know what to do with our babies, at least there are a hundred products to explore. And that is what makes it so hard for us to discard the cot. To do without a crib or a cradle is to deprive the nursery of its advertised centrepiece.

We are encouraged to picture our babies lying in their own rooms at night, surrounded by fluffy bunnies and pastel-coloured alphabets. To deny this image is to destroy the whole vision of motherhood for many women in the West. Decking out a nursery is as important as choosing a white wedding dress. Our culture endorses the ritual of the nursery. And if you have a nursery and a cot, you have to have bedtimes and rules, battles and broken hearts.

There is another way, however. No one wants to return to the poverty-ridden squalor of the Victorian slums, or unlearn all we know about health, infant nutrition and public sanitation. But there are some lessons we can learn from mothers who have never read an advice manual.

In 1943, Margaret Ribble described infant marasmus, a wasting disease in children. It struck many babies in better-class Edwardian homes, at the height of the 'do not over-stimulate your babies' craze. It accounted, she says, for one half of the deaths of babies in Britain:

> . . . babies in the best homes and hospitals, given the most careful attention, often drifted into this condition of slow dying, while infants in the poorest homes, with a good mother, often overcame the handicaps of poverty and unhygienic surroundings and became bouncing babies. It was found that the element lacking in the sterilized lives of the former class . . . was mother love.
>
> (*Rights of Infants*)

Babies need our love and warmth by day and by night. Left alone, most parents are able to provide these things. No amount of well-meant advice should get in their way.

4 | IN TOUCH

It takes only the most elementary observation to see that a
baby needs its mother even more during the night than during
the day, and even more in the dark than in the daylight. In
the dark the baby's predominant sense – sight – is at rest.
Instead the baby needs to use its sense of touch through skin-
to-skin contact, and its sense of smell.

(Michel Odent, *Primal Health*)

Sight may be the predominant sense in children and adults, but touch is
our first connection with the world. The foetus in the womb and the
new-born infant rely on physical contact for information. A new baby
keeps his eyes closed for much of the time, and whatever patterns he
can distinguish in the early weeks cannot mean very much to him.

Maureen Blackman, a nurse from Scunthorpe, spent years working
in special care baby units. She came to realize the importance of
human contact for the premature and ill babies who struggle for life
in incubators:

Years ago, parents looked through the glass at their children,
and we told them 'Do not touch, the baby is too ill.' The
parents accepted that, bless them, and knew no better. Now
we encourage mothers to hold their babies, to stay close to
them. The babies respond to this.

I've looked down on those babies over the years, and I
think, how can you know you're alive if no one touches you?

Therapeutic massage can be traced back to Eastern cultures around 3,000BC. Baby massage has been used for centuries by mothers in India, China and the Eastern bloc and does not consist of kneading and pummelling the body, but of gentle caresses over the babies' skin. These ancient techniques have entered modern medical vocabulary as tac-tic, 'Touching and Caressing-Tender in Caring'. Gentle stroking of premature babies immediately after birth has been demonstrated to have a long-term effect on the children's intelligence.[1]

Massage and faith healing, the Japanese art of Raiki and Californian Rosen techniques all use touch to promote healing and a sense of well-being. Touch techniques often benefit patients with whom other therapies have failed:

> . . . a Scottish hospital stated that patients who had symptoms of tension and anxiety and who had failed to respond to usual psychiatric or drug therapy were treated by use of reflex stimulation using connective tissue massage. 'All patients showed a significant response to treatment in one or more of the psychophysiological parameters,' said the report. Most who had suffered chronic insomnia, despite massive medication, slept normally after the treatment and maintained this improvement.[2]
>
> (Leon Chiatow, *Here's Health*, May 1988)

The importance of touch in healing and sustaining health has been overlooked by the mainstream of Western medical practitioners, says Norman Autton, author of *Pain: An Exploration*:

> Touch is a medium through which persons repeatedly communicate and it is only through communication that man's greatest need as a human being, the need to love and be loved, is fulfilled . . .
>
> Holding hands, putting an arm round the patient, are expressions of affection and friendliness. Kubler-Ross (1969) found that the most expressive relationship during terminal

illness was a gentle pressure of the hand in moments of silence. Physical actions symbolize that someone understands, encourages and comforts. Anna Freud (1952) has described how the youngest blitz victims of the Second World War maintained their morale in the midst of rubble and wreckage when they had a living and helping hand to cling to . . . For a patient in pain touch helps to locate him in time and space.

As with the sufferer of pain, so it is with a new-born baby. Human touch may be the only stabilizing force in a world that is at once foreign and frightening. Physical contact and movement calm the infant, reassuring him that life is not entirely hostile. Through touch, a child comes to value himself. Psychologists say that an infant reared with the loving caresses of his parents is less likely to suffer aches, pains and illnesses later in life:

> One might say that if the baby's body is a joy and a delight in the mother's arms, that same body will become a joy and a delight to its owner later on.
>
> (English and Pearson, *Emotional Problems of Living*)

Parents know for themselves how a child can feel soothed by stroking, patting and cuddling in times of illness or distress. Yet massage expert Gerry Purves believes Western parent are particularly awkward when it comes to touching babies. The all-enclosing womb is replaced by functional contact and quick kisses. These are simply not enough to satisfy our need for physical closeness:

> Caring touch is important for an overall sense of mental well-being. Research has shown that people with heart conditions do better if they have tactile contact with even a pet. Babies starved of touch show extreme distress. Yet from the moment of our birth our quota of touch is reduced from the constant massage of the 'in utero' baby to the less frequent cuddles and nappy changing; from the occasional kiss of a grazed knee to

embarrassed adolescent encounters. Which leaves us with adult sex as our main source of touch, which, (contrary to public 'hype') I suspect leaves much to be desired in terms of simple loving touch.

(*Cahoots*, Summer 1988)

Fear of touch is evident even where small babies are concerned. Luckily the cure is simple – touch itself seems to be the antidote to our fearfulness. British mother Terri Fillary suffered postnatal depression after the birth of her first child. When Robert, her second, was born four months early, he seemed so fragile she was frightened to pick him up. But after he had spent five weeks in an incubator, the nursing team at London's Hammersmith Hospital advised her to hold the baby naked between her breasts.

'He looked a bit like an alien,' said Terri, of her 660g infant. 'I did not touch him; I was frightened to. If I am honest, I felt nothing for him but pity. I did not feel I had had a baby. Instead I felt as if I had lost something.' Skin-to-skin contact immediately transformed her emotions:

'It's lovely to feel him all snuggled up,' she said. 'He's really warm. I can just feel him breathing, his little chest rising and falling . . . Robert really feels like my baby now.'[3]

Fear of holding does not merely affect the individual parent, it has become institutionalized as a tenet of modern babycare. Hospital-based soap operas depict babies segregated in rows behind picture windows, which neither germs nor human hands can penetrate. Health professionals warn of the 'Danger of too much cuddling', a headline in the *Manchester Evening News*: 'Screaming babies may be getting too much love from doting parents' says 'leading North West child specialist' Dr Jay Jayachandra. 'Like adults, all babies are individuals who might just want to be left in peace and not constantly kissed or cuddled.'[4] Dr Jayachandra's view that babies' crying is a condition to be 'cured' is precisely opposed to the instinct and experience of the parent who soothes her baby with skin-to-skin contact. What we do know is that babies reared with a minimum of touching tend to become individuals who cannot stand to be touched. Of course, every baby is an individual, but no baby escapes the context of the all-embracing womb, or the legacy of expectation – which is to be held as much as his carers will allow.

Physical therapist Peter Walker has written many books on the art of natural parenting. He teaches parents how to delight their children with touch therapy, massage being the ancient art of 'rubbing better'. He believes touch has untold benefits for the new baby:

> Both the way in which parents hold and touch their children and the frequency with which they do it are known to have considerable effect on the child's general disposition. Observation has shown that children who are deprived of physical contact generally suffer more from anxiety and its related disorders. They are inclined to be clumsy in their physical relationships with their peers and, as adults, may find difficulty in responding to others. By contrast, more loving secure personalities are seen to emerge from families and cultures who touch and embrace one another frequently as an expression of their love and friendship.
>
> (*The Book of Baby Massage*)

Another researcher[5] has demonstrated that rubbing a baby's feet for five minutes every half hour or so reduces irregularities in the infant's breathing. Touch not only has a calming effect, it also plays an important role in maintaining the health of a young child.

A mother carrying her baby provides him with an all-over massage, coupled with the movement he so enjoys. When I went to interview psychotherapist Jean Liedloff to research this book, she had me jogging around her first-floor flat, dodging the potted plants and the cushions, with Frances bouncing along in my arms. This was the way she had seen the primitive Yequana people carrying their children.

'Hold her by one foot,' she said, 'she'll love it.' I tried not to display my fear as I dangled Frances first from her plump ankle, and then from her hand. There were peals of laughter – at last mum, she was saying – at last, you're holding me right.

'Never treat a baby as if he's delicate,' said Jean, 'or he'll grow up believing you.' Children in primitive tribes start carrying their baby brothers and sisters while they are only toddlers themselves. Nobody rushes in telling them to stop, and they do not let the babies fall.

By way of contrast, it is worth mentioning the practice of swaddling a baby, which was once common in many civilizations. Mothers in early eighteenth-century Britain bound their babies tightly and hung them out of the way:

> Its head was wrapped in 'compresses three, four, or five times doubled', pinned to a cap, and further braced by a tight neck stay. Swaddling was thought to prevent it distorting its supposedly fragile bones by kicking about too much. It also kept babies warm in a draughty age, and was a convenience. While the half-strangled baby hung from a nail, its minder could get on with other tasks. Swaddling slowed down a baby's heartbeat, and encouraged extreme passivity – more sleep, less crying; a swaddled baby made no demands on the adult world around it.
>
> (Hardyment, *Dream Babies*)

Many societies still bind their children today. The tradition is sustained in some hospitals, where new-born babies are wrapped tightly before being presented to their mothers. Nurses in the Eastern bloc handle swaddled new-borns like plates of meat in a restaurant, with the minimum of cuddling.

Swaddled babies are experiencing the close contact they desire, without the benefits of human touch. Societies that practise swaddling have recognized the infant's need for bonding, but they bind the child to itself rather than the mother. It is rather like our assumption earlier in this century, that bottle milk was as good for a baby as the breast, as though nutrition was all a baby received from suckling.

The value of rhythmical movement to a child has been known instinctively by parents throughout history. According to animal and human behaviourist Desmond Morris, if a baby needs comforting, the actions which are most effective are those which 'symbolically return it to the womb':

> In tribal societies, babies were held and carried a great deal of the time . . . Some parents have reverted to the ancient custom of carrying their babies around with them by the use of 'frontpacks' – little slings that support the baby on the adult chest and allow it to remain there, awake or asleep, as they walk about. The body rhythms these fortunate babies experience are primitively reassuring. Such infants are then more able to act in a bold, exploratory way, when the moment arises. They have been 'security-sated' and far from weakening them, this strengthens them and makes them ready for new and novel encounters.
>
> (*Babywatching*)

The Zinacantan baby of South America is rocked rhythmically by his mother's body as she grinds corn. The Nyansongo baby in Kenya bounces along on his mother's back when she goes on long trips. Babies born in traditional villages of Okinawa spend the day strapped to grandmother's or big sister's back while their mothers haul fire-wood or cultivate sweet potatoes. Mothers return frequently to suckle their babies, who are never left alone.

Rural people recognize the infant's need for touch, movement and rhythm and supply it in an infinite variety of ways. In the 1950s, scientists began tentatively to explore the usefulness of rocking, cuddling and holding a baby. Noticing, perhaps, that babies who were rarely carried 'in-arms' resorted to violent rocking or head-banging, they started to examine the value of rhythmic stimulation on babies and other infant animals.

For instance, one study[6] showed that when kittens were rocked, the movement increased their Rapid Eye Movement (REM) sleep.

Loss of REM sleep interferes with memory and the ability to learn.[7] Sleeping tablets reduce our quota of REM sleep.

Other tests have shown that mechanically-breathing teddy bears placed next to babies served to stabilize the infants' breathing patterns. The teddy bears were designed to provide a stimulus similar to the baby sleeping on his parent's chest. This discovery may have direct implications on aspects of Sudden Infant Death Syndrome, as I will explain later.

If teddy bears can be so helpful, imagine the greater rewards of sleeping next to a mother's skin. Babies' motor skills (their ability to co-ordinate themselves in their world) are also honed through body touch and holding.[8]

Another advantage of human contact is the heat exchange between adult and child. Paediatrician Dr Harvey Marcovitch explains why a baby needs special care at night:

> . . . while the average baby weighs 1/20th of an adult, his skin surface area is 1/9th of that of an adult, not 1/20th, so he has twice as much skin in proportion to his body size and loses heat much faster.
>
> (*Mother*, February 1988)

A mother often worries that her baby is not warm enough while he sleeps alone in his nursery. Studies now show that however well-wrapped a baby may be, his temperature can never be maintained as satisfactorily as when he has skin-to-skin contact with another human being. Dr James McKenna reports:

> Fardig (1980) found that for 17 mothers and babies, radiant-heated cribs could not maintain the mean skin and core temperature of human newborns placed on their mothers' bare chests for skin-to-skin contact, even when their ambient temperatures were equivalent.
>
> (*Medical Anthropology*, 1986)

One explanation for the loss of heat may be that a baby separated from its mother produces stress hormones, such as cortisol. These cause a drop in body temperature.

Even without the infant's physiological reaction, it is clear that 'a parent-infant huddle reduces the participants' surface-to-volume ratio and thus conserves energy'. (McKenna) Two people together are warmer than two people alone. Constant warmth helps to keep a baby asleep and breathing regularly.[9] It particularly promotes REM sleep.

Parents in pre-central-heating days had no problems regulating their babies' night-time temperatures – they simply slept with them. But the modern mother, following observations such as these from Dr Marcovitch, struggles to keep her baby warm at night:

> Indoors, babies under three months are happiest when the temperature is about 75°F (24°C) – above the usual setting for central heating . . . These figures are based on the assumption that your baby is in a draught-free room wearing a woollen vest, nappy and a long cotton nightdress or stretch suit covered with a flannelette sheet and two layers of cotton blanket.
>
> Keep your baby in the warmest room overnight and add extra blankets as well as mittens, socks and hat. Calculate that the baby needs two more covers than you yourself would want.
>
> (*Mother*, February 1988)

The arrival of the pram in Victorian Britain added the problem of preserving the baby's warmth in the daytime. Before this, mothers and nannies used to carry their children around – the 'perambulator' was thus a controversial invention. But the editor of *Baby* magazine was all in favour of it:

> Senex writes to the *British Medical Journal* protesting against the use of perambulators in cold weather, and maintaining that every child not old enough to walk should be carried in the

nurse's arms. I cannot agree with this . . . If a child is properly wrapped up and protected in the perambulator, there need be no more danger of cold than if it were carried. On very cold days a hot-water bottle may be placed under the infant's cushion, and in very cold or windy weather the little face should be covered with a thick, but not fluffy, veil.

(Ada Ballin, December 1887)

You can wrap up your baby all you like, but he is still going to drop in temperature, like a dinner taken out of the oven. Frances was a winter baby, but I did not have to worry about extra blankets and hot-water bottles in the pram. I used to go for walks with her tucked under my coat, on her sling. It seemed incredible, but by the time I returned home she was warmer than when we started out.

Whatever else killed British babies before this century, there was no need for them to suffer in the cold. In the Arctic, the Inuit traditionally slept naked next to their children in their igloos. They did not die of frost-bite. In fact, if hypothermia threatens, there is no better solution:

Experts have different opinions on the best way to treat a cold baby. If he has become cold rapidly then he can be safely rewarmed rapidly. The best place is probably next to his mother's skin under her clothes, and in a hot dry room.

(*Mother*, February 1988)

Actually modern babies, wrapped up in woolly layers with blankets and in centrally-heated rooms, are more likely to overheat than to freeze to death. A survey carried out in the north of England studied babies' bedding and clothing, and found that 'by night there was excess bedding, and many babies had too much, a few of them much too much.[10]

Overheating is a problem, as this is one factor related to Sudden Infant Death Syndrome. It is clearly not advisable for a baby to get too hot in the night. The baby on his mother's skin takes her temperature, and she his. If it gets too warm under the duvet, she will feel this herself, and respond by throwing off the cover. Sleeping with his mother, the baby remains at his ideal temperature.

The importance of sensory stimulation to the child may never be fully measured and appreciated. Natural birth pioneer Michel Odent proposes that the brain's thermostat for health is being set during the first few weeks of life, a suggestion which has been vindicated by subsequent research on premature babies.

> Eastern traditions knew that by stimulating the senses, energy was brought to the brain. Western science is now able to prove that this is so. It is as if the brain needs to be recharged like a battery . . . When you stroke a baby's skin it gives energy to the brain at an important stage in its development.
>
> (*Primal Health*)

We do not need to understand the technical reasons for a baby's love of touch in order to fulfil his quite obvious need. And the real beauty of touch-communication is that its benefits are reciprocal. Human contact has a soothing effect on the adult as well as on the child. If it is in the baby's interest to be held throughout infancy, then it makes sense for the pleasure to be mutual. Nature looks after those who serve her needs.

Paediatric nurse Joyce Russell says that, however, small or ill the newborn baby, some form of skin contact is essential 'if the infant's experiences are not to be entirely negative'. She backs up her case:

> Preterm infants are not only deprived of touch such as stroking in the earliest days of life, they are subjected to invasive procedures . . . To protect him or herself from such an environment, the neonate is likely to create a defensive shell . . .
>
> Staff working in intensive care of the newborn will recognise the infant who, after prolonged periods of invasive

procedures, seems no longer to respond but lies apparently indifferent to what is going on and frequently does not cry . . .

Research conducted at Bedford College, London, demonstrates scientifically how massage can help premature babies . . . those who were stroked put on weight faster and developed more quickly. Babies seem to enjoy being stroked and respond with purring and stretching, and this helps to establish strong bonds between mother and baby . . .

Research has also shown more recently that there are other valuable benefits to massage . . . it lessened pain by causing a rise in the production of endorphins . . . and by acting as a distraction technique.

(*Paediatric Nursing*, April 1993)

If, rather than separating mother and baby at night, professionals were to encourage the mutual benefits of contact, babycare would become a positive, uniting force. The nervous mother would be reassured by keeping physically in touch with her baby. Bonding, a topic which concerns many writers on childcare, would occur naturally and in its own good time. Parent and baby would be able to operate as one, supplying and enjoying each others' needs.

A report in *The Lancet* illustrates the value of body contact in providing security for a young child, and better bonding for the mother or other care-giver:

Two groups of women were given a baby carrier or a soft seat (bouncing cradle to be placed on the floor) when they left hospital with their newborn babies. The idea was to find out which group of babies seemed more content after just over a year: those who had spent quite a lot of time strapped to their mother's chest . . . or those who had been left to bounce gently in a seat . . .

The research, carried out in New York, showed that babies who spent more time close to their mothers were more content to be separated from her at 13 months; they cried and

whined less when with a stranger and behaved as if they were
more secure.

(Olivia Timbs, Early Days, January 1988)

So often we hear that babies need to be left alone to learn
independence. The opposite is true. Offer a child security, and he
will grow up to be more secure. Anthropologist Ashley Montagu
puts it this way:

> The infant needs to learn, on the firm foundation of closeness,
> what closeness, proximity, distance and openness mean . . .
>
> To remove the newborn baby from its mother and place it
> on its back or its front on a flat surface, often uncovered, is to
> fail to understand the newborn's great need for enfoldment, to
> be supported, rocked, and covered from all sides, and that the
> infant may only gradually be introduced to the world of more
> open spaces.
>
> (Touching – The Human Significance of the Skin)

He goes on to speculate on some possible long-term effects of
repeated separations of babies from other humans:

> We must ask ourselves here, whether in removing the
> newborn from his mother, as is customary in hospitals, and
> placing him in the open space of a bassinet or crib, we are not
> visiting a seriously disturbing trauma upon the baby, a trauma
> from which, perhaps, he never completely recovers? A trauma,
> moreover, which in the civilized world of the West, and those
> cultures that have been affected by the West's childbirth
> practices, is repeatedly inflicted upon the infant during the
> early years of his life. It may be that fear of open spaces
> (agoraphobia), or of heights (acrophobia), or of sudden drops,
> may have some connection with such early experiences. It may
> also be that a preference for having one's bedclothes about
> one's body rather than tucked in at the foot and sides of the

bed reflects a desire to recreate the conditions enjoyed in the womb, in reaction to the lack of body support experienced in infancy . . .

Montagu's conclusion?

. . . we shall have to consider giving children more tactile attention than they have hitherto received.

There is something magical about holding a baby. It has to do with the beauty of skin-to-skin warmth, the sweet smell of milk-fed breath, and the rare experience of sensuality and innocence wrapped together. Physical contact with a baby is all that it promises to be, because nothing is hidden. A baby lives and communicates through sensation.

It is true that not all babies seem to give themselves easily to our embraces. By the time they are a few months old, some struggle in their parents' arms and refuse to cuddle.

Many parents put this down to temperament, although we often forget that it is almost impossible to distinguish temperament from experience where babies are concerned. What we do know is that babies are accustomed to the rhythm and all-enclosing contact of the womb; most babies are born without defences, body armouring or stiffness; and every baby 'expects' to be carried – at least in the evolutionary sense of the term. Resistance to being held is best learnt during periods of non-holding. However, it might be the way we hold our babies which matters most, as this Western mother suggests:

I lived for three years with the Lobi people of West Africa. West African babies are carried basically until they are weaned; they are generally calmer, cry less and squirm less than American babies . . . My first child was born in Africa. He, too, was carried much of his first year, passed around and held constantly, and not allowed to cry if possible. Our pace of life was slow and calm. He was healthy and grew well. But he was just as jumpy as other American babies, and other American babies there had the same experience.

My conclusion from this is that culture forms our most basic being in ways that we do not understand, and we can almost never separate ourselves from it . . . Many other elements play into the calmness of African children. One is a community consensus about the role and function of children in society . . . Also, Lobi adults are much less worried and nervous than Americans tend to be . . . I don't believe we can say that what is true in one culture will translate easily into our own, much as we might wish it.

('Do We Idolize the Tribe?',
Sherri B. Shanes, *Mothering*, Summer 1989)

The imperfections of our body usage, our upbringing and our social support group may be some of the reasons why we find it hard to get truly in touch with our babies. Try as we might, our infants sometimes seem to resist us, they become colicky in the evenings – perhaps they resist the comfort of the family bed. However, the bonding lesson is learnt by degrees. The often-held child quickly gets used to the care he is given, and his body becomes softer and more pliant for the experience. The aim, in the end, is not to emulate the rural tribes of distant continents, but to increase the two-way flow of pleasure between ourselves and our children. Holding should not be forced, but an available part of our physical vocabulary with our babies from the beginning. Franz Wagner, a Professor of Medical Sociology at the Johannes Kepler University in Austria, reminds us how quickly children respond to physical therapy:

Therapy often has unexpectedly swift results with child patients. Their young bodies are highly receptive to therapeutic stimuli . . . It is also comparatively easy to treat inherited complaints in children, who show a swifter response than their parents!

(*Reflex Zone Massage*)

Parents who hold their babies from birth find it increasingly easy to do. Outsiders look aghast and say 'Isn't he heavy?', and indeed he is, if you only transport him from the pushchair to the baby bouncer and from the bathroom to the nursery. If you carry a baby constantly, your arms accustom themselves to the weight as it increases imperceptibly over the months. Frances felt lighter to me at eight months, than she did at eight days old. She was carried a lot, but Alice, my second daughter, was carried constantly. Within a few weeks, I hardly knew she was there. The older she got, the easier she became, until, suddenly, she crawled off in the 'bold, exploratory way' described by Desmond Morris. A physiotherapist warned me Alice might be seriously delayed in walking, since she did not have the chance to lie on her back and kick her legs. In fact, after a very brief crawling phase, she took her first steps at eight months old.

In this, Alice resembled Bali children who are not allowed to touch the ground before they are six months old. Balinese babies are considered divine and are either carried in-arms or wrapped in a cloth, sleeping on their mother's arm at night. At six months, they undergo an elaborate ceremony when they touch the earth for the first time and are then considered part of the earthly realm.

The crawling stage is even considered impure in Bali culture and discouraged by parents, so children quickly learn to walk if they want to move around. Maya babies in Yucatán also 'skip the crawling stage' according to anthropologist Brigitte Jordan:

> Babies have almost continuous body contact from the time of birth, at first and for the most part with their mothers, but as time progresses, also with other members of the family. A baby is not put down unless it is asleep, at which point it might be laid into a hammock . . . Yucatecan matrimonial hammocks stretch out to a width of eight feet and are designed to sleep several people. The term 'matrimonial' is actually a misnomer. Husband and wife do not normally sleep together at night; rather each one has one or more small children in the hammock with her or him . . .

> In the hammock the baby will be lying on its back or side
> . . . Yucatecan babies never experience lying prone on a flat
> surface (such as a mattress or floor). Perhaps that is why
> Yucatecan babies skip the crawling stage. Before they are able
> to walk, they locomote instead, by scooting in a sitting
> position, using one leg to push themselves along while tucking
> the other one underneath.
>
> (*Birth in Four Cultures*)

Alice crawled for around a month before standing, rather spectacu-
larly and without any support, in a doctor's waiting room while
awaiting her seven-month hearing check. Not long afterwards, she
learnt how to stamp her little foot to assert herself, while balancing
easily on the other. She has always been very 'grounded'. It turned
out that she did not need to 'practise' kicking at all.

People who have not held a child in this way, and who have not
seen it done, tend not to believe it. We tend to imagine that babies, if
carried, are literally a burden, as in this cautionary tale from the States:

> In America recently, a class of schoolgirls were told to carry a
> 5lb bag of flour around with them for a whole week and
> pretend it was a baby. They had to get up in the night to
> 'feed' it and spend each day 'changing' it and caring for it. The
> result: the local pregnancy rate dropped dramatically as the girls
> realised the responsibility.
>
> (*Davina Lloyd, Practical Parenting*, July 1988)

It's a pity babies aren't bags of flour, or our children could be self-raised.
It may be useful for a class of teenagers to realize that babies need a lot of
looking after – but five pounds of flour will always weigh five pounds;
unresponsive and inert in your arms. A real baby bouncing along in
your arms is soft and giving, warm and life-lending.

It is sad that so many people are frightened of holding babies. Once
again, this is merely a problem of experience and conditioning. We
grow up hearing that infants are precious things. People warn us that

we will drop them, so we approach babies with fear and caution. It is a vicious circle, for the baby also learns to be shy of contact with members of his own species.

One way to breake the circle is to sleep alongside a new baby. At night physical closeness is preserved with baby and adult cuddling up together. He sleeps easily, secure in the presence of his mother or other guardian, stirring to feed, waking for a second or two and then slumbering on. Bodily contact with a child allows parents to become more at ease with themselves.

How can it possibly be that carrying a baby around actually makes things easier for the already exhausted parent? We are trained to believe that we should put our infants down at every opportunity, with excuses about their needing to cry things out, kick their legs, exercise their lungs, learn independence and so on. As we have seen, the solitary baby does undergo a range of physiological changes – to his metabolic rate, his hormones, enzyme production, temperature, heartbeat, breathing and sleep patterns.[11]

However, it is hard to prove that these changes are, any of them, actually good for human infants. Aletha Jauch Solter believes that while babies do need to discharge their energies through crying, they can only properly do this when being held:

> Babies need the loving and delighted attention of others in order to discharge effectively. During crying episodes babies should be neither distracted nor ignored, but listened to and held lovingly. Babies can be trusted to do exactly what they need to do. They should therefore be allowed to cry as loudly and as long as they need. This is quite different from 'letting babies cry it out,' because that approach advocates ignoring babies when they cry.
>
> (*The Aware Baby*)

Similarly, Jean Liedloff noticed how, snug in his continuum, the Yequana baby discharged his energy through the motions of those who carried him:

In the infant kept in constant contact with the body of a caretaker, his energy field becomes one with hers and excess energy can be discharged for both of them by her activities alone. The infant can remain relaxed, free of accumulated tension, as his extra energy flows into hers . . .

Yequana babies are soft and easy to handle, unresistant to being held or carried in any convenient position. Our infants, on the other hand, kick their legs out straight, wave their arms violently and stiffen their backs into strained arches . . . They often emit piercing screams when excited by the attention of some person, as well as squirming. Although they are expressing pleasure, the stimulus causes a violent muscular reaction that expends some of the pent-up energy.

(*The Continuum Concept*)

A baby lying alone for a short period does not necessarily kick his legs in frustration, scream or become stiff and unyielding. The key is to watch the child; to sense when he is enjoying his own company; notice his pleasure when he sees his hand free-float before his eyes, or his feet push gently against something new. However, compare this with the stiff, jerking movements of a baby seeking human contact, and you may see that his 'exercises' are not giving him any joy. A frustrated baby moves with tense energy, like a bed-bound adult or someone who works at a desk all day. He is not taking genuine exercise, but winding himself up into a frenzy. So when the mother picks her child up again, he is stiffer, colder and less at ease than when he was being held. For the short time she carries him now, his equilibrium is being restored. His breathing calms, he begins to relax. Bonded together, they make up one energy unit, the adult working off the excess energies of the child.

If parents deny themselves the rejuvenating benefits of contact with their baby the times when they do pick him up are a tremendous effort. It's like starting a car over again, rather than keeping the engine running.

Physical contact with our children is a vastly underestimated benefit of being a parent. Peter Tinniswood captured the tonic effect of babies superbly in his comic novel, *A Touch of Daniel*. Daniel is the new baby in the Brandon household. Every day, he is taken to see the two old men who live in the attic at the top of the house, and gives them a kiss. Miraculously, the ailing old fellows being to radiate good health:

'The funny thing is that they seem to perk up every time I take Daniel to see them,' said Carter Brandon to Pat one evening in the first week of January.

'What's so funny about that?' said Pat. 'I mean to say, the sight of a bonny bouncing baby always acts as a tonic to old folk, doesn't it?'

'Aye, but it's something more than that.'

'What?'

'When Daniel touches them, you can see a sort of red glow comes over their faces.'

'That's happiness.'

'Is it?'

'Like the red glow that comes over me when you kiss me, luv,' said Pat, wrapping her arms around his neck and kissing him on the lips.'

The invalid Corporal Parkinson goes on to grow new hair, teeth and a pair of legs, while his companion Uncle Stavely slips the grip of senility to enjoy a fling with the resident nanny. If that's what a daily kiss can do, think of the benefits of being cuddled up with a baby all night. No wonder politicians and old people love babies.

A Touch of Daniel strikes home, because babies are like that. They do transform our lives. Either we resist them, and leave them to kick alone – or we allow ourselves to be touched by their magic.

To sleep with your baby next to you is – as many parents agree – a most wonderful and uplifting feeling. It may also offset the effects of postnatal depression (PND), a reaction so common in the West that it is considered physiologically 'normal' to suffer from Baby Blues. Zinc supplements and better social support may help to alleviate PND, but no one has yet considered the nocturnal separation of mother and baby as a possible trigger for maternal depression.

Mothers suffering from severe Baby Blues are often advised to get away from the baby for a while, and hand him over to someone else. While this may be necessary in emergencies, it is a strategy which decreases the mother's feelings of confidence with the baby. Taking the baby away, at a time when the mother is hormonally-programmed to be with him as part of the natural bonding process, adds to the pain and anticlimax that so many women feel after giving birth.

Could it be that Western women, high on hormones and alive with instincts, are depressed because they are unfulfilled? So many mothers, sitting up in hospital with the baby sleeping in a cot at the end of the bed, feel that something, somehow, is wrong. 'Depressed?' said Brigid McConville. 'It's only "normal" . . .':

. . . at least one school of thought believes that three–quarters of all women in Britain and in America suffer either depression or acute anxiety after childbirth.

(*Mad to be a Mother*)

Brigid McConville analyses the social pressures behind long–term maternal depression. Dietary and environmental factors also play a large part in the stresses from which Western mothers suffer. But perhaps there is a biological factor, too. If so, the remedy might include a skin-to-skin contact programme, sleeping with baby at night, napping with him in the afternoons and carrying him around in a well-made sling during the day.

Anyone who imagines that having a baby in the bed would be too disruptive should compare the average disturbance caused by a child in the next room with that of a baby in the bed. All babies are prone to night waking, whether or not their parents are aware of it.[12] A baby may stir and resettle many times in the night. But people need to be awake for at least fifteen seconds to realize that they have been disturbed.[13] Neither parent nor child need be bothered by the minimal movements and shifts that the other makes in the night.

97

NORTHFIELD PUBLIC LIBRARY
210 Washington Street
Northfield, MN 55057

Babies are prone to wake more often than adults, as their average sleep cycle (through stages one to four, REM sleep and back again) takes only fifty minutes, compared with a ninety-minute cycle for the mature sleeper.[14]

Every time a person reaches the lightest stage of sleep, he is liable to wake, and may be roused by a light stimulus, or unfavourable conditions. For an infant, such conditions might include hunger, a drop in temperature, or the release of stress hormones because his care-givers are not around.

Few mothers realize that when breastfeeding they do not enter the fourth, or deepest, phase of sleep.[15] This phenomenon is governed by hormonal changes during pregnancy. Whether or not the baby is with her, she will be more prone to disturbance than before. With mother and baby both sleeping so lightly, separating them at night is a recipe for frequent disruption.

The infant may wake during any one of the light-sleep periods during the night. He stirs, and if he does not find the comforter he expects, or the company he craves, he may cry. With every second that passes, he becomes more fully awake. The breastfeeding mother will be woken instantly, tuned in, as she is, to her baby's cries. She is destined for many disturbed nights until the baby has been 'trained' to sleep through in his own cot.

If the parents are in deep sleep (if, perhaps, the baby is bottle-fed), they may take minutes to wake up, and even longer to listen out and decide whether or not to respond to his cry. By the time the parent gets to the nursery, he or she is fully roused (and irritated), while the baby is in complete anguish. No chance for everyone to turn over and doze off to sleep again.

I was once woken in the night by the sound of the doorbell ringing at five in the morning. I dragged myself up to answer it, and when I got back to bed found I was fully awake. Frances, then six months old, had never woken me to that extent, and to my annoyance it took me more than half an hour to get off to sleep again.

Many Western parents experience that degree of disturbance – and much, much worse – for months on end. No wonder they are desperate to persuade their cot-bound children to sleep through the night.

This, by way of comparison, is the night-time pattern of a Yequana baby sleeping with its mother, as described by Jean Liedloff:

> If there is a party while he is asleep, he will be bounced about quite violently while his mother hops and stamps in time to the music. Through daytime sleep, similar adventures befall him. At night his mother sleeps beside him, her skin next to his, as always, while she breathes and moves and sometimes snores a little. She wakes often during the night to tend the fire, holding him close as she rolls out of her hammock and slips to the floor, where he is sandwiched between her thighs and ribs as she rearranges the logs. If he awakens hungry in the night he signals with a soft grunt if he cannot find her breast; she will then give it to him, and again his well-being will be re-established . . .
>
> (*The Continuum Concept*)

When you sleep with a small child, it feels easier to be a parent. You are literally in touch with the infant, not at odds with him. The level of satisfaction and contentment rises, and capability increases, along with a sense of doing the 'right' thing. For both parents, there is an increased tenderness which brings them closer to their child.

As Janine Sternberg, a child psychotherapist with three children, described it, 'We slept with our youngest, Sarah, from the first night. My husband Mike was happy about it in terms of all the pleasures of having a baby in the bed, you know how they smell nice and they feel soft . . . Having the baby there is a tangible expression of our love.' It also gives you a good night's sleep.

The experience of sleeping with a new-born child is strangely comparable with keeping vigil at the bedside of someone who is dying. Rather than easing someone out of life, as many are prepared to do, you are holding the hand of someone slipping into it.

Interestingly the Trobrianders, a tribal people of Papua New Guinea, connect the concepts of birth and death in their language:

> Kopoi, the word used when villagers sit and care for a dead person before burial, also means 'to feed' or 'to nurse an infant'. A woman nurses (kopoi) her baby for about a year and a half.
> (Annette E. Weiner, *The Trobrianders of Papua New Guinea*)

Birth and death are events that require the support of those who care for us. They are the most vulnerable periods of our lives, and no caring society leaves an individual alone at the beginning or at the end of his time. The adult who shares a bed with a child is giving the proper tenderness for someone newly-born, comparable with the experience of this nurse:

> Something happens to you when you're with patients you feel a lot for. I think it's like a wave of gentleness or tenderness. It sweeps over you when you care. I suppose I show it in my voice and hands. I know that inside I feel warm and soft, I'm sure I do something to express that feeling.
> (Davitz and Davitz, *American Journal of Nursing*, 1975)

Carrying a baby, sleeping with a baby and answering its needs, are all in themselves the rewards of mothering. Keep in touch with a child, and his capacity for calm and physical ease enters your body, too. There is less parenting to do, and more time for getting on with other things when the baby comes too.

But social pressure to put baby in a cot is so strong, that parents may not admit that they allow their baby into bed. Many go to great lengths to keep a distance between themselves and their children – even when their instincts prompt them to do otherwise.

Jane Asher, the actress and author, says, 'It's a lovely feeling to have a warm snuggly baby next to you in bed to cuddle,' adding that she has 'no doubt that having the baby next to you is the natural way'. But eventually her baby Alexander was destined to sleep alone:

I have had to put the crib over the other side of the bedroom so that I am forced to get out of bed each time he wakes – by the time I reach him I am just about fully awake and strong minded enough not to take him back into bed.

(Silent Nights)

Parents prefer to be woken up in the night, rather than be weak-willed about sharing their bed with a baby. Ms Asher's strategy was – incredibly – an attempt to secure 'a certain amount of uninterrupted sleep at night'. No wonder *Mother* magazine carried an article in 1986 about the 'Bedroom Farce' of getting children off to sleep. As one mother wrote:

How cheering to know that I'm not alone in being reduced to ridiculous nightly contortions to escape my reluctantly sleeping child's bedroom.

Of course, we could just close the door and let them play or sob themselves to sleep. But how would we fill our evenings?

(Amanda Ferguson, Cardiff, September 1987)

The cunning we employ to trick our children into dreamland makes a nonsense of our genuine concern for their well-being. We tell ourselves it is vital they get their sleep – but it is apparently more important that they get it on our terms. If we could abandon the social stigma of bedsharing, then we could stop playing these games. Children learn from the beginning that their parents are attempting to lull them into a false sense of security every night.

In our consumer-based society, there are many tempting ways of dealing with our children's needs for tactile stimulation and nocturnal security. Manufacturers mass-produce the cot and they even supply accoutrements to take the place of the mother, who can hardly crawl between the bars to soothe her infant.

Many products are designed specifically as night comforters. Baby sheepskin rugs, warm and cosy, can help the baby to settle. Baby bouncers simulate the wonderful feeling of being jogged around in mother's arms. Baby alarms monitor the infant's breathing while parents are at the other end of the house.

But these products don't really do the trick. No teddy bear or cot-jiggler yet invented can simulate all the benefits of a mother's body. According to Dr McKenna, 'mothers' biorhythms physiologically regulate their offspring both prenatally and postnatally'. Babies need their mothers, not machines.

Some of the devices on the market are quite ludicrous. This is what Jane Asher had to say about her two-way baby alarm:

> Some of them have a talk-back switch so that you can comfort the baby by the sound of your voice, but the only time I ever tried to use one Katie nearly leapt out of the cot with shock. I suppose your mother's voice suddenly booming out from a little box must seem a bit strange.
>
> (*Silent Nights*)

Other inventions, equally crude, prove the infant's desperate need for company at night. Nurseries have discovered that a mother's heartbeat, played over a loudspeaker in a hospital nursery, soothes the crying infants. American mothers can buy machines to simulate the noise and movement of a car – well known for its somniferous effects – presumably to save the bother of driving baby round the block.

Hospitals, hooked on new gadgetry, are also experimenting with electronically controlled rocking cots, to soothe colicky babies and premature infants. I talked to Cradlecraft, a company which manufactures a variety of these cribs, for use at home and in hospital. Their automatic crib saves the parent even the trouble of seeing the baby off to sleep. Based on the 'pendulum principle', Cradlecraft's machine will rock the most fretful of babies to contented rest, they say. Salesman Tony Urry told me that paediatricians also believe the invention aids premature babies in tissue accretion.

If an automatic machine can stimulate growth in small babies, think what benefits a premature infant would gain by being kept close to his mother, day and night.

All babies need and expect the kind of contact and comfort that will satisfy them for the rest of their days. If a child has his fill of parental care – even if it does not come from his actual parents – he will be more likely to enter adulthood without hang-ups and neuroses. He will be less hooked on money, or drugs, or the many other objects that promise to bring him happiness but never do. He will know that peace of mind comes from within himself, not from external sources.

Psychologist John Bowlby was concerned with the deprivation of institutionalized children when, in 1953, he wrote *Child Care and the Growth of Love*. His words apply with increasing urgency today, as more and more mothers seek to put distance and comfort-giving objects between themselves and their babies:

> It is exactly the kind of care which a mother gives without thinking that *is* the care which they have lacked. All the cuddling and playing, the intimacies of his mother's body, the rituals of washing and dressing by which through her pride and tenderness towards his little limbs he learns the value of his own, all these have been lacking. His mother's love and pleasure in him are his spiritual nourishment . . .
>
> It is only when nature's gifts are lacking that science must study what they are in order to make the best shift it can to replace them.

Babies need the soft touch of humans in order to thrive. The life-long benefits of sharing the parental bed are beautifully put in this passage by American novelist William Wharton:

> Ben is stretched out, overlapping his cot by the fire, arms hanging over the sides. He sleeps deeply, calmly, no tossing, no teeth grinding, no startled nightmares, no thumb or finger sucking. We like to think it's because we never let him cry

himself to sleep, never left him alone in the dark when he wanted to be with us. Until he was seven, he spent at least half of each night in our bed, usually cuddling with me. I didn't mind, I liked it; I don't think sleeping alone is natural. With our first three we were young and foolish enough, vulnerable to rigid conditioning theories then prevalent, to insist they stay in their own beds, so now each is an erratic sleeper. I myself only became capable of deep, full, refreshing sleep when I was about forty. I can't always manage it, now, even with meditation or Valium, but then things have been hard lately.

(Tidings)

Valium is one of the comforters of our adulthood. Jim Horne, director of Loughborough's Sleep Research Laboratory, describes the placebo effect of hypnotic drugs for people who need a psychological support before they can sleep. A well-chewed blanket contains as much medication as these tablets:

All that many sufferers require . . . is some form of guarantee that they will have a good night's sleep. Taking the tablet each night sees to that, even though it may not be required. In this respect, the best sleeping tablet may be the one that is never taken but placed by the bedside. Knowing that it is there, ready for use just in case, can be very reassuring.

(The Practitioner, October 1985)

Perhaps if we gave more true comfort to our children – the joy of touch, the security of contact at night – then we would begin to satisfy the ancient desires which motivate us all our lives. A child wants nothing but complete acceptance from his parents. When he has had his fill of that, he will move on to other things.

5 | WILL IT BE ALL RIGHT IN THE NIGHT?

It is not uncommon that a baby is found dead in a room away from its parents. In the animal world separating the young from the mother for long periods until weaning has been established is the exception: it is *Homo Sapiens* in western society that provides this exception . . .

(Davies and Gantley, *Archives of Disease in Childhood*, 1994)

Medicine is keeping more babies alive than ever before. A child may be born months before his time, survive a difficult birth, shrug off jaundice, and battle successfully with an infection which a few years ago would have killed him. Improved sanitation and knowledge about nutrition ensure that high infant mortality is no longer a problem in developed countries. But there is still a killer that claims up to 500 children a year under the age of two in the United Kingdom and many hundreds more in industrialized countries from America to Australia, Scandinavia to Canada.[1] And we don't even know what it is.

Many thousands of pounds are channelled into studying the possible reasons for the Sudden Infant Death Syndrome. SIDS, also known as 'cot death', is slightly more likely to affect boys than girls. Ninety per cent of the babies die before they reach the age of nine months.

Stories of how an otherwise healthy infant suddenly stops breathing, often unnoticed in his cot or pram, add to the fears of new parents. This account in a monthly magazine is typical of the cot death experience. Laura was just three and a half months old:

The night before she died was much as usual. Early in the
morning, at around 4.30, she woke for a cuddle, then
Jacqueline put her straight back in her cot which was by the
side of our bed.

At 7 we woke up, and immediately wondered why our
'little alarm clock' hadn't gone off at her normal time of 6.30.
One look and we knew: she was cold and lifeless. I called the
ambulance and tried to resuscitate her but it was too late. She
had been dead for over an hour and there was no hope.

We couldn't believe it was happening to us. We felt angry,
guilty, confused . . . why, why, why? If we'd been awake,
perhaps she wouldn't have died.

(*Practical Parenting*, June 1988)

Guilt and confusion are typical reactions to a death which has no
satisfactory explanation. In the experience of child psychotherapist
Dilys Daws, many parents with healthy children dwell on the subject
to the detriment of their own happiness and that of the family. A
mother's fears may in themselves cause infant sleep difficulties:

With sleep problems it seems to me often that what I am
doing for the mother is directly containing her anxiety so that
she can go back to the baby and contain the baby's anxiety.
There is often some real external cause for anxiety in the
mother: difficulties in the birth or early weeks that she has not
recovered from and not properly absorbed. Mothers worry that
their baby may die in the night and this kind of fear is based
on reality. Everyone has heard, or read in the newspapers, of
such tragic events.

(*Journal of Child Psychotherapy*, 1985)

A mother's fears for her child can grow to horrendous proportions in
the night, when the baby is tucked into a cot in the next room, and
she is sleeping her light, maternal sleep in the big double bed.

There is a telling scene at the beginning of the film *Terms of*

Endearment, when the young mother, played by Shirley Maclaine, tiptoes into the nursery, panicking that her baby is not breathing. She pokes her small, sleeping daughter until she cries. Now the mother is happy. As long as she can hear the screams, she knows her baby is alive.

With all this panic and such little understanding of cot death, it might seem that a nightly vigil is the parents' only option. Apnoea alarms (breathing monitors) are now on sale, claiming to detect when a baby stops breathing in the cot – but the Foundation for the Study of Infant Deaths warns against these expensive items. Manufacturers, say the FSID, make exaggerated claims of success. Undoubtedly the most dramatic advance has been the government's Back To Sleep campaign, inspired by research from the Institute of Child Health in Bristol which demonstrated that babies who were laid face down in their cots were more likely to die from SIDS. The FSID has produced leaflets showing parents how to 'Reduce the Risk of Cot Death', which covers factors such as smoking, overheating and placing a baby on its back to sleep.

During the 1990s, SIDS reduction campaigns took place in countries as diverse as America, Canada, Britain, New Zealand, Norway, Denmark, Sweden, Ireland and France. Without exception, they helped to reduce dramatically the numbers of babies dying. However, the downward trend did not continue indefinitely. In 1995 and 1996, the rate of sudden infant deaths per 1,000 births in Britain steadied at 0.61 and 0.65 respectively. In 1998, it became obvious that unexplained baby deaths were increasing in some parts of the British Isles. The SIDS rate in the Irish Republic rose by seventy per cent in one year. 'We await the new UK figures with apprehension,' said Joyce Epstein, secretary of the Foundation for the Study of Infant Deaths. 'We are concerned parents are still not getting or following the "reduce the risk" message. But we also know that the message isn't the whole answer. Something else is happening; babies are still dying and we need research to find out why.'[2]

The message to parents had been consistent since the early 1990s –

lay baby on his back to sleep; do not smoke around the baby; place him in a feet-to-foot position at the bottom of the cot with sheets or blankets rather than a cot duvet or quilt; do not let baby become overheated and do not cover his head for sleep. From the results of extensive annual reports by CESDE, the British Confidential Enquiry into Stillbirths and Deaths in Infancy, it became clear that prone (face down) sleeping and parental smoking were the main culprits in many cases of infant death.

Health experts were chastened. For more than forty years they had instructed mothers to lay babies prone to sleep. At some time during the 1940s or 1950s, Western babies began universally to be placed on their stomachs in what appeared to be a reasonable imitation of the adult recovery position. The practice was even recommended by Dr Spock, who had previously advised against it: 'I think it is preferable to accustom a baby to sleeping on his stomach from the start if he is willing,' he wrote.

Perhaps there had been something, after all, in the wisdom of a 1729 publication entitled *The Nurse's Guide, or, the Right Method of Bringing Up Young Children* (author unknown). Here was its advice on infant sleep position:

> . . . so long as a Child takes no other nourishment but milk, 'tis better he should be laid to sleep on his back, than either of his sides. For the back is, like the keel of a ship, the basis and foundation of the whole body, upon which the child may therefore rest with safety and ease. But if he be laid on either of his sides, there is danger that his rib-bones, which are as yet very soft and tender, and which are fastened by very short ligaments, may give way, and bend inward, under the weight of the whole body . . .

The CESDI reports also confirmed that back-lying was preferable to side-lying, with the risk of baby rolling over on to his front. But what the statistics could not explain – what no one could explain – was the mechanism for sudden infant death. In the end, the only message the

FSID could offer bereaved parents was the one it had been offering for many years – condolence and reassurance:

> Babies die unexpectedly for many reasons. In some cases the cause is evident at post mortem; but in many others, in whom earlier signs of illness had been absent or trivial, the cause of death is not found . . . the tragedy is world-wide.
>
> (*Support for Parents Bereaved by an Unexpected Infant Death*, September 1983)

Worldwide, perhaps, but not universal. Babies continue to die unexpectedly without cause in many parts of the world. But it appears that children in some societies are far less likely to die from the syndrome than others. Recent studies indicate that SIDS is rare in some countries and among certain ethnic groups. It did not escape the notice of SIDS researchers that these ethnic groups had a vastly different approach to infant sleep. Very broadly speaking, in countries where babies routinely sleep with their parents for the first few years of life, there is usually a very low rate of SIDS. In fact, examples of sudden, unexplained infant death were so rare they did not even warrant a name, let alone an entire syndrome.

French birth pioneer Michel Odent, travelling in China in 1977, asked medical professionals about the phenomenon of cot death. No one knew what he was talking about. Later, in correspondence with *The Lancet*, Dr Odent reported his findings. Even translators, the most Westernized of his hosts, did not recognize his description of a young baby dying suddenly for no apparent reason:

> Nobody understood my questions; the concept of sudden infant death or cot death was apparently unknown among professionals and lay people in such different places as Peking, Hsian, Loyang, Nanking, Shanghai, and Canton. Furthermore I learned that Chinese babies sleep with their mothers, even in the most westernized families, such as the families of interpreters. Ever since then I have held the view that, even if

it happens during the day, cot death is a disease of babies who spend their nights in an atmosphere of loneliness and that cot death is a disease of societies where the nuclear family has taken over.

(The Lancet, 25 January 1986)

Isolation is only possible where people have space and rooms enough to put babies in. In a high-density city such as Hong Kong, where families are crowded into high-rise apartments, infants are rarely alone. Professor D.P. Davies, a paediatrician working in the Prince of Wales Hospital in Hong Kong, is the author of a study demonstrating that cot death is rare among the Chinese community there. He reports:

> Over the 5 years 1980–84 only 15 cases of cot death were documented by forensic pathologists – an approximate incidence of 0.036 per 1000 live births. If the incidence was similar to that in western countries (2–3 per 1000), 800–1200 cot deaths might have been expected over this period.
>
> (The Lancet, 14 December 1985)

Of those fifteen cases, eleven were ethnic Chinese babies, three were British and one Japanese – a higher proportion of Western babies than would be expected from the racial mix on the island (ninety per cent are ethnic Chinese).

The most obvious explanation for the low incidence of SIDS might be that such deaths go unrecorded. Dr Davies does not believe this to be the case. He says that cot death is genuinely rare on the island:

> . . . in this small territory with one of the highest population densities anywhere in the world, where closely knit extended families are common, illegal disposal of a dead body is well nigh impossible, and the system of collecting mortality data is highly efficient . . .

111

The findings are surprising because most babies in Hong Kong are bottle-fed, humidity is high and many children suffer from respiratory illness – factors often considered by SIDS researchers. Professor Davies later turned his attention to the Bangladeshi community living in Cardiff, South Wales, and found that, despite overcrowding, over-heated housing and young mothers with many children, Bangladeshi babies were half as likely to die from SIDS as the average Welsh baby.

It is worth comparing Professor Davies's conclusions from Wales with his earlier speculations from Hong Kong. In 1985, he wrote:

Reflecting further on the living conditions in Hong Kong, I wonder whether there might be some benefit to such high-density living. Babies were left alone much less. Sleep patterns might be different, effecting subtle modulations to physiological responses concerned with ventilatory control. The question 'When can I put baby into his own room?' is virtually never raised. Might closer overall contact with the sleeping baby somehow lessen the risks of sudden death?

In 1993, in his report from the Department of Child Health at the University of Wales, Davies wrote:

Bangladeshi babies are thought to be vulnerable, and they sleep close to other people both day and night; at night they are either in the mother's bed or in a cot next to it . . . It is not simply a question of space, but of a belief that, as one mother put it, 'I like to wake up in the night and see all my family around me.'

He concluded, 'Long periods of lone quiet sleep may be one factor that contributes to a higher rate of sudden deaths in white than in Asian infants.'[3] Robert Tseng, a paediatrician who has worked both in Britain and Hong Kong, is convinced that something in the Chinese lifestyle makes cot death a rare occurrence. Dr Tseng draws a vivid picture of the nightmare of trying to save a dying baby:

An infant who has died suddenly and is brought to a casualty department's resuscitation room with its parents is an experience not easily forgotten. I can recall six such episodes over nine months spent as a paediatric senior house officer at a district hospital in Kingston-on-Thames, UK. Over the past 18 months, at a district general hospital in Hong Kong with on-call duties for paediatric resuscitation in the casualty department, I have not once had this traumatic experience . . .

Perhaps there is a holistic answer to the question 'What causes cot death?' which will not readily be found by a vast volume of research in isolated disciplines of medicine or isolated parts of infants who die of cot death. I echo Dr Odent's view that cot death is largely a disease of societies with certain child rearing cultural practices . . . A closer look into these cultural differences with an open mind might provide better clues.

(The Lancet, 1 March 1986)

In the late 1980s medical anthropologist James McKenna of Pomona College, Claremont, led research into the holistic answer to SIDS. He reported that rates of cot death in non-industrialized countries were notoriously difficult to obtain. Many of these countries do not carry out a thorough post-mortem on infants, or do not record a diagnosis of sudden, unexpected and unexplained death.

Comparisons of urban societies that have standardized their reporting and diagnosis of SIDS are better, but even these can be difficult. For example, SIDS rates are lower in Sweden, the Netherlands, Switzerland, and Israel, where in some segments of society, infants sleep with their parents or in the same room. Moreover, the infant mortality rates in general (rather than just for SIDS) are extremely low in Japan, an urban country in which cosleeping occurs . . .

(Medical Anthropology, 1986)

113

Subsequent studies of ethnic sleep arrangements have tended to concentrate on migrant groups – for instance Bangladeshis in Wales, Africans in America and Asians in England. These have produced some fascinating findings. Where the cultural norm is for babies to be carried in the day and held in the night, SIDS rates are usually low. In Yorkshire, for instance, a twenty-two-month study ending in 1993 demonstrated that babies in the white community were more than three times more likely to die of SIDS than babies in Pakistani families (1.48 per 1,000 live births, compared with 0.46/1,000.)[4]

But this is not the whole story. Further analysis of statistics has shown that *the longer a low-SIDS culture group has lived in the West, the more cot deaths it is likely to experience.* In 1990, researchers considering Chinese, Japanese, Vietnamese and Filipino families in California found that the longer they lived in America, the greater the risk of SIDS.[5] In Birmingham, England, where white babies were at twice the risk of Asian (Indian, Pakistani and Bangladeshi) babies, it was shown that the longer a mother had lived in England, the more likely she was to place her baby prone, or Western-style.[6] Asian mothers were extremely likely to keep their babies in their bedroom for the first year (ninety-four per cent, compared with sixty-one per cent of white mothers) and were also more likely to co-sleep (thirty-six per cent, compared with eleven per cent of whites). In his discussion paper, Sadaf Farooqi of the University Department of Medicine, Dudley Road Hospital in Birmingham, concluded sadly:

> . . . we documented the increasing use of the prone position by Asian mothers born in the UK and those who have lived in the country for longer periods of time. This suggests that better understanding of English, education and the media have played an influential role in modifying the behaviour of these women . . . it is ironical that such factors may have inadvertently placed the infants of British-born Asian mothers at greater risk of SIDS than if their mothers had persisted with the traditional supine positions.
>
> (*Early Human Development*, vol. 38, 1994)

And so to New Zealand, where, by the early 1990s, 95,000 Pacific Islanders formed a substantial minority. For the first time, the Pacific Island community were having to deal with a new phenomenon known as 'cot death'.[7] Ironically, this coincided with the New Zealand Cot Death Prevention Programme.

The programme was based on research from the three main New Zealand populations – the whites, the indigenous Maoris and the Pacific Islanders. Ignoring the fact that the Pacific Island people had the highest rate of co-sleeping and the lowest rate of SIDS, statisticians concentrated on the Maori evidence, which coupled a high rate of co-sleeping with a high rate of SIDS. The researchers weighed in immediately with their advice: Do not, on any account, sleep with your baby. This advice turned out to be premature – a serious exception which prompted other scientists to try even harder to prove the rule.

The New Zealand health warning caused ripples around the world. It was immediately adopted by the New Zealand Cot Death Prevention Programme, although equivalent programmes around the world were more reluctant to draw immediate conclusions. Nevertheless, the message filtered through to Britain via an ITV *This Week* television documentary in October 1991. It was fronted by the high-profile presenter Anne Diamond, whose son Sebastian had died of SIDS, and viewers witnessed her emotional trip to New Zealand. At the end of the programme, the prescription against co-sleeping was included with other known risk factors for cot death.

Parents contacted their health professionals and support groups in dismay – should they oust their contented babies from the family bed?

In London, the Foundation for the Study of Infant Deaths hosted a conference for interested health workers. Ed Mitchell, Associate Professor in Paediatrics at the University of Auckland School of Medicine, handed out documentation telling parents not to co-sleep. I was seated next to Dr Michel Odent. He turned to me and said, 'I am going to Japan tomorrow. There, they sleep with their babies and have never heard of cot death. How can I go to them and say "Do not sleep with your babies – this will reduce your rate of cot death"? They will think I am crazy!'

The New Zealand advice was based on statistics from the Maori population, who still often sleep with their children in the traditional way. Unhappily some not-so-traditional factors have overtaken the Maori lifestyle, including alcoholism and a high incidence of maternal smoking.

In January 1993, the New Zealand researchers came back with a study which corrected their earlier assumption that co-sleeping alone was a factor in cot death. Rather, they conceded, it is the combination of smoking with close-contact nurture which is potentially fatal for the vulnerable baby. (By contrast, smoking was 'very rare' among Bangladeshi mothers in the Cardiff study.[8])

Some damage had already been done, however. Professor James McKenna:

> . . . if accepted uncritically, the New Zealand conclusion will lead some to think quite erroneously (with perhaps tragic consequences) that a mother's body, rather than being a source of nurturance, emotional satisfaction, and infant survival, is no more than a hazard over which neither the mother nor the infant has control.
>
> (*Sudden Infant Death Syndrome.*
> *New Trends in the Nineties*, 1995)

New Zealand's programme caused offence among the indigenous Maori population. One researcher reported the way in which a nurse advised new Maori mothers: 'If you have your baby in bed with you, it will have a cot death.'[9] But even this simplistic, misleading and gross distortion of the facts did not convince Maori mothers. To them, the cot death prevention programme sounded like just another invasion of their culture by the interfering whites:

> Maori health workers point out that advice to sleep infants on their fronts, and to bottle rather than breast feed, came from

white health professionals; similarly smoking was introduced by the white settlers. This has prompted a reaction of 'you were wrong before'; this is the response I met among many Maori people to the advice that infants and parents should not share beds. In this way, cot death has become part of the wider history of Maori–white relations, and of the wider experience of the imposition of western values on indigenous peoples.

(M. Gantley, *Early Human Development*, 1994)

As I write, in Britain and elsewhere, health authorities still err 'on the side of caution' and advise mothers not to keep babies too long in their beds. How they can be sure which side caution lies, is not absolutely clear. In 1993, at the height of the scare caused by the New Zealand research, Joyce Epstein, secretary of FSID, wrote to me that 'we feel the research on bed-sharing is not definitive enough, or compelling enough, to include firm advice in our "Reduce the Risk" campaign leaflet.' Yet she added, 'we have always come down on the side of suggesting parents not co-sleep with babies.' The inevitable result of thinking like this is that health workers become confused and parents are disempowered when they could be making sensible choices for themselves.

In contrast, Jeanine Young, research nurse at the Institute of Child Health, Bristol, suggested that influential agencies should not 'come down' on either side. She offered a plea to midwives to be even-handed in giving information to parents:

. . . the existence of dangerous co-sleeping conditions is no more an argument against the potential benefits of bedsharing with infants than the existence of dangerous solitary infant sleep environments constitutes a valid argument against the safety of all solitary infant sleep. No environment is risk free . . .

The integrated care system which incorporates co-sleeping with parents is the result of millions of years of evolution. One would therefore imagine that it must provide social, physiological and psychological benefits for those involved. The

117

question is therefore not whether we should or shouldn't bedshare, but rather that we should study bedsharing and become more open minded about its potential role in contributing to infant survival . . .

Midwives should be discussing the issue of co-sleeping in their 'parenthood preparation' classes and dispelling common misconceptions about the practice. Until midwives inform mothers of the potential benefits of bedsharing with their babies, we are not meeting [the] recommendation ['to give all necessary advice to the mother on infant care to enable her to ensure the optimum progress of the new-born infant', The Midwife's Code of Practice].

('Bedsharing with Babies: The Facts', RCM *Midwives Journal*, 1998)

The 'potential benefits' of bedsharing have only recently attracted the attention of scientists. In the 1980s, it became increasingly obvious that SIDS affects each population differently. But epidemiology – statistical analysis of the incidence, geography and circumstances of a disease – does not explain why certain environments may be protective, neutral or dangerous. It does not give us cause and effect or offer a holistic understanding of why so many babies are vulnerable to dying in their sleep.

So scientists embarked on a new strand of laboratory research. McKenna was the first to video mother and babies sleeping together and apart in laboratory conditions. Earlier, in his paper *An Anthropological Perspective on SIDS*, he had gathered a wealth of supporting data for his theories on sudden infant death. It is important to examine the major points of his academic discussion.

The foetus in its mother's womb begins to breathe rhythmically up to three months before birth. Studies have shown that sensory stimulation (e.g. the rocking of the mother as she walks, and the sounds she makes) keeps the unborn child breathing regularly. All these stimuli are felt and heard by the foetus, who has advanced hearing even in the womb.

At birth, the infant has a natural immunity to cot death. This may be because of a natural gasping reflex, which gets the baby breathing when in danger of suffocation. The reflex is lost after a few weeks, however, as the higher brain takes over and begins to control the child's development. As this happens, the baby 're-engages' with the mother, becoming more dependent on her. The child is vulnerable to errors in brain-controlled functions (such as breathing), especially during the shifts from reflexive behaviour to controlled behaviour.

As one doctor explains, the heartbeat of a normal, healthy baby sleeping alone is notoriously irregular:

> Workers making 24-hour recordings of heart-beat in a large number of normal infants have shown that occasional abnormalities of rhythm are unexpectedly common. It has been suggested that immaturity of heart-beat and breathing regulation may result in arrest of heart or breathing under circumstances which would not normally cause such an event.
> (Dr Andrew Evans, *Nursery World*, 31 July 1980)

One of the most important changes a human baby has to make is in the way it breathes, in order to vocalize speech. This is a major difference between humans and other mammals, which do not speak, and are not susceptible to sudden death syndrome.

The baby has to learn how to make purposeful, non-crying noises before he can learn languages. In the first year of life, his breathing slows from 87 to around 47 breaths per minute. And between two and four months of age, the time when a baby is changing his breathing patterns, he is at his most susceptible to SIDS. He is also most responsive at this time to the benefits of touch.[10]

I have already described in the previous chapter how sleeping next to an adult can stimulate regular breathing in a baby. Dr McKenna works on the theory that if a baby is stimulated to breathe by movement in the womb, then a new-born child will be similarly stimulated by the parent at his side. We really are a carrying species, and the infant expects to be always with his mother or guardian.

McKenna demonstrates that vestibular stimulation (e.g. breathing movements of the adult's chest when asleep), rocking, touch and heat exchange all help to promote the health and easy breathing of the infant. Gas exchange may also be an important factor. The baby sleeping next to his parents is likely to breathe in carbon dioxide, a chemical stimulant to take the next breath.

> When parents sleep with or near an infant, it is likely, at least for much of the night, that not only will their body heat be exchanged but also will their expelled carbon dioxide gases. Recently, Sullivan (1984) suggested that during REM sleep, infants can smell carbon dioxide . . . If this is so, then in the microenvironment created by its parent [in their bed], the infant could respond to the parent's exhaled carbon dioxide by breathing in some of it. That is, the infant's upper nasal chemo-receptors may receive enough of its parent's CO_2 to increase the chance of a brain stem-inspired inspiration.
>
> (*Medical Anthropology*, 1986)

It is ironic that gas exchange was the very reason why the Victorians felt mother and baby should *not* sleep together. We may recall the words of *Baby* magazine:

> For the first few weeks animal heat is maintained by sleeping with the mother; but on no account should a child of any later age sleep between two persons, as by so doing it must of necessity breathe the emanations from their bodies.
>
> (*Baby*, 1888)

The author would have the child taken from the bed at precisely the age when he is most dependent on the mother for external stimuli to keep him breathing. The rationale for using a pram was the same:

> I think a young child can lie much more at ease in a berceaunette-perambulator than in the arms of a nurse who

cramps its movements and causes it to inhale her breath and the exhalations of her clothes.

(Baby, December 1887)

It might be that the regular chest movement of the sleeping parent, coupled with the rhythmic flow of air, reminds the vulnerable baby to keep breathing. If there is a problem, author Dr Penny Stanway believes the baby is bound to be safer in his mother's arms than in his own room.

'If you have a baby prone to having its heart simply stop, it's going to start wriggling,' she told me. 'The mother will wake up and feed the baby, which will stimulate the system again. It's far better than relying on cot alarms.'

Dr Stanway also points out that the common night-time feeding position of resting the baby's head in the crook of the arm reduces the chance of the baby choking on his own vomit. Even in terms of basic safety, a baby is better in his parents' bed than out of it.

Dr McKenna does not present co-sleeping of baby and parents as a complete solution to cot death, any more than solitary sleeping is the cause of it. But he says that the human baby's dependence on his mother is a compelling reason for not separating them at night. When a baby is at risk of Sudden Infant Death Syndrome, his constitutional weakness may combine with his solitary sleeping habits to make death more likely.

> My reasoning is that solitary-sleeping infants will breathe differently (less stably) than will social-sleeping infants, and of course, the parents themselves will be in a better position to respond to changes in their infants, such as serious apneas [interruptions in breathing] or breathing silence.
>
> (Medical Anthropology, 1986)

Dr McKenna has studied the breathing patterns of babies when they sleep with their mothers, and when they sleep alone. His studies of Latino mother and infant pairs sleeping together and apart show that, when sleeping together, mother and baby naturally gravitate to a position less than 30 cm apart. McKenna has suggested that co-sleeping babies always take the supine position – otherwise it would be difficult to sleep-feed. And, most interestingly, he has shown that mothers are aroused to a lighter state of sleep (not fully awake) in synchrony with their babies.[11]

McKenna suggests that the more frequent arousals of babies may strengthen, co-ordinate and integrate the baby's system – waking up, even slightly, means more work for the heart, the brain, the muscles, reflexes and the entire breathing system. Long periods of deep, solitary sleep, the idealized state for babies in the twentieth century, could be a dangerous routine for the vulnerable infant.

On the other side of the Atlantic, Professor Peter Fleming and his team at the Anne Diamond Sleep Laboratory in Bristol began video-taping mothers and babies at night. In contrast to McKenna's experiments, Fleming's laboratory was designed to be as unlike a lab as possible, resembling a family bedroom with pretty duvet and double bed. Fleming's babies were wired up, but, for freedom of movement, his mothers were not. On solitary sleeping nights, the baby was observed in a cot in the mother's room, rather than down a corridor, allowing for subtle observations on the differences between rooming-in and actual bedsharing.

Analysis of hundreds of hours of video material and physical measurements produced a number of interesting findings. There was a marked coincidence of sleep states for mothers and babies – especially for those who routinely slept together at home. Routine bedsharers breastfed almost twice as many times in the night as the routine room-sharers, although the feeds were almost half as long, producing a similar total feeding time. Some mothers 'appeared to fall back to sleep during a breastfeed'.

Mothers' responses to their babies' movements and sounds in the night tended to be swifter when they were bedsharing. 'Even when asleep,' said researcher Jeanine Young, 'mothers appeared to be aware or sense the presence of their baby in bed with them, and at no time was a mother ever observed to roll on her infant, even when sleeping very close together.'[12]

Mothers were more likely to communicate through touch than through speech with their babies at night. Most also lay awake occasionally 'just watching their infant'. Mothers checked babies' temperatures and rearranged bedding accordingly.

Routine bedsharers usually faced their babies and lay within 20 cm of them. The only prone sleeping occurred when babies were placed on their mothers' stomachs – 'generally, this position was only used for short periods to settle the infant to sleep'.[12]

Finally, bedsharing babies were sometimes discovered under the mother's duvet 'although no apparent deleterious effects were observed'. Since overheating has been identified as a factor in cot death syndrome, this could be highly significant. Dr Andrew Sawczenko, also working in Fleming's team, analysed the thermal and CO_2 environments of the co-sleeping baby and uncovered a fascinating phenomenon. Although the babies' environment was warmer when bedsharing – and their forehead, stomach and shin temperatures were higher – their core temperatures were actually lower than when they slept alone. Dr Sawczenko attempts to explain his results:

We found that on the bed-sharing nights the infants were covered with more insulation, in a warmer environment, and had higher peripheral temperatures than on the room-sharing nights, suggesting peripheral vasodilatation [expansion of blood vessels] to increase heat loss. However, surprisingly, the nadir of rectal temperature was significantly lower on the bed-sharing nights and was not raised for any significant portion of the night. This finding suggests one of two possibilities: a) the infants were mildly cold stressed on the room-sharing nights, with, as a result, a slightly higher metabolic rate and thus higher core temperature, or b) that when bed-sharing, despite being in an environment in the upper thermoneutral range [warmer], peripheral vasodilatation and increased insensible losses [ie. which were too small to be noticed] were more effective in heat dissipation despite a constant metabolic rate. The environmental conditions observed in the room-sharing nights do not support the former suggestion, as all infants were well within the predicted thermoneutral range. The results of our study suggest that under our experimental conditions infants can effectively thermoregulate whilst bedsharing.

(Sawczenko, Young, Galland, Fleming: 'Observations of the effects of nocturnal bedsharing on the sleeping, microenvironment and physiology of healthy infants aged 2–5 months', in press 1998)

In other words, the baby's system compensates for the warm family bed. Could it be his body contact with another human which facilitates this physical response? There may be more to the infant–parent sleeping relationship than we have yet dared to imagine.

A full understanding of co-sleeping could revolutionize our view of the relationship between mother and baby, and change our assumptions about the level of independence an infant can tolerate. Meanwhile, there is no sign that co-sleeping, practised carefully and within a given range of precautions, does any harm. In fact, doctors have noted the benefits for families which fear sudden infant death. Dr Hugh Jolly, for instance, wrote:

Many parents say that they sleep better in a family bed because they are not frightened about what is happening to their young children. One mother told me she could not sleep unless her baby was beside her. Parents who are particularly frightened about 'cot death' have been relieved to have their babies in bed with them.

(Book of Child Care)

Parents who take their babies to bed do not need to worry about whether their child is still alive, as, with bodies touching, they can tangibly feel the life within. If the baby does stop breathing, they are on hand to deal with it in the shortest possible time. Picking up a baby, rocking or feeding him are all known ways of reviving him after apnoea (the cessation of breathing).

Sometimes cot death is confused with mechanical suffocation. People say they are frightened to have a baby in the bed, because they might smother him in the night. There is even an official word – 'overlaying' – which refers to babies who suffocate while in the parental bed.

The phenomenon is not new. There is a reference to 'overlaying' in the Old Testament's First Book of Kings, a document which dates back to around 500BC: 'and this woman's child died in the night;' says the commentator, 'because she overlaid it'. However, we have to remember that for many hundreds of years, overlaying was the given explanation for sudden, unexpected infant death. Because everyone slept with their babies and SIDS occurs in sleep, 'overlaying' was simply a pseudonym for cot death.

One English textbook from the seventeenth century contains a dire warning about wet-nurses who drink too much and accidentally smother their charges in the night. Ironically, these women were apparently drinking 'to encrease their milk'.[13]

In the nineteenth century, Europeans adopted a new explanation for SIDS: a condition called 'Status thymo-lymphaticus'. Infants were diagnosed (in autopsy) to have an enlarged thymus which was thought to hinder breathing. The idea persisted into the twentieth century, even though it did not explain all cot deaths. New theories began to emerge, and still abound. Most recently these include concerns about chemicals in cot mattresses, links with snoring, reductions in oxygen following air flights, 'inattentive' mothers, vaccination programmes and respiratory infections. Included in these has always been – and always will be – the charge of overlaying.

It is, of course, possible to smother a baby, though highly unlikely when the co-sleeper is healthy, aware of safety details and his faculties are unimpaired.

Numerous studies have shown that there is no connection between cot death and overlaying. Dr David Haslam, author of *Sleepless Children*, says the idea that parents suffocate their children in bed is

125

'nonsense'. Dr Hugh Jolly also dismisses the connection between cot death and mechanical suffocation:

> Guilt and misunderstanding are still the penalty of our hazy ideas of the cause of cot deaths, and only now is some light beginning to dawn on this difficult subject. For example, suffocation used to be made the scapegoat for many sudden infant deaths. Parents felt they were at fault for providing the 'wrong' kind of bedding or, worse still, for letting the baby sleep in their bed. At worst, the suspicion of deliberate suffocation arose. Yet at the age when cot deaths are most common – two to six months – a normal baby can lift his head and change his position if he cannot breathe easily.
>
> (*Book of Child Care*)

Any suggestion that breathing is more difficult for the baby while suckling during sleep is quashed by evidence from the John Radcliffe Hospital in Oxford. Dr Paul Johnson, consultant clinical physiologist, reports in FSID's newsletter of August 1986 that the descent of the larynx during early infancy poses no problems for babies:

> The newborn infant is thus able to breathe effectively while swallowing at 3–4 times per second – a reflex act which most adults cannot match.

One prevailing myth about babies is that they are unable to breathe through their mouths, and that this increases their chances of suffocation. Dr Johnson demonstrates that babies are perfectly able to mouth breathe by choice:

> . . . the human newborn (in common with most mammals) contrary to the published statements is not an obligate nose breather. This was a popular but unproven view which followed 'tests' in which the noses of babies were obstructed and the infants were observed to attempt to breathe without

opening their mouths. However, for ethical rather than physiological reasons the nose was only obstructed for a few breaths. It has now been shown by two independent groups in Belgium and the USA that not only do some newborn babies normally mouth breathe but that they will switch automatically to mouth breathing if their noses are obstructed without waking up.

This is the kind of evidence a mother sees for herself whenever her baby has a cold. He will attempt to nose breathe, but failing this, opens his mouth. Meanwhile, Prof. McKenna says that even a one-day-old baby will complain if he has difficulty in breathing:

> Overlying is, of course, possible, but it is not likely, just as strangulation by defective cribs, while known to have happened, also is not common . . . soft mattresses, as opposed to hard mats, may change the overall safety picture of parent-infant cosleeping. Nevertheless, even day-old infants will struggle violently and protest vocally in response to obstruction of their air passages.
>
> (*Medical Anthropology*, 1986)

Accidental mechanical suffocation is, in fact, extremely rare. Figures published by the Office of Population, Census and Surveys in 1985 show that the total number of deaths of British babies of less than one year was 6,141. Of these, 1,165 were diagnosed as victims of SIDS. Only six babies during the year actually suffocated – four in their parents' beds, and two in their own cots.

Apparent instances of smothering tend to reach the national press. A one-year-old child from Wiltshire was suffocated under his parents' duvet after his mother moved him into her room, 'in an effort to get him to sleep'. According to this newspaper report:

> A verdict of accidental death was recorded on Leon Forsey, of Bishops Cannings, Devizes. A spokesman for the Royal Society

for the Prevention of Accidents commented afterwards: 'Our advice is that babies are best off in their own cots at that age. We don't recommend they should go into an adult bed alone or with adults.'

(*Daily Telegraph*, 1 October 1988)

Without knowing the exact circumstances, it is impossible to say why a healthy, mobile one-year-old was unable to wriggle free from his parents' duvet during the night. Incidents of this sort make the headlines precisely because they are so rare, while cot death goes largely unreported.

The Foundation for Infant Deaths in Britain has itself reported cases of babies dying of cot death while sleeping with their parents. From data available to the Foundation, information officer Tracy Curds confirmed that 'of the very few babies who were found dead in their parents' beds (and registered as SIDS) there was NO evidence of overlaying.'[14]

Interestingly, the same researchers found that SIDS families had moved house almost twice as often before the infant's death as had control families. This further corroborates the idea that disruption and separation – likely consequences of the trauma of moving house – are critical in a baby's life.

If a baby is to sleep with his parents, there are a few very simple precautions to take. The baby should feel free to move. The co-sleepers (adults or children) should all be well. They should not be drunk, or drugged, or excessively overweight. No one should smoke in the bed, or near the baby. Water beds should be avoided, and pillows arranged so that they cannot fall and smother the child.

Modern parents tend to be overprotective of their babies, not careless. These essential preparations will seem obvious and common sense. In poor households at the end of the century, not all parents took as much care. More babies suffocated in their parents' bed at weekends – presumably when mother or father came home drunk.

Since 1908 there has been a law in Britain to safeguard against parents' going to bed drunk with their children. The Children's Act provision was incorporated into the Children and Young Persons Act of 1933, and is still in force today. It reads:

> . . . where it is proved that the death of an infant under three years of age was caused by suffocation (not being suffocation caused by disease or the presence of any foreign body in the throat or air passages of the infant) while the infant was in bed with some other person who has attained the age of sixteen years, that other person shall, if he was, when he went to bed, under the influence of drink, be deemed to have neglected the infant in a manner likely to cause injury to its health.[15]

The far-ranging CESDI report in Britain has failed to uncover any added risk to babies of sleeping with their parents in a bed (sofa-sharing brings its own hazards because of awkward corners and cushions). CESDI has established, however, that parental smoking is even more poisonous for bedsharing babies than it is for babies in cots. It makes sense that if the 'micro-' or immediate environment of the baby is at all important, it should not be polluted with smoke. Information like this demonstrates just how important the micro-environment of the sleeping baby can be to his overall health. By implication, a baby's place of sleep, his proximity to other bodies, access to breast milk and to adult care-giving are all vital components of the cot death picture.

Researchers from Zimbabwe go further: 'Sudden infant death may result from trivial embarrassments, upper respiratory tract infections . . . and so on. It may begin with remarkable episodes of distress, which, if they had been witnessed, might have been simply attended to and thought little of.'[16]

This, after all, may be the scenario in millions of homes across the world, where mothers and fathers co-sleep so that they can safely attend to their vulnerable babies. In Britain, three years of CESDI reports finally showed that room-sharing with a baby was 'strongly protective' against the risks of cot death, including when baby was brought into the family bed.[17]

This instinct to reach out to our infants at night is very powerful. As Michel Odent pointed out, co-sleeping is often the last practice to be abandoned by non-Western peoples, even where bottle feeding and high-tech births are introduced. It is sad and ironic that some cultures, impressed by Western arguments for cots and sleep-training, are now experiencing SIDS for the first time. Perhaps it is not too late for us to learn a little from them.

6 | THE MIDNIGHT FEAST

> Most of us smile at a yawning colleague who has spent time in nocturnal lovemaking, drinking or setting the world to rights, yet a mother and baby who suckle at night are objects of pity and concern. The mother is seen as a slave to her child and she is criticised for this, but slaving for other people during the day is taken for granted.
>
> (Gabrielle Palmer, *The Politics of Breastfeeding*)

When my grandmother wanted to breastfeed, the midwife told her: 'You wouldn't want to eat a beef steak in the middle of the night, so why should your baby want milk?' She followed the advice, feeding her baby only during the day, at the prescribed four-hourly intervals. Within a few weeks, her daughter was losing weight, and my grandmother gave up. Like most mothers of her time, she was told she did not have enough milk for her baby. The fault, apparently, was hers.

Thousands of British women tell similar stories today. Childcare books imply that breastfeeding is a specialized art, which is difficult to perfect. Friends say it is a struggle which they did not enjoy. Many give up because they have 'insufficient milk'. Meanwhile, rather than support the breastfeeding woman, food companies promote artificial feeds and encourage early weaning on to solids.

The British government's Committee on Medical Aspects of Food Policy found that breastfeeding was the best nutrition for babies, and that it should be provided for at least a year. But the Committee also accepted that most babies in Britain are likely to be bottle-fed by the

131

age of four weeks.[1] Whatever the experts tell us about the benefits of breastfeeding, fashion still favours the bottle.

It should be no surprise to learn that for millions of years all babies were breastfed, whether by their mothers' milk or by that of a wet nurse. Some tribes and cultures, including our own, believed that the pre-milk, colostrum, was bad or dirty, and so separated the baby from its mother in the first few days. Colostrum was known as 'witch milk', until the English doctor, William Cadogan, pronounced its virtues in the mid-eighteenth century. Cadogan was an advocate of unrestricted feeding:

> Nature, if she be not interrupted, will do the whole business perfectly well; and there seems to be nothing left for a Nurse to do, but to keep the child sweet and clean, and to tumble and toss it about a good deal, play with it, and keep it in good Humour.
>
> (*Essay on the Nursing and Management of Children*, 1748)

Mothers' milk was the obvious nourishment for a child, and without it, a baby would probably starve.

By the middle of the nineteenth century, however, alternatives to mothers' milk were being sold alongside the cures for baldness and linctuses in the classified ads. Babies could now be spoon-fed, or reared from bottles with leather teats. In 1882, the edition of *Enquire Within Upon Everything* made these suggestions:

> Children who are brought up by hand, that is to say, who are not nursed by mother or wet nurse, require an occasional change of diet, and thin gruel affords a wholesome alternation to milk. When cow's milk is used it should be obtained, if possible, from one and the same cow, and diluted with boiled water. Swiss milk is recommended by some medical men. The Aylesbury Dairy Company furnish a speciality for young children under the name of 'Artificial Human Milk', which is recommended.

It was around this time that doctors and other experts began to prescribe the best methods and formulas for feeding infants. At first, their recommendations were merely an attempt to bring order to the apparently *ad hoc* way in which most mothers fed their babies. Constant feeding in the day and at night was seen as a messy (and unmedical) way of doing things:

> The time of taking food is not a matter of indifference; very young infants made an exception; for as their consumption of vital power is more rapid, they may be more frequently indulged with aliment.
>
> It is, however, advisable to accustom even them to a certain regularity, so as to allow them their victuals at stated periods of the day; for it has been observed that those children which are fed indiscriminately through the whole day, are subject to debility and disease.
>
> *(Enquire Within Upon Everything, 1882)*

The 'discriminating' mother introduced a system to her breastfeeding technique. The laws of mothering were no longer to follow the mood of mother and child – rules were made by the doctors, equipped with new, scientific theories on nutrition.

Community midwife Chloe Fisher has pored over many early textbooks in an attempt to discover where we lost the art of successful breastfeeding. She found that doctors imposed several types of restriction on lactating mothers: (1) an insistence on regular feeding times; (2) control of the frequency of feeding; (3) a limit on initial sucking at the breast; (4) limits on the total duration of each feed; and finally, (5) a complete ban on night feeding.[2]

To this list we might now add the social pressure to wean as early as possible. The trend in Britain is to introduce new foods to the baby at three months – or even earlier, if the baby seems especially hungry and constantly at the nipple. It is fashionable to express distaste at seeing toddlers breastfed, and most women who do breastfeed stop after a few months. The most common reasons for weaning are lack of maternal milk, discomfort, social pressure and the return to work – not rejection of the breast by baby.

In the 1920s, pioneers such as New Zealander Truby King were to influence a whole generation of medical professionals throughout the English-speaking dominions. While King's intentions (to rear well-nourished babies and educate women on matters of hygiene) were honourable, his recommendations created a breastfeeding timetable of the most rigorous kind.

Victorian doctors said new-born babies should be fed every one and a half hours. This was more or less an observation based on common practice. As doctors revised their opinions, the gaps between feeds widened. Edmund Owen, writing in the 1880s, suggested:

> For the first month a baby should be fed every two hours, and if he be a good sleeper he may be woke up for his meals, at any rate he should not be allowed to pass the third hour without food. If he be allowed to sleep on, he wakes up at last so desperately hungry that he overfeeds, and, by an attack of vomiting, much of his meal is wasted . . . Regular and frequent feeding is a great thing for little children.
>
> (*Baby*, 1888)

But Truby King and his disciples of the 1920s believed the new-born to be made of sterner stuff. They introduced the four-hourly feeding rule. Mabel Liddiard, an Englishwoman and a devoted fan of King, wrote:

> Public opinion has changed very rapidly on this subject – not many years ago the mother was asked to feed two-hourly, night and day. What wonder that breast-feeding went out of fashion! Then the three-hourly interval was recognised as best, while now the four-hourly has been approved.
>
> (*The Mothercraft Manual*, 1924–1948)

Liddiard recommended an eight-hour feeding ban at night for even the new-born.

The horrors of breastfeeding were to be found in every manual on mothering. The words of the Victorian authority, Mrs Jane Ellen Panton, set the tone for a hundred years of breastfeeding advice: 'Let no mother condemn herself to be a common or ordinary "cow" unless she has a real desire to nurse . . .'[3]

The message to mothers and midwives was clear – breastfeeding was an unpleasant task. It was not realized at this time that one of the greatest reasons for the unpleasantness was that the baby was limited in his feeding. The truth belies the theory. The long gaps now usual between feeds are the times when engorgement and potential damage set in. Intermittent snacking by a baby held constantly at the breast does no damage to mother or child – the breast does not need a rest.

Despite the Baby-Friendly Initiative, Ms Liddiard's methods still apply in many modern hospitals, where most breastfeeding begins. According to *Mother* magazine, the average new-born baby has six feeds a day – which means that four-hourly feeding is the current practice.[4]

Frances weighed 6 lb 1 ½ oz (2.73kg) when she was born. As she was on the border of being a 'tiny' baby, I was instructed to feed her at three-hourly intervals, rather than every four hours.

Although I chose to feed her almost constantly instead, I did keep a record of the gaps between feeds for a while, until I tired of writing down '20 mins', '10 mins', '30 mins' and so on. One young trainee midwife mentioned that the reason I did not suffer from cracked nipples, engorgement, blisters or soreness was the constant feeding. But that was not part of the standard advice.

There was a slight problem when it came to weighing Frances before going home. I was supposed to wait for at least an hour after a 'feed' to put her on the scales, but as I always held her in my arms, and as she suckled frequently from the breast, no such interval conveniently arose. We went home regardless. Three weeks later, she had gained a rapid two and a half pounds in weight. I had no idea that

Frances' frequent-interval snack-style breastfeeds were similar to those of the !Kung hunter-gatherers of Botswana and Namibia. These traditional people have been the subject of outside research because of the long intervals between the births of their babies – an average of forty-four months. Researchers from Harvard University noted that:

> We now report that the !Kung have an unusual temporal pattern of nursing, characterized by highly frequent nursing bouts with short inter-bout intervals . . . Observations from dawn to dusk revealed that nursing occurred for a few minutes at a time, several times an hour, throughout the daylight hours . . . No systematic observations were made at night. However, it is customary and apparently universal for !Kung infants to sleep on the same skin mat with their mothers until they are weaned. Interviews with 21 mothers nursing infants as old as 3 years old indicated that nursing during the night is universal . . . All 21 reported that the infant nursed during the night without waking the mother, from two to 'many' times or 'all night'.
>
> (*Science*, vol. 207, 15 February 1980)

Recent evidence from Thailand shows that even the test-weighing of babies in the night interferes with their intake of breast milk.[5] (This is when babies sleep with their mothers.) The practice of weighing a baby in the first few days when the milk comes in, is in itself a disruption to the establishment of breastfeeding.

But there are many other reasons why women fail to feed their own offspring. In the first place, the new mother may not expect to succeed. All around her is evidence that others have failed.

From those early hours, when the midwife forces the baby's mouth on to the nipple, to the final act three weeks later, when the woman, battered and sore, finally says 'I've given up', our breastfeeding experiences are a shambles. Those women who do go on to enjoy and succeed in this mysterious art are seen as weird, earthy types, clinging to their babies in an 'unhealthy' way.

In the relatively poor valleys of South Wales, social stigma is the greatest bar to breastfeeding. Having a night-life is important to most young women – and that means going to pubs and clubs, not pacing the landing with an unsettled baby.

Midwife Gail Pritchard from the Rhondda Valley in South Wales, slept with and breastfed her two daughters, and gives talks on the subject. Her toughest audience is a class of teenage valley schoolgirls: 'In the Rhondda,' she says, 'only one in a hundred women breast-feed. It is absolutely unheard of to suckle a baby past four months old. None of the fourteen and fifteen-year-olds I talk to want to breastfeed, because it means they can't go out at night.'

The same objection was presented to me in Manchester, by the young doctor who came to treat me for a flu bug. He was amazed that I was still breastfeeding a ten-month-old child, as his wife was tired of feeding their new baby after ten days. When he heard that I fed Frances without limitation, he quizzed me on the scientific evidence for my method, and then said 'So you were housebound for six months?' I told him that from Frances' earliest days, we had gone to the theatre, out to meals and even abroad, with as little fuss as if the bundle in the corduroy sling were a cabbage patch doll.

'Engorgement is normal, isn't it?' the doctor hazarded, echoing the words of Dr Hugh Jolly in his *Book of Child Care*:

Some aspects of breastfeeding that might cause problems if misunderstood [are] after-pains and engorgement, which are really normal stages in the establishment of feeding.

My doctor had no idea that it was possible to escape the discomfort of swollen breasts, cracked nipples and the pain of the infant gums clamping down over the areola. Luckily, I was able to show him the draft copy of a new publication, *Successful Breastfeeding*, produced by a team of midwives and health visitors (no doctors) for the Royal College of Midwives. Many childcare professionals prefer to see the scientific evidence in a medical journal, rather than trust the experience of a mother.

Successful Breastfeeding was a practical guide distributed free to the 32,000 members of the Royal College of Midwives. 'In future,' said Chloe Fisher, one of the document's co-authors, 'midwives who are not practising the methods shown in this book will have to justify themselves'.

The book is not so much a list of rules for mothers and midwives, as an untangling of the mess which constitutes modern breastfeeding advice. It debunks many of the myths about restricted feeding. For instance on engorgement, the commonest problem in early feeding, it says:

> Milk production continues as efficiently at night as by day, and if the milk is not removed as it is formed (as regulated by baby's needs to go to the breast) the volume of milk in the breast will rapidly exceed the capacity of the alveoli [milk-producing sacs inside the breast]. The consequent engorgement is not only uncomfortable for the mother, but it will begin the process of lactation suppression. Feeding the baby at night will minimise or prevent the potential problem of engorgement.

My doctor left vowing to persuade his wife to take their little boy into bed to feed.

Professionals seem to be at as much of a loss as mothers themselves. Deprived of successful examples, even doctors do not know for sure what is the normal experience of the breastfeeding mother and baby. Chloe Fisher believes our ideas of normality are severely impaired. Two generations of women have witnessed a nearly universal failure to breastfeed and the apparent success of bottle-feeding. She says this is why mothers and midwives mistakenly treat the nipple like a plastic teat when teaching a baby to suck.

Neo-natal weight loss and excessive weight gain are always a cause of worry for the professionals, who are on the look-out for signs of illness or crisis when they examine babies. As all mothers know, it is easy to become weight-obsessed, both with your own figure and that of your child. Every trip to the clinic revolves around a pair of scales. ('He hasn't gained today, Mrs Jones' – exit one mother with 'failure' tattooed on her heart.)

One friend with a bonny breastfed baby was reprimanded by the health visitors because his weight was off the top of their chart. They wanted her five-month-old son to go on a diet, ignoring the fact that a staple diet of breast milk was his best insurance against being an overweight adult.

I, too, was often accused of 'overfeeding' my child, though she was never force-fed. Sometimes it felt as though the word meant 'over-mothering' or 'mollycoddling'. It is a sentiment that harks back once more to the beginning of the century:

> The intervention of imposing a limitation on the ultimate duration of a feed when lactation has become established originally occurred because of a fear, widespread in the medical profession at that time, of a condition which they labelled 'overfeeding' and which was said to cause such serious problems as failure to thrive and diarrhoea. A French doctor wrote 'nothing is further from my thoughts than the advocacy of overfeeding.' He then describes how mothers fed their babies frequently, and that by test weighing he discovered that the baby was taking '. . . far too much. We are forced to keep them apart from their mothers.' (Budin, 1907)
>
> (Chloe Fisher, *Midwifery*, vol. I, 1985)

By contrast, Jean Liedloff told me that the babies of the Yequana tribe in South America were far fatter and softer than the average British baby. They feed constantly, and are never far from the breast, night or day. Overfeeding is not possible when the baby is on breast milk alone.

Successful breastfeeding is not unknown around the world, especially in regions untouched by Western culture. But armies, missionaries and multi-national companies have done their best over the years to impose Westernized methods on impressionable parents in developing nations. Not content with ruining the relationship between mother and child in this country, we have exported our restrictive suckling practices, often with disastrous results.

A friend who worked in Malawi in central Africa told me how the women there scrape together precious coins to pay for bottle milk, because it is the Western, and therefore the modern, thing to do. In the 1970s, when the slogan 'Coke is good for you' was broadcast worldwide, African mothers actually put cola in bottles and fed it to their infants. Health workers are still trying desperately to undo the damage caused by the methods and messages of the sophisticated, industrialized world.

In India, where only thirteen per cent of homes have a continuous water supply, many babies fall ill and die from complications in bottle-feeding. Chloe Fisher bitterly regrets the British part in spreading unreliable advice:

> In the developed world, slavish adherence to the earlier
> theories probably did as much harm to human lactation as did
> the promotion of artificial feeds. But that we should have been
> guilty of taking these ideas to the developing countries, where
> artificial feeding can cause gross malnutrition, if not death,
> should make us pause for serious thought.
>
> (*Oxford Medical School Gazette*, 1982)

Chloe Fisher delivered a paper to the International Conference of Midwives, in which she quoted a textbook for Nigerian student midwives. It was written by Victoria Ajayi, a Nigerian midwife trained in Britain:

> 'First day – 2 min at each breast.
> Second day – 5 min at each breast.
> Third day – 7 min at each breast.
> Fourth day – 10 min at each breast making 20 min feeding time.

Twenty minutes altogether is the maximum time from then on.'

These instructions contain three of the commonest interventions which still exist; to limit very severely the duration of the early feeds, to restrict the ultimate duration of the feed, and requiring that both breasts are used at each feed. In practice this can result in the baby and the breast being out of phase and engorgement occurring, with the mother believing that she does not have enough milk, and the baby being denied the high fat hind milk.

(*Midwifery*, 1985)

The baby allowed to suckle as he wants will feed for an average total of three hours in the twenty-four[6] – that is, if he sleeps with his mother at night. Immediate access to the breast has many benefits for mother and baby, as we shall see later.

But midwives continue to recommend that mothers put their babies in the nursery overnight. Other hospital practices – such as the administering of drugs during labour – may have short-term effects on the baby's ability to suck, yet we know that the first few days are crucial to establishing a feeding pattern, and for allowing the baby to drink the maximum amount of colostrum.

Sally Inch, author of *Birthrights*, examines the problems which sometimes arise after the use of pethidine during labour. (Its use is extremely common in British hospitals):

It may also make the baby dopey, sleepy and slow to breathe, and the effects on sucking may last for up to two weeks.

Pethidine delays the development of the ability to habituate for at least two months and the overall effect of pethidine on the newborn may be the unfortunately familiar sight in some maternity hospitals of the baby who is at the same time jumpy and sleepy and a poor feeder in addition!

My Manchester doctor complained that his baby slept so much he never seemed to want to feed. He could not, therefore, understand what I meant by unlimited feeding, or how 'demand feeding' could be put into practice. The baby who cries a lot is a better communicator than the baby who sleeps a lot in such a case. At least the mother of the crying child knows she can soothe him by carrying him and allowing him to suckle frequently. My doctor's new baby was hardly making any demands at all.

The answer is to keep mother and baby together, day and night. The baby who sleeps near the breast will suckle in his sleep. During REM sleep, he will move his jaw as if feeding – every mother will have seen her baby doing this. If the baby is on the breast, this action stimulates milk to come through and the baby receives nourishment without waking. He will therefore relieve the breast of heaviness between more serious feeds, and stimulate the breast into constant and long-lasting milk production.

Unlimited feeding is not merely a matter of 'demand' (waiting for the baby to wake and cry), but of symbiosis – the 'association of two different organisms living attached to each other to their mutual advantage'.[7] Clearly, the presence of the mother at night is crucial to the success of the symbiotic relationship. Such freedom was far from the minds of the educators of the Victorian age:

> It is improper and pernicious to keep infants continually at the breast; and it would be less hurtful, nay even judicious, to let them cry for a few nights, rather than to fill them incessantly with milk, which readily turns sour on the stomach, weakens the digestive organs, and ultimately generates scrofulus affections [forms of tuberculosis].
>
> (*Enquire Within Upon Everything*, 1882)

We now know that sour milk in the stomach is not the cause of TB. The ban on night-feeding was an essential part of the restrictions placed on breastfeeding mothers. If frequent feeding in the day was a nuisance, then how much more demanding was the baby who cried at night. Now that there were larger homes, with airy nurseries, babies could sleep well away from their parents, and be trained to 'sleep through'.

Children can be conditioned to sleep through the night, but it is rare for a baby to take a regular ten hours or so of slumber throughout infancy. The easiest way to avoid disturbance is for the breastfeeding child to sleep with the mother. Not only does this create the minimum of noise and fuss, but it may, according to new evidence, allow the mother to get a better night's sleep:

> The quality of sleep the newly-delivered mother experiences may be improved by breastfeeding at night. Although there is no direct experimental evidence to suggest a role for oxytocin in the control of cortical [brain] activity, there is a suggestion that dopamine receptors in the brain mediate sedation and sleep, and that dopamine may be involved in the mechanism of oxytocin release. If this is the case, it may account for the often reported and observed sleepiness that many women experience when they breastfeed, which facilitates a rapid return to sleep at night.
>
> (*Successful Breastfeeding*)

It is this natural drowsiness that results in many babies sleeping in the big bed. Although the mother may not have originally intended it, she falls asleep on the job.

Child psychotherapist Janine Sternberg slept with her first two children on and off this way, until she realized – with the birth of her third child – that it was not worth dragging herself out of bed at night: 'So often at night you'd feed the baby and it would appear to fall asleep sucking and you'd very gently get up, and just as you put it in the crib, it would wake up again.

'Eventually it dawned on me – why bother? Sometimes the baby would just stay with us by default, or out of sheer exhaustion. You'd be feeding, and the next thing you know you'd find you'd been asleep, and had woken up and that the baby was asleep next to you all the time.'

Babies, too, fall asleep as they feed. Doctors in Sweden have now identified chemicals in breast milk which are similar to those found in commonly prescribed tranquillizers. 'It appears,' said the magazine *Practical Parenting*, 'that mother's milk has been soothing babies for centuries, long before the pharmaceutical industry discovered artificial chemicals to produce a similar type of effect.'[8]

Given the mutual drowsiness of mother and child, it seems amazing that fashion should fight so hard against co-sleeping. The late childcare expert Dr Hugh Jolly used to tell mothers not to sleep with their infants. Then he saw the practice at first hand and realized how relaxing, reassuring and easy it was to 'sleep-feed'. Babies were permitted to sleep with their mothers at Charing Cross Hospital where Dr Jolly was consultant paediatrician:

> I always used to advise parents against bringing their children into bed with them but I have now changed . . . Everything is much simpler if [the baby] is allowed to 'sleep-feed', meaning that he sleeps alongside you in bed and feeds when he wants, often without waking you. This is a controversial practice both in the United Kingdom and the United States, but it is perfectly safe provided the mother has not had a sedative. In the hospital where I work we have practised this method for years without problems. Many mothers have told me they cannot sleep if their baby is not in the bed. Many others have had their babies in their beds for years but felt guilty until recently when they were told it is safe.
>
> (*Book of Child Care*, revised edition, 1985)

On night-feeding itself, Dr Jolly remarks:

> Because you have slept beforehand and are warm and relaxed, it is likely to be a satisfying feed for the baby . . .

In other words, sleep-feeding may be a cosier and less stressful experience than day-feeding, especially for the new and nervous mother. Rather than insisting that the new-born sleeps in a cot, hospital midwives might consider leaving him in his mother's arms, from where, in the unpressurized quiet of the night, he will naturally take to the breast.

Mike Woolridge, a lactation physiologist at Bristol University, develops the idea that night-time feeds are often happier for mother and baby than day-time sessions. He writes:

> Intriguingly, for many mothers who attend the breastfeeding clinic, and who are having difficulties feeding (e.g. breast refusal at day-time feeds) the night-time may be the only ones which go well.
> (Woolridge and Jones, *Bristol NCT newsletter*, June 1988)

A friend of mine who was careful – on advice from the experts – never to take her baby into bed, breastfed in agony for four months until her milk supply finally dried up. Her first experiences of breastfeeding were in a bright and noisy hospital ward, as unlike home as possible, with two midwives cramming the baby's jaws around the nipple at feeding time. The baby screamed, and she felt like doing the same. She never enjoyed the feeds, nor felt relaxed enough to lie down or walk around while feeding, and always associated the event with that first, raw bite of the baby's gums against her breast. Had she been able to breastfeed in the drowsy domain of the bed; had she fed and held her baby constantly, the pain, embarrassment and feelings of failure may never have dogged her determined efforts. Even at the end, she bitterly regretted not being able to carry on.

One has to admire the selfless way in which many Western women tackle breastfeeding, which they believe to be best for their babies. But if they had better counselling and support in the first place, their suffering would be unnecessary.

One mother wrote to a national newspaper:

> The saddest thing of all is that if only you can learn to do it properly, breastfeeding can be very pleasant for both the

145

mother and the baby. Nobody who switches to bottle-feeding because they can't stand the pain should feel guilty: it's the people who should be showing them how to do it who ought to take the blame.

(Patricia Finney, London, *Independent*, 2 August 1988)

Unfortunately the people 'showing us how to do it' are not always trained in the art of knowing when to help and when to stand back. A survey of eighty-eight maternity nurses in three British hospitals criticized their knowledge as often outdated or inadequate – researchers said they relied on personal beliefs when giving breastfeeding information.[9] Sometimes professional interference can be emotionally undermining – occasionally it is physical. Mother Alisa Washington recalls how an over-zealous midwife turned her happily-feeding new-born into a screaming baby who rejected the breast:

. . . he [Ben] fed perfectly every three or four hours. I felt so proud of myself . . . That evening Ben seemed fidgety and I presumed he had wind so I offered him the breast again but he refused. So I just cuddled him. One of the midwives . . . said he was still hungry, let's try him again . . . I thought that she was the professional and knew best so I let her help me. That was my biggest mistake.

For over an hour she held Ben tightly by the head forcing him on to my breast, he was screaming by this stage and I felt totally helpless. Whatever I said to her she would not listen. I felt as though she was raping me the way she was pulling at my breast. Thankfully another midwife, Chloe, took Ben away to give him a bath to calm down. Then she suggested that she tried him to the breast again but he just started screaming. So after a bottle he went to sleep.

('How to Wreck Breastfeeding', *AIMS Journal*, Spring 1995)

Despite his mother's many efforts, Ben lost so much weight in two weeks that she decided to put him on the bottle.[10] The extreme disappointment of mothers who desperately want to breastfeed is often compounded by their own (and others') labels of 'failure'. Alisa did not 'fail' her son in any way – she was battling against impossible odds.

It is unnecessary and intrusive for a midwife to stand over the uninitiated couple (mother and baby), positioning the infant jaw around the nipple. Only if there is an acknowledged failure to feed need she offer her expertise, and even then her role should be one of helping the mother to relax, rather than engineering the mechanics of the first bite.

Ironically, the latest debates on breastfeeding have concentrated on preparing the nipples, a preliminary which may not even be required when mother and baby are constantly together. Patricia Finney writes:

> Most babies, given the chance, would like to suckle all day and night and the effect on the mother's nipples can be like suddenly walking thirty miles in bare feet.

Remedies such as massaging the nipples with surgical spirit, or tucking cabbage leaves inside your bra, leave many women wincing – and rightly so. Breasts do not normally need to be toughened up for feeding. Constant suckling, especially at night, keeps the areola moist and supple; and a baby who is offered the breast as often as he wants is unlikely to approach the scene like Jaws Junior, ready for the kill.

Many mothers complain about the ferocity of their baby's bite. This may be the result of the long gaps they are imposing between feeds. Ashley Montagu describes the 'unloved life' of the Mundugumor child. The Mundugumor are a river people of New Guinea, who – in the 1930s at least – were discovered to be 'an aggressive, hostile people who live by themselves in a state of mutual distrust'. Montagu summarizes their breastfeeding techniques:

> From birth on the infant is carried in a rough-plaited basket, semicircular in profile, suspended from the mother's forehead.

The basket is harsh, stiff and opaque. No warmth from the
mother's body can penetrate it . . . At home the infant in its
basket is hung up. When it cries, without touching its body,
the mother or other female scratches the outside of the basket
with her fingernail, making a harsh grating sound . . . If . . .
the crying does not stop the infant is suckled – the mother
standing up while doing so. There is no playful fondling
between mother and child. The moment suckling stops, the
child is returned to his prison. Children therefore develop a
strong fighting attitude, holding on to the nipple as firmly as
possible, frequently choking from swallowing too rapidly. The
choking angers the mother and infuriates the child, thus further
turning the suckling experience into one of anger and
frustration . . .

(*Touching – The Human Significance of the Skin*)

As Edmund Owen said back in the 1880s, the new-born is rave-
nously hungry after three hours without food.[11] The unwitting child
thinks that if he chomps harder, he'll get more milk out – especially if
he knows he is going to be whisked off the breast before he has
properly finished.

Chloe Fisher advises all mothers to let the baby choose when he
comes off the breast, however long that takes. A baby eventually
stops suckling of his own accord.

Current advice leads the mother into a downward spiral: her
breasts become engorged, baby cannot fix properly on the areola, her
nipples become cracked, feeding is painful, mother limits feeds even
more to avoid pain, baby sucks even harder next time . . .

It would have helped, for instance, if the midwives attending my
friend had read this paragraph about allowing mother and baby to
feed and sleep together:

. . . the mother needs to be able to put the baby to the breast
at night, not only to stimulate her breasts, but to '*practice*'
attaching the baby to the breast while it is still soft, in

preparation for effective milk removal. Furthermore a woman delivered in hospital needs to have experienced her baby's feeding patterns '*round the clock*' (which is something that women delivered at home will do automatically), so that she does not feel that there are any confidence-sapping gaps in her knowledge when she goes home.

(Successful Breastfeeding)

The immediate effects of constant suckling from the first few hours and in the first few days further reveal the symbiosis of mother and baby. The uterus returns to shape more quickly, while baby receives the maximum amount of the valuable pre-milk (colostrum), so rich in protein and anti-bodies.

A mother's milk will still come in, even if her baby does not suck at the breast for twenty-four hours after the birth,[12] but this does not mean the first days are of no value for breastfeeding. They allow the mother and baby to establish a rhythm that will set them up for months.

Engorgement often sets in by the end of the first week. This may be a sign that the baby is not milking the areola properly (he has only the nipple in his mouth), or that he has not been allowed to suckle freely. Ideally, the baby needs to be allowed to feed for as long as he chooses, with no time restrictions or swapping of sides, unless he spontaneously asks for more. Studies show that prolonged feeding from one breast at a time is less likely to lead to engorgement and infant colic.[13] Swollen, painful breasts are a sign of insufficient feeding, and this is one step towards running down the mother's milk supply. Mothers who are allowed to feed their babies unrestrictedly from the beginning are the ones least likely to suffer with breastfeeding problems later on. The early 'colostrum days' are their chance to get a pattern going before the milk flows.

Dr Michel Odent believes that if there is no interruption in the early phase of feeding, babies may gain weight from the outset. He questions the assumption that a new-born baby 'normally' loses weight immediately after the birth. His findings are based on studies of women he assisted at home births in Britain, ninety per cent of whom slept with their babies.

'. . . the amount of colostrum a baby can consume in the first days after birth is generally underestimated, as is the extreme importance of colostrum itself,' he writes. 'I know of babies who have spent two of their first three hours of life suckling at the breast.'[14] This, of course, is only possible given a range of conducive conditions, most of which relate to privacy and the initial intimacy of mother and baby.

According to Dr Odent, an instinctive approach to feeding, coupled with the relaxed atmosphere of a home delivery, enables women to satisfy their babies' needs. Hospitals, he says, including his own at Pithiviers near Paris, cannot completely capture the calming effect of giving birth at home. His neo-natal weight charts for home-delivered babies who feed without limitation night and day do not dip as you might expect, but rise steadily from birth.

An American study conducted in the 1970s further suggests the importance of bringing mother and baby together at the very beginning:

> . . . two groups of mothers had expressed a desire to breast-feed. One group were given their babies to suckle shortly after birth, and the other had no contact with theirs till some sixteen hours later. No mother in either group had to stop breast-feeding for physical reasons. However, two months later, those mothers who had had their infants to suckle immediately after birth were still all breastfeeding, while of the others five out of six had stopped.
>
> (Aidan Macfarlane, *The Psychology of Childbirth*)

Jacquie, a mother from South Wales who wanted to breastfeed, had a particularly long and difficult labour in hospital. An hour after the birth, she fed her son and was then left to rest. She slept off the effects of two painful nights and an epidural. Eight hours later, a midwife came to see her, asking 'When was this child last fed?'

Nobody had suggested to her that the baby needed to feed. Jacquie had read books about breastfeeding that told her that the milk didn't come in for three days, and that the baby would not be hungry for twenty-four hours in any case. She suffered terribly from cracked nipples and severe engorgement, and it was only her own persever-ance that enabled her finally to breastfeed her baby.

Once a breastfeeding pattern has been established, a mother and baby need each other to maintain the rhythm of symbiotic suckling. It makes sense that a baby should be able to stimulate the optimum amount of food for himself at night as well as during the day:

> Once lactation is established, night feeds provide the infant
> with a substantial proportion of his 24 hour intake. The
> younger the baby, the more likely he is to consume the same
> volume of milk during the 12 hours from 5 pm and 5 am as
> between 5 am and 5pm; i.e. 50 per cent on average. It is
> therefore to be expected that the baby will be hungry at
> night . . .

> (*Successful Breastfeeding*)

Before Frances was born, I had invested in a large pack of breast pads, to mop up the leaks, also a set of plastic breast shells to catch the drips of milk to store them in bottles to freeze, for those 'essential' nights off. When, in the first week, I clearly had enough milk for my baby, the community midwife was very excited, as she wanted me to send any spare milk to the hospital's bottle bank. But I only ever dripped a few measly drops, and these ceased to flow within two weeks.

Frances suckled a lot at first, though not constantly. She did not need a dummy, nor did she suck her thumb, except briefly in the early days as a sign that she wanted the breast. Feeding at all times, both night and day, meant that Frances and I were attuned to each other. Frances took as much as she needed, and stimulated my breasts to manufacture just the required amount – no more, no less. I was not blighted by the problem my mother, my mother-in-law, my grandmother and my friends had had – insufficient milk. Nor was I over-producing.

The baby who gets his fill of the breast will not need to suck on anything else. This is good news for his tender gums. The human breast is soft and yielding, and does no damage.

The modern Western attitude to breastfeeding is that it is probably a Good Thing, but who wants too much of a Good Thing? The mood is captured perfectly in this *Times* article by Dr Thomas Stuttaford:

> Women should be given every encouragement and help to breast-feed but some find it repugnant and others have physical problems that prevent it. These mothers should be reassured that it is the cuddling while feeding that is the most important factor in establishing bonding and that careful bottle-feeding will to a large extent alleviate any problems caused by lack of breast milk . . .
>
> A family has to develop as a unit. The role of the father in the modern family is becoming less prominent than it should be for some men because of the hours they have to spend away from home, at work and commuting. If a child becomes even more attached to the mother than is necessary because of prolonged breast-feeding, the father's essential position in the household may be further undermined.
>
> ('When breast is no longer best
> for the loving mother and child', 21 May 1997)

We want to increase the appalling breastfeeding rates in industrialized countries, yet seem not to realize that the single major problem is society's ambivalent attitude towards the breast. Our reluctance to allow babies to feed in public, our preference for them to be rapidly and prematurely weaned, our expectation that mothers will leave the nearly new-born baby at home to join the workplace – these are the factors which contribute to the repugnance and 'physical problems' which Dr Stuttaford describes. The lessons about attachment we learnt in the 1950s are conveniently forgotten by those who would like to place limitations on the feeding patterns of babies by day and by night.

So we need to understand the Art of Breastfeeding, to borrow the title of probably the best book on the subject.[15] In order to breastfeed for any length of time, a mother must be convinced of her ability to feed and be supported by those who share her conviction. She needs to enter the breastfeeding relationship as openly as she can – open, perhaps, to the possibility of an intimate long-term relationship with her baby.

When Alice, my second baby, was born in Manchester, I helped to organize a pregnancy and mother support group. Those of us who had the greatest emotional postnatal worries were undoubtedly those anticipating their return to work. The early breastfeeding relationship is easily marred by fears about weaning. These fears often lead to mothers weaning much earlier than they had originally intended.

Breastfeeding, which requires mental calm and confidence, is not easy under such conditions. Fathers who fear their family authority will be undermined by the mother–infant dyad may unintentionally add to the atmosphere of tension. They may, of course, be reassured that this intimate start to life will render their children more – not less – independent. And feeding at night is one of the best ways to create the intimacy necessary for successfully breastfeeding at all.

Not only does night-feeding keep the baby satisfied, it also releases a higher level of prolactin, which sustains breast-milk production in the long term:

A recent study has demonstrated that prolactin release in response to night-time suckling is greater than during the day; thus milk production may get its greatest '*boost*' when the baby feeds at night.

(*Successful Breastfeeding*)

Long-term lactation is not achieved by four-hourly feeding routines. The areola needs frequent and regular stimulation. If this is provided, almost any woman can breastfeed a baby, even if she has never given birth. Many experts[16] quote examples of women who have breastfed adopted babies.

The women of the Pitjandjara, a desert people from Australia, breastfeed their babies for at least two years. Their adult women are milk-producing throughout their fertile lives, and are able to breast-feed each other's children.[17] A grandmother may breastfeed an infant of the third generation, when mother falls ill or is absent.

Another value of night-feeding is its role in suppressing ovulation. Round-the-clock suckling is invaluable to women relying on the contraceptive qualities of breastfeeding. According to birth cam-paigner Sheila Kitzinger:

> Breast-feeding tends to reduce fertility but it is not an effective contraceptive unless you are suckling the baby intermittently right through the 24 hours and are giving him or her no other food or fluid at all.

> *(Pregnancy and Childbirth)*

Successful Breastfeeding makes a connection between a woman's fertility and the milk-release hormone, prolactin:

> The frequent suckling, which results in elevated prolactin levels, also suppresses ovulation – although the exact mechanism is not yet clear. The contraceptive effect of breastfeeding, although not 100 per cent reliable, may be of great importance to those who for personal or religious reasons do not wish to use conventional (western) methods, and it is therefore vital that these women are not subjected to any restrictions on feeds, especially at night.

We should consider the effects of modern breastfeeding management on millions of families across the non-industrialized world. Many people, dependent on natural family spacing, have found their families unexpectedly enlarged because fertility returned too soon.

If left to feed unhindered, a woman may go for a year or more before the return of her monthly period.

In fact, most women in the West feed their new-born babies according to such strict routines that their periods return almost immediately, and accidental pregnancies leave mothers with babies only 10 or 11 months apart. The swift onset of menstruation is directly linked to our universal failure to breastfeed for any length of time.

A study carried out in Scotland[18] has demonstrated that supplementing breast milk with other feeds, and reducing the amount of time allowed for suckling, have a direct effect on the monthly cycle. Researchers say that no mothers in their study ovulated during unsupplemented breastfeeding, although the women were well nourished.

It is little wonder that Western women, having few children and little respite from periods, tend to be anaemic. Even more worrying are studies which show that the monthly drag on the reproductive system, for years on end, may make women more prone to degenerative diseases, such as cancer. Night-feeds would help to stem menstruation for many months.

When a mother sleeps with her baby, she is truly demand-feeding, because the infant takes exactly what he needs. Even if feeds are initiated by the mother during the day, by night they are baby-led. And as he and his mother are asleep, there is no emotional pressure for him to feed for shorter, or longer, periods than he wants to.

A baby who is allowed to suckle in the bed takes consistently the same amount of milk every night for twelve months, the crucial period highlighted by the government's report published in 1980. Night-feeding provides an opportunity for nature to take control:

Data show that nocturnal breast feeding was not restricted at any age. As weaning foods were introduced, 'day' time breast feeding was reduced, but night time feeding remained unaffected, and thus made up a higher proportion of 24 hour milk intake in older infants.

> . . . the amount of breast milk consumed at 'night' was not
> related to infant age and remained constant over the first year
> of life.
>
> (Imong et al., Proc. 5th Asian Congress of Nutrition,
> October 1987)

Once the breastfeeding pattern is established to include night-feeds, it is hard to destroy. But there was one occasion in the early days, when I almost upset the rhythm between Frances and myself.

A friend lent me a breast pump to express milk for storage, as she had done. I spent half an hour pumping away with pitifully little result. The nipple rapidly became sore, and two days later the breast started to over-produce. Just one intervention meant a lot of work to regain our symmetry.

One nationwide survey[19] showed that forty per cent of British mothers chose to breastfeed their babies because it was 'convenient'. And so it is, offering simplicity – an easy way of carrying the perfect infant food, stored at a perfect temperature, everywhere you and your baby go. But society conspires to make things difficult.

The breastfeeding mother is not encouraged to suckle her baby in public, and other women are often her worst critics for this. (Edwardian mothers could buy an 'anti-embarrassment device', which fed baby via a tube concealed in their clothing.) In private, the 'norm' is to try to breastfeed at night camping in separate rooms.

While the baby in the cot cries into the night and learns either the futility of expressing his needs, or how to make his parents come running, the baby in the bed is learning the value of hope. The breast is always there. He sucks on it, and at first nothing happens, but he knows that if he keeps sucking, *through his own endeavours*, the milk will come through.

He does not need to scream, or become angry, or ruin anyone else's sleep. And he is rewarded with just as much milk as he needs and wants – because in the early days, need and desire are the same. The analogy with a beef steak in the middle of the night does not hold. The foetus in the womb is on constant tap to nourishment via the placenta, and a new-born baby weans himself very gradually from this uninterrupted flow. He certainly does not differentiate between night and day in his feeding requirements.

We enter the twenty-first century with a vastly improved knowledge of nutrition and obstetrics. We can see the foetus floating in the womb, and we can keep tiny premature babies alive – yet we are so far from restoring confidence in women, that thousands are still unable to feed their own young.

According to some figures, breastfeeding is an art in decline. The 1990 Infant Feeding Survey for England and Wales, reported in October 1992 by HMSO, records that while sixty-four per cent of mothers begin breastfeeding, only thirty-nine per cent continue for two weeks or more and by four months, eighty per cent of babies are fully weaned.

All of these figures are worse than previous years, but positive change is not impossible. In Norway, ninety-eight per cent of babies are breastfed at birth, with sixty per cent still breastfed at six months.[20] The reason, according to Norwegian mother Vigdis Wold, is the universal social acceptance of breastfeeding in that country:

> . . . it will take more than a ban on promotions in maternity wards or even a great official publicity campaign to encourage British mothers to breastfeed their babies for months rather than a day or two. There is a cultural difference involved.
>
> In Norway a mother can breastfeed her baby anywhere, without embarrassment – at work, on the train, in a restaurant, even in parliament. It is assumed that she will prefer to breastfeed as long as possible, it's convenient and she is surrounded by friends, family and professionals whose experience and advice support her in that choice.
>
> My own experience as a breastfeeding mother in London was very different.

('Food Thoughts', *The Guardian*, 25 March 1995)

When breastfeeding is acceptable during the day, it is usually found to be acceptable at night, too. After all, if we don't feed at night, we jeopardize the whole picture – as scientists discovered in New Zealand, when they analysed the factors which were associated with 'a shorter overall duration of breastfeeding'. Next to 'maternal smoking' and 'dummy use' is the factor 'mother not bedsharing'.[21] Similar research from south-east England concluded that: 'Bed sharing was associated with a longer duration of breastfeeding.' However, they added, 'This may not necessarily be a causal relationship because breastfeeding may promote bedsharing.'[22] Either way, it's a causal relationship – it's just that the breastfeeding seems to be considered a desirable outcome, while co-sleeping is not.

Lone voices throughout the century have questioned the medical management of breastfeeding. They have gone largely unheeded. In 1953, one writer proclaimed the virtues of instinct-led feeding:

> When this regime becomes universally adopted, as surely it will, so the last chapter on the history of infant feeding will be concluded.
>
> (I.G. Wickes, *A History of Infant Feeding*)

Some of us feel the last chapter is taking a long time to write.

7 | NOMADS AND NANNIES

> I was brought up in the time when women were the mana
> [power] of the family home. They were the sacred house of
> the people, the foundation of life, the silver-haired
> knowledge, an encyclopaedia of all the values of Maoridom. I
> slept as all the other brothers and sisters did, between our
> parents, and our mother was the greatest teacher I know, of
> my life.
>
> (A Maori remembers)

It's time we put ourselves into perspective. Babies who scream in the night, breasts that blister from misuse and electronic cot alarms are the trappings of modern mothering in the developed world. History and anthropology show us that not all societies suffer like this with their children.

It would be wrong to assume that every non-industrialized culture has child-rearing methods that are superior to our own. This glance across centuries and continents is not intended to be a brochure of beautiful babycare ideas. It may, however, be useful to be aware of what other people are doing, if only to reassure ourselves that yet another 'difficult' phase of civilization is likely to pass.

Many of the habits of primitive man (or of people without a written language) are still practised by the hunter-gatherer tribes which roam every continent. Such groups are often labelled as outcasts in their own lands, and find their traditional lifestyle open to attack. Governments want to pin people down, missionaries want to convert them, roving camera crews want to record the last glimpses of uncivilized man in his environment.

The hostility of our own society towards the gypsy community is a typical example of our impulse to socialize others according to our own rules. In the words of an anthropologist from Granada Television:

> . . . nomads are feared and despised by those who govern them. People who cannot be confined to one place throughout the year are difficult to control for purposes of education, health and, most important of all, taxation.
>
> (André Singer, *Disappearing World*)

Despite the difficulties, some nomadic tribes survive. The G/wi, a people numbering around 2,000, wander in bands through the Kalahari Desert in southern Africa. Theirs is an egalitarian and loose-structured society, where men and women work together in all but a few tasks (men hunt, women prepare the food). Most marriages are stable; spouses are chosen on the wishes of the couple as well as of other family members. Mutual affection tends to be warm but not showy.

Anthropologist George B. Silberbauer explains how the G/wi bushmen raise their children:

> A baby is never left alone, but is carried everywhere on its mother's hip or slung in her cloak. If the child cries, it is given the breast immediately. When the mother is sitting in a group, the baby is passed around and rocked in the arms of anybody old enough to do so without dropping it. Men and boys show the same fondness for babies as do women and girls. Babies are not parted from their mothers at night, but sleep held in their mothers' arms . . . A baby thus spends its first years in the secure affection of an attentive band of colleagues.
>
> (*Hunters and Gatherers Today*)

A similar pattern is found among the Paliyans of southern India, who move in groups through the rain shadow of the Palni and Anaimalais mountain ranges. The Paliyans value individuality and personal independence above all else. Equality is so important to them that individuals always share their good fortune with others in the group, but other co-operation between group members is rare. Minimal assistance is offered to the weakest among them, and men strive to avoid violence or competition. Husband and wife have an equal say in all matters relating to their marriage. This is how they treat their children for the first two years of life – a view by anthropologist Peter M. Gardner:

> The child spends most of its sleeping and waking hours in direct physical contact with its mother's body. In the daytime, it rests on her left hip in a sling formed from a swath of her upper sari cloth. At night, it sleeps by her side. The mother gives her breast to the child at the slightest whimper, as often as four or five times an hour; denial even at night would be inconceivable, because, as they put it, the child's throat would become dry. Infants over a year regularly ask for these night feeds. There is a great deal of maternal warmth during the first two years, and much concern is expressed for the infant.
> Unless a child is ill, prolonged crying is unlikely. Outbursts of anger are rare; they are averted or appeased quickly, if possible.
>
> (*Hunters and Gatherers Today*)

A third example comes from Africa:

> Night sleep was quantified in a study of infants of the Kipsigis, a Kenyan people. They slept beside their mothers, awakened often, and suckled during the night. They slept less in 24 hours than did a comparison group of American infants.
>
> (Elias, Nicolson, Bora and Johnston, *Paediatrics*, March 1986)

Pat Gray, co-founder of CRY-SIS, a British support group for the mothers of crying children, told me about her travels on the Indian continent. 'I went to Sri Lanka,' she said, 'where the people live in simple houses, made of mud with dried cow dung on the floor and palm leaves for a roof. They sleep on rush mats made out of coconut fibre, and the babies sleep on the floor near their parents.'

Parents belonging to non-industrial cultures are far more likely to sleep with their infants than not. One survey[1] shows that co-sleeping is or may be practised in seventy-one out of ninety societies. McKenna's table of co-sleeping cultures (opposite) illustrates a variety of ways in which parents sleep alongside their young children.

The Copper Eskimo and the Dogrib Indian, the Guayaki of Paraguay and the Walmadjeri bushmen of Australia all sleep with their children. The anthropologists who write about these tribes never fail to mention the apparent 'indulgence' of parents towards their offspring. But not all primitive tribes are so generous. Not all sleep with their babies.

The Nootka, an Indian tribe on the north-west coast of India, are known for their aggression. Within the group, violence rarely goes beyond swearing and hair-pulling, but tribal warfare is a regular and savage occurrence. Their practice is to raid other tribes during the night, or during a ceremony, with the aim of beheading as many men as possible and bringing home the women and children as slaves. Victorious warriors return home singing, with the heads of the slain on poles. They publicly torture and humiliate any prisoner chief before killing him.

The Nootkan baby is separated from his mother at birth, so that his head can be elongated according to the group's ideals of beauty. (A neighbouring tribe flatten the heads of their new-born for the same reason.) This is how a baby spends his first months:

> During these four days following the delivery, the woman placed and kept the baby in a temporary cradle consisting of a mat suspended on either side between a pair of poles, with a crossbar to hold up the neck, bark mats for bedding, and a head-pressing device of cedar bark running over the forehead plus bark pads on either side of the head . . .

Culture	HRAF ID	Where Do They Sleep?	Upon What Do They Sleep	Comments
Ganda	FK7	Infant with parents	Bed, with bark cloth, laced with cowhide thongs	Teenagers & single adults in same-sex groups
Flores	OF9	Infant with parents	Bamboo sleeping bench (hale-hale)	Children with friends in same-sex group
Lau	OQ6	Infant with owner & wife	Pile of mats; Tongan tapa as covers; bed called palang	At 7 to 10 years, boys move to other huts
Maori	OZ4	Families sleep together, several to a hut	Special sleeping huts for summer & for winter	Winter huts have sunken floors & are heaped over with dirt for warmth
Bushmen	FX10	Infant with parents	Scooped-out area in hut, in grass	At 7, girls sleep with grandparents or relative
Yap	OR22	Infant with parents until 2 or 3, sometimes in hanging basket		At 5, child moves from parents' room
Garo	AR5	Infant with parents	Mats from bark of trees	Bachelor quarters
Katab	FF38	Mothers with infants, husband, siblings	Mattress of rags	Bachelor & maiden co-sleep dorms; sleep during times of scarcity
Mauri	MS12	Infant with parents	Sleeping mat. Kathari mattress of rags	
Tiwi	O120	Children with parents	Mats of paper bark (melaleuca)	
Cuna	SB5	Infant with mother in same hammock: father in same room	Handmats – cotton of ciba tree covered with plantain leaves	
Tzeltal	NV9	Youngest infants on parents' mats (patates)		At 5, sleep with same-sex sibling
Bhil	AW25	Infant with mother		Sisters & brothers separated past childhood

(Table of co-sleeping practices, *Medical Anthropology*, 1986)

163

After four days in the temporary cradle the baby was moved to a one-piece wooden one, hollowed like a canoe, with a projecting headpiece and a footpiece flush with the sides. The baby was bound into this cradle, which was carried vertically. A girl baby's cradle had three holes bored in the footboard for urine to leak through, but a boy baby's cradle did not; he was left with his penis exposed.

(Carleton S. Coon, *The Hunting Peoples*)

An interesting comparison may be made between the habits of two tribes from the South Seas – the New Guinea Arapesh and the Mundugumor. While the Arapesh, an extremely gentle people, nurse their children on demand and sleep with them at night, the Mundugumor are 'exactly the opposite':

They despise the pregnant woman. When a child is born, he is placed in a hard, uncomfortable basket. He is nursed only when he simply will not stop crying. His mother stands while she nurses him, and as soon as he stops sucking, if only for a second, the baby is put down. Instead of letting the child wean when he is ready, the security-seeking child is pushed away from his mother. She forces him to wean long before he is ready, but at a time when he can survive on other foods.

These people lack all trust in one another. Until the government outlawed it, they actively practiced head-hunting. They are hateful and distrustful. Sexual foreplay is performed with biting and scratching one's partner to the point of bleeding.

(Tine Thevenin, *The Family Bed*)

For good or for bad, the traditions of isolated tribes are fast disappearing. Peoples who for centuries shared bedspace with their children have been urged to abandon the practice, and to adopt Western ways.

The Mistassini Cree are one of the groups of big hunters living on

the Labrador Peninsula, on the remote east coast of Canada. They
have had contact with Europeans for three hundred years, although
this was limited until prospectors built a railroad in the 1950s.

Today most Mistassini have converted to Christianity and are
registered as Anglicans, but as each member of the group is free to
choose his own religion, ancient shamanism is still practised. Mothering techniques are similarly a mixture of old and new: babies are
breastfed on demand for at least a year, but these days they are
expected to sleep alone:

> Bedding is derived from European sources and consists mostly
> of woollen blankets and occasionally sleeping bags . . . Infants
> are placed in moss sacks and sleep in hammocks. The latter are
> most likely a European inspiration. Cradle boards are known
> and said to be occasionally used . . .
>
> (*The Hunting Peoples*)

The modern Japanese family may no longer take its children to bed as
is still the tradition in rural parts; mothers on the Indian continent are
persuaded to try the cot along with the bottle; the Inuit who used to
sleep naked together in their Arctic igloos now tend to cover up their
babies and put them in cradles.

It is now considered normal in many societies to separate mother
and baby at birth. But why depart from nature's needs at all? Why
should any civilization, at any time, decide that mother and baby
should sleep in separate beds?

Natural-childbirth pioneer Michel Odent is fascinated by the
question. He travelled to China to observe mothering practices
there, and was amazed by what he saw.

'I was studying the conditions of birth,' he says, 'and found that
Chinese hospitals tried to copy the West by having delivery tables,
with stirrups and so on. They were very proud of their modern
equipment. But something they had forgotten to copy was to
separate the mother from her baby.

'I found this out quite by chance. We were in a village visiting a

165

house, and I asked who slept in the bedroom. The woman said, "I sleep here with my baby because he is just six months old." '

Many cultures consider bedsharing, hammock- or mat-sharing with their children to be normal behaviour. Of the societies for whom the practice is anti-social, the United States and the former Soviet Union are the prime examples. North American theorists and psychologists lead the field in Western childcare, but the former Communist countries also separate mother and baby with regimental efficiency from birth.

'In Russia, Czechoslovakia and East Germany, it's worse,' says Odent. 'In one maternity unit, I saw a huge nursery, with babies wrapped like parcels. At feeding time, the baby is brought to the mother, and then taken straight back to the cot. This applies to hospitals throughout the Communist bloc, and that is a great part of humanity.'

Dr Odent has his own theory as to why certain societies choose to separate mother and child at night: 'The only cultures we can study are those which have survived, and which have eliminated the others,' he says. 'So even the most primitive societies surviving today are likely to be the most aggressive ones.

'Perhaps to separate mother and baby at birth is to create an aggressive civilization. And if we look at the two most successful and aggressive cultures of all – Russia and America – we can see that there mother and baby are kept apart.'

Studies have shown that when babies are deprived of physical contact, they are more likely to grow into aggressive adults. One survey[2] of primitive cultures illustrates that lack of touch in infancy produces individuals disposed towards violence. A warring tribe will harden its offspring by separating babies from their mothers for the first few days, or at night-time. It may not be coincidence that American and Russian babies are also kept in cots.

Despite the spread of 'modern' practices, sleeping next to babies is still taken for granted by many social groups. Paediatrician Betsy Lozoff begins her study on sleep-management in North American families with this point:

Pediatric health professionals often advise parents not to sleep with their children . . . This approach to sleep is different from the practices that one of the authors (B.L.) observed in Latin America and Asia while conducting medical and anthropologic research projects. Infants were generally not expected to go to bed by themselves at a regular time or place or to sleep alone during the night. Instead, they were held until asleep and slept with their parents or other family members. Bedtime struggles and crying in the night were not apparent. These observations led to a search of the anthropologic literature, which confirmed that the practices currently recommended by pediatricians differ from those generally found in other cultures. In addition, in one sample of more than 100 societies, the American middle class was 'unique in putting the baby to sleep in a room of his own'.

(Lozoff, Wolf and Davis, *Pediatrics*)

For 'American', read British, European, or any country which encourages competition and harbours aggression. The separation of mother and baby at night is supported by taboo in some primitive cultures and by medical say-so in ours, but the effect is the same.

Societies which attempt – abruptly and prematurely – to wean, train or otherwise mould the baby (sometimes in physical ways, like the Nootkan Indians), tend towards violence. This is turn leads to 'success' in world terms. We did not get where we are today by showing indulgence to our children.

Throughout history civilizations have sometimes favoured, sometimes banned co-sleeping. A letter from one mother to another in the third or second century BC offers childcare advice based on the Pythagorean theorics of which the Greeks were so proud. This emphasized balance and measure in all things:

Myia to Phyllis, greetings. Here is my advice to you now that you have become a mother. Choose a proper and clean wet-

167

nurse, a modest woman who is inclined neither to drowsiness nor to drunkenness . . .

The nurse will give him the nipple and breast not at whim, but after due consideration. In this way she will encourage the baby's health. She will not succumb to sleep when *she* is tired, but when the newborn wants to rest. She will offer the child no small relief . . .

It is best, if the baby is put down to sleep when it is well fed with milk. Such rest is sweet for little ones and such feeding most effective . . . Moreover his water should not be too hard nor too soft, nor his bed too rough – rather, it should fall comfortably on his skin. In each of these areas, Nature desires what is rightfully hers, not luxuries.

(Lefkowitz and Fant, *Women's Life in Greece and Rome*)

Whereas Myia implies that a baby has its own bed or cradle, a second letter – from a first-century Roman household – indicates that a wet nurse was expected to sleep with her charge:

The wet-nurse should be self-controlled so as to abstain from coitus, drinking, lewdness, and any other such pleasure and incontinence . . .

In regard to drinking, first the wet-nurse is harmed in soul as well as in body and for this reason the milk is also spoiled. Secondly, seized by a sleep from which she is hard to awaken, she leaves the newborn untended or even falls down upon it in a dangerous way . . .

(*Women's Life in Greece and Rome*)

Fears of smothering the child were always paramount. Historian Diana Dick believes this is why co-sleeping with babies was considered 'a grievous sin' by the Church in the ninth century. 'I think there was the worry about overlaying the child,' she said, 'although you must remember that babies were swaddled in those days. They would only have their eyes and nose free – so the baby would be unable to move if he was being smothered.'

The French dauphin, Louis XIII, was tucked in at night with official 'bedfellows'. On his first night, so the story goes, the young prince disgraced himself by wetting the bed. This may be another reason why rich folk in civilized societies, cultivated in personal cleanliness and outward neatness, would not always tolerate having a baby in the bed. The modern nappy does away with this particular objection.

But if well-to-do European parents were reluctant to sleep with their babies, they did not expect them to sleep alone.

American mother Tine Thevenin charts the history of bedsharing, which often meant couples, children or servants sleeping together. In the days before central heating and electric lights, neither adult nor child was expected to pass the night alone in a separate bedroom:

> During the sixteenth century in England, the so-called Trinity bed was developed. It consisted of a large bed upon which the immediate family slept. Two smaller beds, often referred to as trundle beds, rolled out from underneath the large bed. The older children, servants, or relatives slept on this.
>
> In the seventeenth century, perhaps the largest of all beds was designed by John Fosbrooke for the royal family. It could sleep 102 persons! Obviously the 'luxury' of separate beds and bedrooms of which we boast today was not at all considered to be a sign of wealth or prosperity at that time.
>
> (*The Family Bed*)

With the rise of the middle classes and the creation of the concept of childhood – previously children were considered to be little adults and not given any special treatment – the practice of co-sleeping began to wane. Christian moralists of the eighteenth century urged people not to share beds unless married, and children of the opposite sex were taught to hide their bodies from each other. All manner of touching and sexual exploration by children was to be discouraged.

In the late eighteenth century, the idea of independence training was put forward: children must learn early self-reliance. This meant toilet-training from three weeks, and sleeping alone at a few weeks old.

Cleanliness being next to godliness, it was not long before hygiene was peddled as a reason for sleeping apart. Sanitary conditions in the poorest part of London were a disgrace, as this extract from Dr Wilan, a late eighteenth-century observer, reveals. There was a lot for the doctors to worry about:

It will scarcely appear credible, though it is precisely true, that persons of the lowest class do not put clean sheets on their beds three times a year; that even where no sheets are used they never wash or scour their blankets or coverlets, nor renew them until they are no longer tenable . . . that from three to eight individuals of different ages often sleep in the same bed; there being in general but one room and one bed for each family . . . The room occupied is either a deep cellar, almost inaccessible to the light, and admitting no change of air; or a

garret with a low roof and small windows, the passage to
which is close, kept dark, and filled not only with bad air, but
with putrid excremental effluvia from a vault at the bottom of
the staircase. Washing of linen, or some other disagreeable
business, is carried on, while infants are left dozing and
children more advanced kept at play whole days on the tainted
bed . . .

(*Diseases in London*, 1801)[3]

Sickness and disease were killing the poorest inner-city dwellers, a
situation which worsened in the Victorian and Edwardian eras,
before the introduction of the Welfare State. What was needed
was a major spending programme to prevent London from becoming
a sewer. Instead the people were warned against the dangers of
sharing a bed.

The middle classes, who were increasing in number, were able to
follow the professionals' advice. Now that they could afford it, they
were being sold the newly valuable commodity of privacy – privacy
from one's neighbours, and privacy within each house from the
servants and from the children. In your clean-air suburb, you could
have a villa with separate bedrooms (a vast improvement on the
traditional curtained-off bed which dominated the living room a
hundred years earlier).

The greatly increased number of bedrooms in Victorian as
compared to Georgian houses of the same class is eloquent
testimony to the value placed on privacy within the family.
The *Builder* in 1864 was quite smug on this point: '. . . When
we reflect upon the scanty supply of sleeping apartments which
it was usual to construct in an ordinary London house of the
annual value of from £80 to £120 a year, at the time when
Regent Street was built, and which scarcely ever exceeded in
number two principal bedrooms and three or four attics, it
becomes difficult to conceive how the last generation bestowed
themselves in their sleeping arrangements.

'. . . our present ideas on the subject render increased accommodation in this respect absolutely necessary.' Smaller houses had smaller rooms, but nearly as many of them.

(Olsen, *The Growth of Victorian London*)

The late Victorians separated even man and wife in the search for wholesome living:

In 1893, *Scribner's Magazine* carried what was probably the first twin-bed advertisement to appear in the United States. It read 'Our English cousins are now sleeping in separate beds. The reason is: *never breathe the breath of another.*'

(*The Family Bed*)

The Edwardians took separation of mother and child to its limits. A baby's life in middle- and upper-class Britain was by now one of solitary confinement. Nanny took charge of all the children, allowing them plenty of fresh air, but not much else in the way of live entertainment. The young Queen Victoria, besotted with Albert, but not a great fan of babies, introduced the perambulator to fashionable society, and soon everyone was wheeling their infants around in mini carriages. Older children were sent away to boarding schools and military academies. Parents delegated most of the upbringing and education of their offspring to professionals. When babies cried, mothers and nannies were encouraged to ignore the screams until the child fell off to sleep. According to Jessica Markwell:

Crying babies were less intrusive than they are today, because the fashion then was to leave them in their prams for long periods, well out of earshot.

(*Practical Parenting*, June 1988)

In 1882, *Enquire Within Upon Everything* described the perfect nursery. It could not be less like the squalid conditions of inner-city slums.

A Bedroom or Night Nursery ought to be spacious and lofty, dry, airy, and not inhabited through the day. No servants, if possible, should be suffered to sleep in the same room, and no linen or washed clothes should ever be hung there to dry, as they contaminate the air in which so considerable a portion of infantile life must be spent.

You can imagine the difficulties the majority of people would have encountered following this prescription. Townsfolk and villagers throughout Britain were still crammed into undersized accommodation. The poorest families had just one room. Only the rich could afford the luxury of an airing room, a nursery, a schoolroom and a playroom, not to mention the servants' quarters.

In Britain and America poor parents were the last to sleep with their babies on a full-time basis. The following describes the typical arrangement in a pre-war London household:

Besides Mother and Father there were five sons and five daughters. Our parents had the top front bedroom, sharing this with the baby and the next youngest child. The girls had the top back bedroom and the boys the ground-floor bedroom. It was mostly two at the top and two at the bottom of a double bed and the odd one in a little truckle bed, the 'iron' bed we called that . . .

Mother had her priorities right, children must have love and food, food for their growing bodies and love to make them secure . . .

(Scannell, *Mother Knew Best – An East End Childhood*)

It was thought that order, cleanliness and moral exactitude would alter the face of Britain. But the separation of infants at night did not bring harmony to all homes. If anything, the frustrations of parents and children created new problems.

The temper tantrum is a phenomenon that is not mentioned in medical literature before 1800. Children were now depicted as wilful, rebellious and in need of severe punishment. 'Spare the rod and spoil the child' – a saying taken from the Bible – was often invoked. For the first time the generation gap revealed the unsavoury truth about Victorian society – the more children were treated as if they were naughty, the naughtier they became. The puritan ethic did not stem behavioural problems; rather it created them.

Children themselves had few rights. Child abuse often went unrecognized, and until the establishment of the NSPCC in 1884, doctors were likely to blame babies' broken bones on congenital disease. Nobody admitted that children were being battered, especially in the nicer homes. In the words of an early NSPCC annual report:

> The average age of victims shows that cruelty is chiefly practised on little children; small babies come in for a large share.
>
> Cruelty is not confined to wretched dwellings. Pianos and bric-a-brac may be in the drawing rooms of people who behave like brute beasts to their offspring.[4]

In 1885, a certain Mrs Montague locked her child in a cupboard as a punishment. The child suffocated. In court, her lawyer argued that parents had absolute rights over their children, and that therefore Mrs Montague was beyond criticism.

The era of the despotic parent, starched-apron nanny and distant child is over. But in Western societies, an increasing number of women work full time, leaving their children in care. It is good that women are returning to work in large numbers, but when the mother comes home at night, she does not take the child into her bed to enjoy his tactile company. Instead, she gets embroiled in the recommended bedtime routine, with a song, a bath, a story and a firm good-night.

Baby may or may not respond to this treatment, but I would envisage a new and dangerous generation gap emerging as a result of our mothering practices. As mother Julie Whitfield wrote in her article 'Listening to our "Stone-Age" Babies':

Something has gone wrong. Here we are mothers . . . we have come a long way. Most of us go out to work, and it's not menial jobs for us any more. We've got important jobs. We've got nannies, childminders, creches, daycare, pre-schools, kindergartens, schools and even after-school activities . . .

Things have really changed for us, it's not like it was . . . except unfortunately for one thing – we keep on giving birth to stone-age babies. These little twenty-first century creatures want to be held, all the time if possible, against our bodies, close to our hearts to hear that familiar beat . . . it's not just during the day they follow their ancient instincts, but it goes on into the night, when they need to be snuggled down between the two bodies who first gave them life. We have come a long way. Let's go back to our babies.

(LLL GB News, no. 85, Jan/Feb 1995)

If working parents could drop the formalities and take their babies into bed, they would be more in touch with their children. There could be a crisis looming, as children grow up more closely bonded to their minders than to their parents.

The idea of taking a baby into bed all night, every night, as a matter of course, is relatively new to parents in the West. Before the late 1980s, the subject was taboo – now it is a viable alternative, gaining slow acceptance among the legions of childcare experts. The possibility of sleeping with my first child would not have occurred to me, had I not spent those few prenatal nights in hospital. Yet, for every parent who says she would never try it, there is another who 'confesses' to sharing bedspace with her children occasionally. In 1988, when I first wrote this book, I estimated that about three-quarters of the parents I spoke to during my research said they slept with their children at some time or other. In 1995, a random study by the Institute of Child Health in London revealed that seventy per cent of four to sixteen-year-olds came into their parents' beds regularly – at least once a week.[5] We might imagine the figure to be higher among younger children, and yet an NOP poll conducted in 1998 by the women's magazine *Bella* found that under-threes were actually less likely to be co-sleeping than the four to sixteen-year-olds in the 1995 study. Countrywide, sixty-one per cent of parents said they had never let their small children into their bed. The vast majority (eighty-four per cent) said they did not believe in letting a baby under one into the family bed. Parents in Scotland were strictest of all on this point – ninety-one per cent were against co-sleeping.[6]

This creates a fascinating picture of modern Britain – of parents determined to keep their babies away from them at night but relenting to the comfort needs of their school-age children. In primitive cultures, the reverse pattern is seen: children who have had their fill of adult company in infancy are expected to emerge with great reserves of independence and to move away from co-sleeping.

A recent shift in sleep trends has been to bring baby (in his cot) out of the nursery and into the family bedroom. Advice on reducing the risks of cot death has encouraged parents to keep their babies near, (if not too near) at night. A PhD thesis conducted at the University of Bristol in 1998 established that around fifty per cent of British parents room-share with their under-ones, while thirty-five per cent of babies sleep in a separate room.[7] Analysis of data from New Zealand and the CESDI reports in Britain has shown room-sharing strongly protective against the risk of cot death – including where mothers take their babies into bed.[8]

Those who are keen not to co-sleep on any account create strategies of their own. Many opt for a bedside vigil with their babies, rather than actually getting into bed with them. Parents are getting as close as they can to their children without breaking society's rules about bedsharing. This is how one mother coped with her three-and-a-half-year-old's reluctance to sleep alone:

> 'She asked me why Mummies and Daddies slept together as they were big people,' said Penny. 'When I tried to explain that all her friends' Mummies and Daddies slept together, she simply declared that there must be lots of lonely children

about. I found it hard to argue with that, so for the last 18 months, we've been sitting by her bedside till she drops off.

'Yes it is tedious, but my doctor agreed that it would be very cruel to let her get worked up every night.'

(*Mother*, June 1988)

No wonder many parents choose the more practical solution, and sleep with their children. A fascinating study made in the US by Betsy Lozoff and her team[9] reveals that many people bedshare on a temporary basis. It is a cross-cultural report, which shows a marked difference between white and black families in their attitudes to bedsharing.

Ms Lozoff found that, contrary to the advice of Dr Spock and other childcare experts, thirty-five per cent of white families and seventy per cent of black families routinely took their children into bed. While white families tended to allow bedsharing at times of stress, or when the children had sleep problems, black parents were more likely to sleep with their children as a matter of course (see table overleaf).

More than half (fifty-six per cent) of white children who came into their parents' bed were rated as having overall disruptive sleep problems. 'Among black children,' however, 'there was no association between co-sleeping and stress, maternal ambivalence, or sleep problems.'

It is impossible to say whether the white children's sleep problems were caused by being taken into bed, or whether white parents were sleeping with their children because of the problems. But as co-sleeping was far less likely to occur in the cases of parents who were educated and highly trained, it could be concluded that white middle-class families do attempt to follow the advice of the childcare books. Only when this advice does not work do parents respond to the needs of the children by taking them into bed.

In another report by Americans Hanks and Rebelsky,[10] it was shown that only eighteen per cent of middle-class mothers who slept with their children actually admitted the fact to their doctors. The modern mother who sleeps with her child knows she is going against the trend, and is unlikely to admit to her 'unacceptable' behaviour.

Many mothers who told me that they took their babies into bed also expressed their relief at talking to someone who did not condemn them for it, yet said it was hard to throw off feelings of guilt. Nurse Maureen Blackman said, 'My daughter Hannah is two. We call her Hannah the horrible. A couple of nights a week she'll howl at three a.m. I'm afraid we have given up as parents and taken her into bed. She sleeps beautifully with us.'

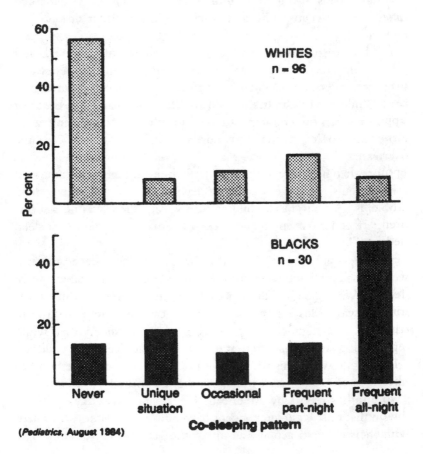

(*Pediatrics*, August 1984)

It is an enormous self-condemnation to say you have given up as a parent, especially when it's for something that is obviously working for you and for your family. But this is how parents are made to feel in our society when they sleep with their children. Co-sleeping is recognized as a sign of failure, not of success.

Maureen Blackman added another explanation for her guilt: 'Bed has such nasty sexual connotations,' she said. 'The media has done it. Parents are afraid to admit that children are in bed with them, because health visitors may think "aha".'

It comforted Maureen to think that Elvis Presley slept with his mother until he was fourteen – apparently the done thing in parts of Kentucky.[11] Girls there may graduate straight from their parents' bed to that of their husband's.

While most mothers see bedsharing as a sign of failure, there is a growing movement – which is strongest in America – that endorses the practice. Groups like the La Leche League, the breastfeeding support network, now advocate that parents sleep with their babies. Many of the mothers in London who give birth at home with Michel Odent automatically take their babies to bed. Betsy Lozoff, in her report, mentions the 'subgroup' of white families who deliberately abandon the cot.

Mothers who keep their babies close to them day and night are often regarded as an oddity in Western society. However, the medical perception of such practices is changing all the time. Research from the Department of Family Medicine at the University of North Carolina concluded that 'La Leche League mothers re-present a subset of nursing mothers who have a life-style of which the primary care physician must be aware in order to provide optimal maternal – infant care.'[12] Eighty per cent of mothers in this study slept with their babies.

Parents all over the world love their children and want to do what is best for them. No one has a monopoly over all the good ideas, and it would be facile to condemn the practice of co-sleeping when it so obviously works for millions of families. Think of all the babies out there for whom night-waking is simply not a problem, because mum and dad – or siblings, or grandma, or aunt – are there. As Marjorie Elias comments, it is all a question of attitude:

> Sharing a bed and late weaning are the common practice of many societies in the world and probably throughout most of human history, although relatively uncommon in our own society. Yet, night waking has been called a 'disease of the so-called developed world'. Where infants share their parents' beds, night waking is not reported to be a problem.
>
> It seems ironic that, although night waking is so much less frequent in infants cared for in Western style, it presents so much more of a problem for parents.
>
> (Elias, Nicolson, Bora and Johnston, *Pediatrics*, March 1986)

For whatever reasons, civilized or not, babies need comfort and company at night; and some parents are determined not to let social conditioning get in the way.

8 | NOT IN FRONT OF THE CHILDREN

For some reason Mum had dreams of Sardinia, so we came; to widows in black, cold churches, candles and heat. We had escaped an England of husbands, fathers, almost-fathers and an upper-middle-class regime of cosmetic alcoholism. I was happy here because once again I slept in my mother's bed, hot against her sunburnt body.

(Tiffany Murray, 'Suddenly One Summer',
Independent on Sunday, 3 May 1998)

Sex after childbirth is complicated enough, without the extra dimension of babies in the bed. For many parents, the prospect of children interrupting their sex life is enough to put them off the idea of bedsharing. Even those who are genuinely interested in the idea take me to one side, whispering, 'How do you do *it?*' Not at all, if you feel like this mother quoted in the tabloid press:

TURNED OFF SEX
Since my little girl caught my husband and I making love, I freeze every time he touches me. We have three children and the youngest, who's three, has to share our bedroom.
    She is a poor sleeper and most nights she gets into our bed. When she gets in, my husband usually goes to sleep in her bed.
    We cope with that, but one night she woke as we were making love, and said out loud, 'Mummy, why are you wriggling about?'

> It's put me right off sex. My husband thinks I'm making
> excuses but I'm not, as I like sex very much and enjoy making
> love with him. I just can't respond for fear of her waking.
>
> (Letter to the agony column of the *Sun* newspaper,
> 25 July 1988)

Others worry that bedsharing may be connected in some way with sex abuse, a recurring and apparently growing crisis in the industrialized world. In the late 1970s, the National Society for the Prevention of Cruelty to Children (NSPCC) in Britain had only a few recorded cases of sexually abused children. In 1987, 7,119 cases were registered and between 1983 and 1988, the numbers of under-fives registered as being sexually abused rose twelve-fold.[1] By 1995, the NSPCC was claiming that one adult in six had suffered 'sexual interference' as a child – a statistic which attracted considerable scepticism and the *Daily Mail* headline 'The survey on sex abuse that just can't be true'.[2]

True or not, the fear of unsuitable intimacy with children has become a focus of public concern. If we believe the headlines, sexual abuse seems to blot the history of every other children's home or orphanage; rock stars are arrested along with their child porn collections; released paedophiles find themselves under siege at police stations; entire countries and communities are paralysed by the removal of children from their parents as officials try to uncover exactly who is doing what to whom. There's even a counter-movement: False Memory Syndrome, which throws the accusation neatly back at the accuser and leaves us all feeling uncomfortable and confused.

The sudden rise in figures may be partly explained by our growing awareness of the existence and dangers of child sex abuse. Child abuse of all sorts has been a feature of many civilizations for as far back as we can tell. In ancient Greece, young boys were routinely molested by men. 'Today,' said Brett Kahr, lecturer in psychotherapy at Regent's College, London, 'we would refer to this as child sexual abuse or male rape, whereas in former times this practice would have been regarded as a type of educational instruction. We know that little girls suffered abuse as well . . .'[3] If the problem is not new, public outrage is. The present climate makes it all the more difficult to discuss sleeping with our children as many people associate sex with the bed.

If we examine Western attitudes to sex, we find a tendency to confuse it with intimacy of other types. Men cannot hold hands in public without being considered homosexual; 'going to bed' with someone means much more than sleeping with them. This was not always so. As Tine Thevenin describes, 200 years ago casual household guests might be invited to bed-down for the night:

> . . . before the steady decline of co-family sleeping gained full momentum, it enjoyed one final triumph. The custom of bundling came nearest to being a world-wide custom, including its practice in America, during the period from 1750–1780. The usual definition of bundling is a man and woman lying on the same bed with their clothes on. They may be either conversing or sleeping. Usually, they were covered with a blanket or a quilt.
>
> This practice was even accepted among the sex-conscious Puritans, who would never have allowed such a practice to prevail had it proven to be a subtle cover-up for sex.
>
> (*The Family Bed*)

Sexual repression is usually the product of a civilized society. Primitive groups are too busy trying to procreate and survive to stop people expressing their physical needs. Our own history shows swings from the liberalism of the Middle Ages to the repression of the Puritans, the libertinism of the Restoration era to the sober strictness of the Victorians. Every age reacts against the attitudes of the previous generation.

We can thank the Victorians for our particular range of hang-ups. First attempts to deal with the initial AIDS crisis in 1980s Britain were hampered when campaigners found that words like 'condom' and 'climax' were more likely to offend than to inform. Sex is the butt of our adult humour, and the filling of our tabloid newspapers.

After the birth of a baby, sex becomes even more problematic. Once the act of intercourse has achieved its procreative purpose, couples are expected to muddle through with the remains of their sex life. Unsurprisingly, studies of postnatal parents find they have less sex after birth than they did before the arrival of a baby. In one survey, organized by *Mother* magazine and analysed by Dr Maurice Yaffe from Guy's Hospital in London, only fifty per cent of responding mothers admitted to any interest in sex after birth. Fewer (forty-five per cent) said they often had orgasms when they did make love. Fifteen per cent said they made love once a month after the baby was born. In this study, breastfeeding made no apparent difference to desire, nor to the frequency of sexual activity after the birth.

The first few months of a baby's life can bring enormous tension to the nuclear family, which may have been quite stable previously. The mother devotes most of her energies to caring for the baby, and sex may take a low priority, even if she is in a physically fit state for it. The only advice and solace a woman finds at this point is a cursory post-natal check-up by a doctor who pronounces her – usually – sexually available once more.

However, researchers from the University of Minnesota in Minneapolis found that sexual intercourse may be physically difficult for months following birth – longer than most doctors realize:

> They found that three months after childbirth, 40 per cent of women still had problems, including discomfort during intercourse and difficulty reaching orgasm. Many women do not return to 'pre-pregnancy levels of sexual experience' even one year after giving birth.
>
> ('Post-natal blues', *Independent*, 23 March 1993)

With so little relief from her soreness, support for her tiredness, and understanding of her emotional upheaval, a new mother might feel quite panicky about her first postnatal sexual encounter.[4] And so might her partner.

Michel Odent says that thirty per cent of men experience some form of impotence immediately after childbirth, especially if they have been a witness to the birth. The arrival of the baby possibly signals a time for parents to take a short natural break from sexual activity, helped by hormonal and other biological interference. The satisfaction a breastfeeding mother experiences may in itself be a mechanism that relieves her desire for sexual intercourse.

But our society does not allow for this settling-in period. Partners may be impatient to return to their usual pattern of sexual intercourse soon after the baby has arrived. While many primitive groups have built-in taboos for sex after the birth of a baby[5], nothing interrupts our media's flow of romantic and sexual imagery. No one says it's OK to wait a while. Certainly not columnist Julie Burchill, who is concerned that some mothers are over-catering for their babies and neglecting their marriages:

> The New Age recipe for bringing up baby – carry it about constantly and breastfeed it till it can open beercans with its teeth and have it sleep between you and hubby until it reaches voting age – seems to me to be disastrous for a romantic and happy marriage.
>
> The Born Again Cows who advise such a regime may well be responsible for a generation of split families ten years from now. For nothing turns a man off faster than making him feel he is married to a womb rather than a woman.
>
> ('Smother Love', *Mail on Sunday*, 26 August 1990)

Penny Mansfield, deputy director of the Marriage Research Council, says that whatever the individual reactions of the couple to sex, this is likely to be a time of tension. She conducted a survey in which forty-nine couples were interviewed after six years of marriage, comparing their responses with their eve-of-wedding hopes.

'A group of men found the waiting quite difficult. Wives tended to go off sex during pregnancy, and things did not get better with the arrival of the baby. What's more, women found their husbands unsatisfying in terms of emotional reward, and they would find more affection and emotion from the baby.'

Couples who were unable to talk about their different needs were those most likely to be heading for difficulty or divorce.

Sex immediately after the arrival of the new-born is not nature's priority, whether we sleep with our babies or not. But if couples think love-making will automatically be easier with the baby in a cot, away from the bed, they could be mistaken.

Trying to train a baby to sleep through the night on his own can be an exhausting experience. The tiredness and the headaches that go with it are probably the greatest dampeners of the sexual libido. And if the baby is crying in the next room, it can be hard to concentrate on feeling sexy.

The couple that brings a baby to bed addresses all these problems head-on. There is evidence that sleeping with your baby is more likely to promote intimacy and desire – and sexual activity, if it is wanted.

A baby is an extremely sensual being, and both parents can enjoy the innocent thrill of holding their new baby at night, cuddling up close to the warm skin. When the child wakes in the morning, it is with a stretch and a smile, teasing the parents slowly out of their sleep – not a rude awakening three or four times in the night, and again at five in the morning.

Actor Richard E. Grant describes his own experience:

Around 2am Olivia crawls into our bed; I'm not even conscious of her coming in. I really don't care what the books say; the amount of time your child will want to snuggle into bed with you is so short, I'm enjoying it while it lasts. Besides, she has very sweet breath in the morning.

(*The Times*, 1995)

When parents want to be alone together, they do not have to banish the child from the room. When the baby is asleep nearby, there is nothing whatsoever to prevent intimacy. There is no need to whisper unless you want to, because a baby is used to sleeping through noise in the womb.

In fact, it is a good idea not to tiptoe around babies, but to let them sleep in family rooms and wherever there is activity. When we cosset new-borns, creating laboratory-style conditions for their sleep, they quickly become dependent on such conditions to get to sleep at all. American Leslie Jacobs makes these observations about co-sleeping in southern India:

> The usual practice in an Indian family is to sleep side by side in the largest bedroom or the living room . . . Indian parents feel that sleeping with their children strengthens the nerves and calms the child . . . Because children know that they are going to fall asleep next to their mother or father, bedtime is never a problem. Indian children do not resist going to bed, and they tend to fall into a sound sleep very quickly. To my surprise, neither music nor conversation in the same room ever prevented a child from falling asleep.
>
> ('The Family Bed in India', *Mothering*, Fall 1989)

Actress Jane Asher, who slept with her baby Alexander from his birth, writes:

> There is the common worry that a couple's sex life will suffer, but in practice this is rarely a problem – a deeply sleeping baby is pretty oblivious to everything going on around him, and in the words of the song 'love will find a way!'
>
> (*Silent Nights*)

Parents in many cultures[6] make love when their babies are awake alongside them, a practice which – contrary to Western belief – does not scar them for life, and makes a nonsense of our embarrassment over sexual education. Jean Liedloff writes:

187

There is concern, too, about the infant being present when his parents make love. Among the Yequana, his presence is taken as a matter of course, and must have been so as well during the hundreds of millennia before us.

It may even be that in *not* being present he is missing an important psycho-biological link with his parents, which leaves him with a sense of longing for it that turns later into a repressed, guilt-laden Oedipus (or Electra) wish to make love to the parent of the opposite sex, when in fact he really wanted the infant's passive role in the first place . . .

(*The Continuum Concept*)

Perhaps this is why sex is something that brings out the child in us. Instead of forming a part of our growing experience, love-making has always been pushed aside, something we have had to discover for ourselves. It is difficult to take a mature attitude about something which our parents treated with secrecy. Jealousy of the parents is something child psychotherapist Dilys Daws has encountered in her work with babies and young children who refuse to sleep. The child senses his exclusion from the couple's intimacy and interrupts them:

. . . the meaning of the baby or child's not sleeping seems to be in a non-resolution of Oedipal feelings: that is, where the reason for not sleeping seems to be an anxiety about the parents being together and excluding the child. Often the taking up of the parent's evening together can be as detrimental to a marriage as intrusion into their night.

(*Sleep Problems in Babies and Young Children*)

This is certainly true in experience of most parents I know. We do not live in the relaxed sexual environment of the hunter-gatherer tribe and require some privacy for our love-making. Our problem, generally, is not babies who cuddle us in the middle of the night while we are asleep ourselves. It is generating the time and space we need at other times of the day – particularly the evening – to be alone, to be a couple again. And for that all parents need strategies.

Daphne, a mother from Leeds, told me the wonderful story of her toddler announcing to his grandparents that 'mummy and daddy were playing gee-gees in bed last night'. You may feel this is the kind of intimate experience our society isn't quite ready for. So hold your horses, if you prefer, and wait until the little ones are slumbering – and invest in a squeak-free, non-bouncy bed.

Once the baby is asleep, the only limits to time and place are in the parents' imagination. Many couples rediscover the excitement of their early relationship, as they enjoy cuddles by the fire, and make secret rendezvous around the house.

According to William F. Van Wert, American author of books like *Tales for Expectant Fathers*, the 'postpartum rift' between parents is perfectly normal. It is best healed, not with a swift return to genital sex, but a variety of other intimacies, including extended foreplay, massage, talking, preparing food for one another and laughing together. He even suggests 'forming a ménage à trois' . . .

> With baby, that is. Falling asleep or taking a bath as a threesome is a powerful way of bonding and rediscovering the relationship. Most men operate on visual cues, and nakedness can create an erotic fulfillment in itself . . .
>
> There is no crime in feeling non-sexual after a birth experience. The crime is in holding those non-sexual feelings to oneself, making lame excuses or telling lies to one's partner and eventually killing the relationship. Whatever you do, don't throw out the parents with the bathwater.
>
> ('Sex After Children', *Mothering*, Summer 1991)

All studies show that the most important indicator for a happy relationship is the level of communication between the couple. No two couples will have the same needs or desires, and no amount of sex will repair what is otherwise an uncommunicative relationship.

Rather than banishing sex to one corner of our lives, we need to admit our need for sensuality in many ways. In our touch-starved lives, sex takes on an inflated importance. The more we suppress it, the more it nags us. However,

> Sex, like breastfeeding, is ninety per cent mental attitude and ten per cent technique.
>
> (*The Womanly Art of Breastfeeding*)

The success of our sex lives is mainly in our minds. If what you are doing – or not doing – feels right, then it probably is.

Doctors Andrew and Penny Stanway show how blurred the lines between sexuality and sensuality have become and how reluctant we are to admit our desires. They even put the act of giving birth into a sexual context, reporting on birthing centres in America where parents are encouraged to make love (though not have full sexual intercourse), during labour. Afterwards:

> The couple then cuddle together with their baby. Left to their own devices, they will soon sleep with their baby between them, especially if the labour has been long or if it is in the middle of the night.
>
> (*Choices in Childbirth*)

Without suggesting that every woman wants to have an orgasm during labour, the Stanways reveal an aspect of the birth experience that most Westerners deny. They also explore the sexuality that underlies breastfeeding – symbiotic breastfeeding that is, and not the restricted method which brings pain to the mother as the infant takes every gulp.

A mother who is constantly suckling her child may find that breastfeeding has a mixed effect on her sexual libido. Prolactin, the hormone that controls milk production, sometimes prevents sexual arousal. But the Stanways show that many women find that the gentle stimulation of the breast during feeding arouses them:

Breastfeeding is widely experienced by many women as pleasurable, yet this is a largely undiscussed or taboo subject. In a survey we made of 300 women, 64 per cent said that breastfeeding was 'sexually pleasant' or 'sensual', and many said they had orgasms during breastfeeding . . . Several women have told us that they felt guilty feeling 'so sexy' during breastfeeding and some have even given up because of guilt over this: this applies especially if the baby is a boy.

(Choices in Childbirth)

Perhaps breastfeeding is meant to be a satisfaction in itself, soothing and stimulating the woman who may not be ready for full sexual intercourse.

We are so deprived of the joys of human touch, that it is little wonder our sexual inclinations turn sour. For many, this means our sensual capacity is vastly underused, and desire becomes suppressed. For others, the need to satisfy the senses becomes an overwhelming sexual urge. Often, because of sexual conditioning, it is women who fall into the first category, and men who adopt the latter.

Jean Liedloff believes the overspilling of sexual desire in our society is connected to our infant desire for mother-love. She says we carry our unfulfilled needs with us from babyhood into adulthood:

. . . the confusion between the need for sex and the need for affection, a maternal kind of physical contact, the confusion that gives rise to phrases like 'red-hot mama', is important to resolve . . . The vast reservoir of longing for physical comforting might be significantly reduced if it became socially acceptable to hold hands with a walking companion of either sex, to sit touching, not just near, talking companions, to sit on people's laps in public as well as in private, to stroke a tempting head of hair when the mood takes one, to hug more freely and more publicly, and in general not to curb one's affectionate impulses unless they would be unwelcome.

(The Continuum Concept)

But how can we realistically start stroking our friends' hair, or sit on their laps, in a world so full of social barriers and innuendo? While many Eastern cultures allow for hand-holding, touching and extensive hugging, even for men, in the West such behaviour between adults signifies a sexual relationship. Open kissing and cuddling, whether hetero- or homosexual, can occasionally be seen, but is usually frowned upon as excessive and juvenile.

What frightens many parents is that natural interactions between themselves and their children have also been affected by this climate of suspicion. In a fascinating article entitled 'So what is child abuse?', Rosie Waterhouse examines the trail of neurosis which has followed famous sex abuse scandals and the subsequent public outcries. 'Hugging, kissing, bathing, even sleeping with your children – are these natural patterns of behaviour,' she asks, 'or are they inappropriate, over-sexualised acts of abuse?'[7]

The answer, of course, is that bodily freedom is a neutral act, made good or harmful by the adults involved. But whatever adults offer them, all children crave the intimate body knowledge which helps them to know themselves, to bond with others and to become who they are going to be.

In answer to the *Sun*'s correspondent, it is clear that her problem lies in her feelings about her own sexuality. Many adults are simply not ready to have their babies with them all the time.

An innocent question about wriggling (which could have been answered easily and modestly to the satisfaction of the three-year-old observer), was enough to put this mother 'right off' sex.

Such attitudes are at the root of our current problem with child sex abuse. Some parents, still looking for comfort in their old age, mistakenly interpret the sensuality and passivity of a child as a sexual signal. Some severely emotionally deprived individuals are so unused to experiencing innocent physical intimacy, that they become sexually aroused when they find it. Sex may be the only way they know of expressing deep emotion. It may even be their way of loving their own children.

One newspaper article written during the British 'Cleveland sex-abuse crisis' of 1988, in which many families were split up in a panic by over-zealous social workers, made this comment:

> . . . psychiatrists and therapists . . . who are studying the problem are increasingly finding patients – both as adults and children – whose feelings of affection, fear, love, violence and intimacy have been hopelessly confused.
>
> (*Sunday Times*, 19 July 1988)

This confusion is the result of unresolved mothering. The child who has been excluded from his parents' affections may grow up to be a victim or a bully in his turn. The parent who rapes his child is stealing many things from him: the child's right to choose, the child's physical privacy, the child's peace of mind. And as we know, many sexually abused children take that secret into adulthood, with the danger of becoming sexual abusers themselves.

As Jean Liedloff says, 'No one wins in such a game; no one is the villain. All one can discover from horizon to horizon are victims of victims.'[8]

But there is a way out of the downward spiral, and I do not believe it lies merely in the hands of the courts and social services and lobby groups. We desperately need to restore the balance between parent and child – to bring our babies back into our arms, to welcome them into our presence at night – as a first step towards ending the daily damage we do to them.

American writer Robert Wright points out cogently that it is 'abnormal separation' between parent and child which is most likely to trigger abnormal responses. He poses the question curious parents have asked him:

> Doesn't weird Oedipal stuff happen? . . .
>
> If you're talking about kids 2 or 3 years old – well, the very fact that people ask this question is a sign of how bizarrely obsessed our culture has become with childhood sexual abuse. The fact is that sexual abuse between children and their

biological parents (as opposed to stepparents) is exceedingly
rare. And when it does happen, it's often because the
biological parent was absent during the child's early years, so
that the normal instinctive prohibitions against incestuous
sexual attraction weren't triggered.

(*Slate* magazine, www.slate.com, March 1997)

If a person has been convicted or is suspected of raping a child, then
clearly it would be unthinkable to allow the two to sleep in the same
bed. The success of bedsharing depends on the adult being mature
enough, responsible for his or her actions, and happy enough in his or
her own sexuality not to endanger someone else's.

But since Cleveland in the 1980s and the Belgium crisis of the mid-
1990s, the panic button has been pressed, and there will be many who
believe that sexual abuse results from *too much* intimacy with our
babies, rather than a lack of it. They will not sense the crucial difference
between types of closeness: one type which is essential for the infant,
the other which is a violation. As one nurse put it:

> . . . it seems that problems encountered in sleep in child
> rearing would perhaps be best solved by bedsharing. However
> in the present climate of interest in incest in this country it
> seems ludicrous to mention it.
> (Kathryn Conder, *Midwife, HV and Community Nurse*, April 1988)

Some critics believe that even the desire to sleep next to your child
may be abnormal. One of these detractors is Dr Richard Ferber,
director of the Sleep Laboratory and of the Center for Pediatric Sleep
Disorders at the Children's Hospital in Boston, Massachusetts. He
writes:

> If you find that you actually prefer to have your child in your
> bed, you should examine your own feelings very carefully . . .
> If there is tension between parents, then taking a child into
> their bed may help them avoid confrontation and sexual

intimacy. If any of this applies to you, then instead of helping your child you are using him to avoid facing and solving your own problems. As long as such a pattern continues, not only your child but your whole family will suffer.

(*Solve Your Child's Sleep Problems*)

While I was examining my own feelings very carefully, I stumbled on a suitable reply from Dr David Haslam's book, *Sleepless Children*.

Occasionally claims are also made that only couples with sexual or marital problems share their bed with a child. For example, a writer in the journal of the American Medical Association in 1980 went so far as to state that because most children in our society do not sleep with their parents, 'the physician should consider exploring underlying motives with the parents, as to whose needs are being served by this arrangement.'

Thankfully a few weeks later another paediatrician wrote to express an opposite opinion. An American study in 1974 claimed that bedsharing is an indicator of a disturbed parental relationship. This much-quoted study suggested that the mother often used the child's presence as a shield against her husband's sexual demands. However, a 1982 study from Sweden disagreed with this; it did not reveal any increase in divorce rates in families who shared beds with four- to eight-year-olds. As the Swedes concluded, 'The habit is too widespread among ordinary families for it to serve as a sign that the parents are in the process of separating.'

Parents all over the world use their children as pawns in the games they play. No doubt, some use their baby as a physical barrier. But the best barriers are not made of flesh and blood. A baby between two people is more likely to be the greatest bond they will ever know. And even if parents were to use their baby as a cover-up for their marital tensions, the baby would come out the winner, with all his emotional and physical needs being so obviously met.

Many of the criticisms about baby bedsharing are rooted in fear. People are afraid the balance of their old lives will be upset. Sex will not be as it was. Touching a baby may be the kind of physical intimacy they have been avoiding all their lives. Either they can give in to these fears, or they can rediscover sensuality through the child.

In his book *Primal Health*, Michel Odent connects the well-being of a species with its ability to love (form attachments), reproduce (fulfil all the requirements of the sexual act, the gestation period and the birth) and nurture (feed its young). Our society manifests problems in all three areas. We have trouble making lasting relationships, both sexes suffer from infertility and lapses in sexual desire, and after mechanistic and painful childbirth, we suffer immense distress when we try to suckle our babies. The obvious crisis in our reproductive lives is a sure sign that we are on the wrong track.

'Difficulties in breastfeeding, just as difficulties in childbirth and sexual difficulties, are diseases of civilization,' writes Odent. 'And each in their turn is creating disease. Love; sexuality; health. These are words which only our Western analytical brain can consider as separate entities.'

The problem is not whether or not our babies are beside us when we make love. It is that society does not know where to draw the line between 'healthy' loving, constructive, reproductive relationships – and violent, abusive, uncontrolled desire.

Once again, we need to look back at our own infancy, when all we needed was our mother's loving touch. That is where a healthy sex education begins.

9 | TIME FOR BED

The world is ruled by letting things take their course. It cannot be ruled by interfering.

(*Tao Te Ching*)

There never was a child so lovely but his mother was glad to get him asleep.

(Ralph Waldo Emerson)

Some nights, it's wonderful. You are sleeping, your child is sleeping and the fact that you're all sleeping on a mattress in the middle of the floor is no one's business but your own. At other times, it doesn't seem so great. You've been doing this for a long time, perhaps your child takes up the centre of the bed to himself, a symbolic gesture of the way his needs seem to dominate your life. Sometimes your child seems just too big for your queen-size mattress and cushion arrangement.

Perhaps you have reached a stage where you feel it's time to move on.

Before setting out, many people want to know where their adventure is likely to end. When will the baby leave the bed? Should the child find his own way to independence, or should he be shown the door? Can parents do anything to speed up the process?

These are questions that encompass all our notions about independence and clinginess, strictness and permissiveness, weaning, spoiling and training our children.

Weaning is a pivotal moment for many parents – the moment when we must first make some very adult decisions; the moment when childrearing really begins. All around us, other families have been weaning their babies from the very beginning, through sleep-training, bottle-feeding and the many other enforced transitions from infancy to independence. Perhaps it seems to us that other parents have it easier, that they do not dwell for too long on the dilemmas of letting go. Whether or not this is actually true, parents who wean early usually do have the support and encouragement of health professionals, friends and relations.

After all, we live in a 'weaning society', a culture unable to enjoy fully the moment, to accept that change is inevitable, and to look neither forward nor back. We are programmed to interfere – we want a part in the action. Because we are so aware of the various phases through which a baby passes on the route to adulthood, we tend to urge him towards the next stage, weaning him hurriedly out of the last.

The weaning impulse affects every aspect of a baby's life. 'Can he sit/crawl/walk yet?' we ask other mothers. 'When are you going to take him off the breast?' Doctors tell us to go gently on the weaning process, but we can't help worrying about it. Will he ever be potty-trained? When will he tie his own shoe laces?

Every parental attempt to steer a baby in one direction inevitably has an effect on his overall development. I met one mother who was proud that her little boy was able to stand – with a little help – at five months. 'We didn't want him to crawl,' she told me, 'so we bought him a baby walker from the beginning and always put him in it.'

Unfortunately, prolonged periods strapped in the artificially up-right position had made the poor lad very stiff. He was 'early' in walking, but was unable to fall over without hurting himself. His mother spent many months chasing after him to stop him doing himself severe damage.

The annual report of the Chartered Society of Physiotherapists published in 1988 confirmed that baby walkers may not be as useful to motor development as parents expect:

. . . far too many babies are put into walkers from the age of four months. At this age, muscles are not strong enough to bear the weight, and may cause toes to turn inwards or outwards. Parents often believe that baby walkers will encourage their infant to walk earlier but, says physiotherapist Jill Breckon, the reverse is often true.

(Liz Hodgkinson, *Early Days*, Summer 1988)

We interfere at our children's peril. By rushing them through the natural stages of development, we may alter the processes a baby goes through, the way he learns things, and even the order in which they come. Nurse Kathryn Conder reports:

Babies who are constantly carried around, as South Indians do in Gopalur for example, acquire language and social skills before motor development.

(*Midwife, HV and Community Nurse*, April 1988)

We, who think we know it all, may not understand a fraction of the capabilities of the human child. Take the example of the Ugandan baby, observed by anthropologist Marcelle Geber. Geber's task was to study the effects of malnutrition on babies, but she was amazed to discover that

these babies were more advanced and smiled more than babies she had seen before in industrialized countries.

She found that around the age of six or seven months the Ugandan baby was able to pick up a toy which was outside its vision. With American and European babies, this is usually possible only at around fifteen months of age. Her test evaluated motor development, and the development of a form of reasoning. One big difference between the two groups was that the Ugandan babies belonged to a culture in which the period of dependence on the mother is not disturbed.

(Michel Odent, *Primal Health*)

Why are Ugandan babies more advanced than our own? Could it be because they spend their infancy in their mothers' arms, crawling in their own time, and walking only when they are ready? Observers working in rural villages in Malawi report that the African children there are more advanced than Western babies at every stage. Such babies sleep with the whole family in mud and straw huts, and are carried on their mothers' backs by day.

Different peoples have radically different approaches to the weaning process. The trend has changed drastically in our own culture, from infant training in the 1890s to permissiveness in the 1960s. Among primitive groups, we find the full range of weaning procedures, from the most gradual to the most sudden. The G/wi bushmen of the Kalahari Desert take it slowly:

> It appears to be a fundamental tenet of G/wi philosophy that man is an essentially reasonable being and is well disposed towards his fellows. This belief is consistent with the form that the processes of child training and socialisation take . . .
>
> The weaning process is described as 'the child's growing tired of the breast'. Solids are introduced into the infant's diet at an early stage as supplementary feeding and as material on which to cut emerging teeth. The supplementary component is gradually increased until, before his third year, the child is feeding himself and is given the breast only at fairly long intervals or when he needs comforting. The diminishing nutritional dependence on breast feeding and the desire to imitate older, weaned colleagues are probably the main factors terminating a child's desire for breast feeding. The initiative appears to come as much from the child as from the mother.
>
> (*Hunters and Gatherers*)

This is an arrangement whereby the needs of the mother and of the baby are considered, and whereby things are allowed to take their course. In fact, it does not resemble weaning at all, for it requires no effort or struggle from either the child or the parent. It only takes time and patience, neither of which is conspicuously available in our society.

In the West, the initiatives of mother and baby are suppressed by the expectations of professionals, and other mothers who are following modern advice. Just because we know when a baby crawls, does not mean we should anticipate that stage and hurry it on, or save him the trouble of bothering with it. We do not know – professionals do not know – the many ways in which the body and mind are connected. It is dangerous to assume that we completely understand early human development, and it may be foolish to interfere.

> . . . deprivation of any well precedented detail of experience will cost the individual some degree of well-being, perhaps one too subtle for us to notice, perhaps one so commonly lost that we do not recognise it as a loss. Research has already shown . . . that deprivation of the experience of creeping about on hands and knees has deleterious effects upon verbal abilities when they develop at a later stage.
>
> (*The Continuum Concept*)

This is fascinating, because, as we saw in chapter 4, in cultures where babies are carried continuously, the crawling stage may be brief or nearly non-existent. The point, perhaps, is not that all babies need all stages, but that no baby should be deprived of a stage for which he shows an inclination. If we stop a crawling baby to put him for long periods into a baby walker or bouncer, we should be aware of the possible long-term consequences of our actions.

If not being allowed to crawl can leave a baby speech-impaired, there may be enormous consequences for babies who are not allowed their fill of sleeping by their mother's side. For all we know, co-sleeping may enable a baby to be more supple, or to see further. There might be many minute differences between a child who sleeps with others, and one who sleeps alone. Yet our society considers it reasonable to deprive all babies of that experience.

Many of the professionals who agree with the principles of bedsharing insist that there will be difficulties in weaning the child away. Western society's great fear is that the older child will undermine parental power. In effect, we are frightened to wean at all, and so we try to get it out of the way as early as we can. And society supports us in this premature endeavour.

Introduce solids to a three-month-old infant, and you will find a wealth of literature with tips on how to get him to ingest meat and two veg followed by something for his sweet tooth. You will also be able to galvanize the help of friends, health visitors and your mother-in-law. Keep a baby purely breastfed for six months (the period suggested by La Leche League and the World Health Organisation) and you'll attract weird looks and even weirder suggestions about your child not learning to talk properly and lack of iron.[1] It's the same with co-sleeping. Rather than supporting your (well-informed? and private) decision, many health professionals worry about the future on your behalf. They thoughtfully point out that you'll be making a rod for your own back and ask how it will feel when you're still sleeping with a twelve year-old.

It would be a poor show if we only started things which we did not have to finish. Our babies would never wear nappies, or be breastfed at all.

The minority of parents who choose to let their babies set the pace at first, may later find it hard to change emphasis. Overwhelmed with weaning advice from the beginning, they find it impossible to take advice when they are, finally, ready for it. This is a mother who wrote to me about weaning her three-year-old from the breast:

> I spoke to my GP who recommended that I just stop, and tell her there is no more. I think this is barbaric. Leila would definitely understand if I explained, but I feel that this is just too harsh a way of dealing with things. I don't want it to be a traumatic experience for either of us.

The advice itself – while not exactly gentle – is not necessarily barbaric. It's just that it doesn't come from a position of empathy. I wrote back with a recalled weaning experience of my own. Four months pregnant with Alice, I had been finding it painful to feed my two-year-old daughter, Frances:

> I came back to my mother-in-law's house and cried with tiredness and the strain of everything. My mother-in-law had always been completely supportive of my breastfeeding and everything we were doing with Frances. As I was packing to leave, she came into the bedroom and just said, out of the blue, 'You know, if you need someone to give you permission to stop breastfeeding, it's OK. I'll give you permission.' I can still remember the relief that flooded over me. I now realize that weaning needs more strength than a woman has on her own. It requires society's support. But if society isn't giving you support to feed in the first place, how can it give you permission to stop? Most people who are telling you to give up aren't really on your side at all. You sense this, and you know that what they are saying can't be helpful.[2]

It's OK to wean. It's especially OK when you've devoted months or years to fulfilling the needs of your baby. Ideally, I wanted my children to move spontaneously from my breast and my bed. I wanted my children to give *me* permission, like this wise four-year-old, who decided she had had enough of her mother's milk:

> 'Well, I really should quit. You know, Bill quit.' After a pause, during which Brie no doubt thought about her best friend Bill, she continued, 'I really should stop, but I just don't know . . . I don't know if I can.'
>
> I laughed to myself, thinking maybe I should start a Nursing Anonymous group. 'Brie, you'll be able to stop when you are ready,' I replied.
>
> Over the next few weeks, she mentioned quitting several times. Then one night, she nursed for just a few moments

before pulling away to sleep. The next morning, I said, 'Brie, you didn't nurse much last night. Did you get any milk?'

'No.'

'Are you still going to nurse, even if there is no milk?'

'No. I'm quitting. I don't want to do that anymore.'

A gigantic smile spread across her face as she said, 'No, I'm done.'

(Rosemary Risley, 'A Child-led Weaning',
Mothering, Winter 1991)

It does happen. Nine-month-old babies spontaneously reject the breast they have lovingly suckled. One-year-olds indicate they'd rather sleep nearby, but not with you. Two-year-olds demand their own room (a luxury not everyone can afford). But while primitive tribes offer a framework within which all children are expected to operate, there is nothing except disapproval to steer the Western parent through the maze.

Unsupported, yet still functioning in the 'real' world, many parents reach the point where they have had enough before children reach the point where they have taken all they really need. So we need strategies. We need to be reassured that our actions will do as little harm as possible, while achieving the end result. We need to feel good about asserting our needs. The starting point for weaning is self-appreciation. Give yourself the pat on the back which society has failed to offer. Imagine yourself an honoured and worthy parent, accorded the high status of someone who is rearing the next generation to the best of her own ability, and beyond the expectations of the tribe:

When you have done enough, when you can stand outside your own life and say 'I have been a good parent, I have done many wonderful things with and for my child,' then you will be ready to lead your child without fear. All weaning requires is your ability to trust in the unknown. Imagine you are taking Leila's hand and leading her through a dark tunnel. She is not old enough to have the resources to walk in the dark alone. You may be a little frightened, too, but as the adult you know that you must step out in order to reach the other end. So you give her your hand, and somehow find new strengths you were not sure you had. This is turn nourishes your baby. And at the moment, your child is still a baby. She will be ready to grow when you take the lead.[2]

If we can be, simultaneously, sensitive to our children and to ourselves, then parents are more likely to embrace all stages positively and to see them through successfully to the end. Armed with this self-knowledge, we are then equipped to decide whether or not to wean. Are we forcing something which our children are not ready for and which we ourselves are not prepared to see through? Or have we reached a crossroads which demands we take the adult initiative? Giving yourself the permission to wean now, or at some time in the future, may be all you need to see your own situation more clearly.

Next comes the question of when and how to do it. The older your child is, the greater the chances that all his needs have been met, and that bedsharing has settled into a very comfortable habit. There is nothing wrong with habit, of course, so long as all parties are happy. When they are not, habits can be altered to fit.

Problems need only arise for the parents, if they do not have the strength of their convictions and the confidence to be firm and kind at the same time. Problems need only arise for the child if he or she is weaned too soon and without a framework of total acceptance. We cannot make our children independent, we can only encourage them to take the independence that they are ready for. Like Rosemary Risley, we need to empower: 'With my help, you'll be able to cope,' is our underlying message.

Denying our children's needs for dependency may only result in dependency of another kind. In the next chapter I shall examine some useful strategies for weaning the child from the bed. But first we should perhaps examine what happens when children are weaned too young or somehow experience their parents' boundary-setting as a rejection.

One very common sign of weak progression towards independence is a child's reliance on a transitional object. Most Western doctors believe the comfort toy is a normal phase of development, and some actively promote its use:

> Better than lying with your toddler or young child until he falls asleep at night is for him to fall asleep with a 'transitional object' – a stuffed animal, a doll, a toy, a special blanket.
> (Ferber, *Solve Your Child's Sleep Problems*)

Stuffed animals and special blankets are easy to come by in our society, and once a child becomes attached to a comforter, a mother is advised to buy two or more of the beloved article, in case one gets lost. But in primitive cultures, an entire family's belongings may not extend beyond a sleeping mat. Needless to say, in such groups the use of a transitional object is unknown.

> In many cultures where bed-sharing is the norm notably less sleep problems are found. There is no evidence either that it causes the child psychological harm. In fact in non-literate societies where because of bed-sharing the children have much more tactile stimulation, the use of transitional objects such as pieces of blanket, etc, is almost unknown.
> (Conder, *Midwifery, HV and Community Nurse*)

Michel Odent has conducted his own research among mothers who had home deliveries – an atypical group in London. Babies who were breastfed at night for more than a year did not resort to transitional objects for comfort. At the other end of the scale, it has been shown that children who are severely deprived of love and affection (for instance those kept in old-style children's homes) do not seek transitional objects either. He concludes that 'the need for a transitional object is the healthy reaction of a normal child to a special situation.'

One obvious example of a child's difficulty in becoming independent is when he displays shyness, or fear of strangers. It is a trait so common in our society that we almost expect it in some measure from our children – especially from the girls, according to a five-year study from Cambridge.

Psychologist Joan Stevenson-Hyde assessed a group of children aged between two-and-a-half and seven years when separated from their mothers. She found that the children's security was affected by parental problems. Children were more prone to shyness, for instance, after the arrival of a new brother or sister:

> Anything that might make the mother less responsive, such as the demands of a new baby, which suddenly makes her a different mother to the child, may affect how secure the child feels.
>
> (Gillian Mercer, *Independent*, 12 July 1988)

A tendency to shyness may be inherited, said the report, but Dr Stevenson-Hyde confirmed that the child's experiences were by far the most crucial factor:

> 2½-year-olds who were warmly and confidently attached to their mothers showed only low or moderate fear of strangers, never high fear. These children cope with a noisy new environment such as a playgroup, given time and encouragement . . .
>
> In her unselected sample . . . about one child in ten remained shy, causing difficulties at the transition to nursery or primary school.
>
> (*Independent*, 12 July 1988)

Of course, some shyness is useful. Children who have been reared close to mum sometimes appear clingy for longer than the average, while they assess new situations from a safe place – often with arms wrapped around the calves of her legs. But in the long term any reluctance to join in always melts. The key – and this is a tough one for new parents – is to trust that children will come out of their shells eventually. Left to their own devices, they always do.

The South American Yequana baby, with all his needs fulfilled, has progressed to a stable level of independence by the time he crawls out of his mother's arms. In fact, the movement away from the mother is the child's own statement about his personal confidence. If he is unsure, he returns to the safety of the maternal zone. She does not push him in any direction, knowing instinctively that this will warp his behaviour, either to rebel against her, or to please her and thereby win her attention.

Likewise G/wi and Paliyan children do not develop patterns of shyness. However, the Paliyan people change their tactics when a child reaches two years of age. Noted for their extreme individualism, and the lack of co-operation between adults, the Paliyans fulfil a child's needs for his first two years, and then precipitously abandon him to his own devices:

> The comforting world of the child undergoes a series of rapid changes at the time of weaning at about two and a half years of age. The mother not only denies the child her breast or deters it with bitter paste on the nipples, but she puts it down now for increasingly long periods . . . Facing situations without continuous maternal guidance for the first time, the child is suddenly introduced to new kinds of experiences – misbehaviour and punishment . . .
>
> Although the punishment will not go beyond an angry word or at most a mild slap, this is a distinct change of tone, especially if it comes from the mother. During this period the mother frequently attempts to ignore her child's demands . . . If the child is not already crying, it becomes enraged at its mother's lack of response; it cries spasmodically, pulls its hair, and stamps its feet . . . it seldom calms down in less than ten to twenty minutes. Such tantrums continue until the child is

four or five; in one case the episodes persisted until ten years of age.

(Hunters and Gatherers Today)

This portrait of an Indian people provides an excellent example of the effect of sudden weaning. It is easy to see why the child becomes enraged at such an uncompromising withdrawal of affection. This translates into the fierce independence of adult tribe members.

Another society noted for the temper tantrums of its toddlers is the modern, industrialized world. Current thinking is that babies need to be educated, and that parents should put down their collective foot to stop any nonsense. Failure to do this, say the professionals, will result in households being ruled by the whims of two-year-old tyrants. Here is a typical assessment from American Leo Madow, in his book entitled *Anger*:

> . . . as the child grows older and is no longer considered completely helpless, demands begin to be made on him. One of the first of these is weaning.
>
> Thus mother, by insisting that he do things for himself and restricting the total freedom he had enjoyed, frustrates him. The result is anger that he cannot fully express and that begins to accumulate. The process is normal; mother must frustrate the child, if he is to grow up and become acceptable to society. You might ask, 'Do little babies really have so much feeling?' Have you ever seen a baby have a temper tantrum, or hold its breath, or bang its head against the wall?
>
> . . . This is only the beginning in the frustration taking place in the process known as 'growing up'. Growing up consists of increasing limitations of direct, immediate satisfaction of needs, which the child must learn to satisfy in what he feels is a less pleasant way, or to put off satisfying for a while.

In America and Europe, babies begin to have tantrums at about eighteen months old, and this behaviour may continue for four or five years. Child and parent are reduced to behaving like animal and trainer, in order to continue the battle which began at birth.

In an attempt to capture the maximum amount of a parent's attention – the result of basic needs not being fulfilled – the desperate child sometimes holds his breath. It's a classic warning sign, like the adult who threatens suicide. Here is a common example from the problem page of a parents' magazine:

> I'm having a real battle of wills with my very stubborn 18-month-old daughter. If she decides she doesn't want to do something, she stiffens, refuses to move and holds her breath until she turns blue.
>
> (*Young Additions*, Autumn 1987)

The doctor replies that 'breath holding is a common symptom in toddlers and is a version of "tantruming". She won't come to any harm doing this, so your best approach is to ignore it. It is important however, to talk to her about it afterwards and to try to find out if there is anything that's upsetting her.'

He offers useful interim advice, but it would clearly be preferable to avoid this level of conflict altogether. If we accept tantrums as a normal phase of growing up, they are not going to disappear. Most parents blame themselves ('She's got her dad's temper'), or the child for these regular outbursts. But we should remember that serious tantrums are unknown in societies where weaning is not imposed on the child.

Furthermore, by laying the blame for bad behaviour on genetics, and refusing to listen to the urgent message of a baby who is headbanging, thumb-sucking or throwing tantrums, we imprint the child with negative ideas for the future. Family therapist Steve Biddulph, author of *The Secret of Happy Children*, has written at length on the dangers of negative programming. This is the sort of thing he warns against:

> 'You're hopeless.' 'God, you're a nuisance.' 'You'll be sorry, just you see.' 'You're as bad as your Uncle Merv' (who's in jail). 'You're just like your Auntie Eve' (who's fond of a drink) . . .
>
> This is the kind of programming that many youngsters grow up with; it is passed on unwittingly by overwrought parents and continues as a kind of family curse down the generations . . .
>
> What we have discovered is that these kind of comments don't only have the effect of making the child feel bad momentarily. Put-downs also have a *hypnotic effect* and act unconsciously, like seeds in the mind, seeds which will grow and shape the person's self-image, eventually becoming true facts about the child's personality.

Weaning is all about training, and training is preparation for competition. Though they may make desperate attempts to avoid the trap, most parents find themselves finds herself making comparisons between one child and the next. It is easy to become obsessed with 'norms' as laid down by paediatricians in the 1950s and 1960s, and to chart our children's development according to them: she's talking early, he's walking late, and so on.

Regular development checks by the health visitor reinforce the feeling that we should somehow encourage progress in our children. But this has not always been so. Older generations criticize the young for 'over-stimulating' the child, a phrase that was fashionable in the 'no-nonsense' 1920s. They also say our children grow up too quickly.

In sixty years, we have passed from deliberate isolation of the baby, to an American-style hot-house treatment, whereby children are forced into early brilliance like seedlings for a show. Forcing the child on enables him to attain excellence in his specialization (hence headlines like 'Boy, 9, is new maths genius[5]). But this narrow education may be achieved at the expense of the development of many other aspects of the personality and overall capabilities.

On the one hand, there was great-grandma who left her new-born child for hours alone in the cot or pram to get used to his own company, and on the other, there is the mother who plays Mozart to her four-month-old foetus, and wields a pack of flash-cards in her nappy bag. Our practice in recent decades has been the result of fashions dictated by various authorities. The need is to restore authority to the instincts of parents; then books like this will no longer be required. I do not wish to add to the clutter of conflicting advice, but to point to a way out of it.

Parents in America – and latterly in Britain – talk of 'quality time' with their children. This means not getting on with the washing up, or mowing the lawn, but sitting in a room with the child, poring over books and toys, trying to 'teach' him something. If a child's early experience consists of playing in a room while adults sit and stare at him, then he is getting an extremely warped view of the world. At the very least, he is likely to grow up self-centred.

Surely it's better to educate a child – literally, lead him out – by example rather than say-so. But this method requires participation, and parents are often frightened to allow their children to participate in the real world, because of its apparent dangers. Yet experience in many other cultures shows us that children are well-equipped with their own safety mechanisms, and will not readily fall downstairs or cut themselves if left to their own devices. Among the Paliyans, for instance:

> Nobody pays attention to a two- or three-year-old who runs about with a razor-sharp billhook or who climbs on a house top. A five-year-old is permitted to make fires for preparing food.
>
> *(Hunters and Gatherers Today)*

If a Paliyan child is capable of doing these things without hurting himself, then so can any other. But stories of domestic accidents with kettles and scissors are the stuff of consumer programmes. They set us worrying. And the more household gadgets we invent, the more reason parents feel they have to be protective.

Children do not need protecting in a well-ordered home. If there is visible physical danger around, they can cope with it. Often, they will choose not to confront it until ready. If the danger is invisible, such as electricity, parents need only cover the plug socket. We merely confuse and anger our children by shouting 'no!' at every opportunity. It is also a sure sign to him that the danger point is extremely interesting, and that returning to it will excite the attention of grown-ups.

Musician and Suzuki teacher Ron Colyer made this point in a talk addressed to the conference of teachers of the Alexander Technique in 1988. 'Children like to do what they can do,' he said.[6] 'They develop the ability to say "no" inside themselves.'

Instead of growing up constituting a 'series of frustrations' – to use Leo Madow's phrase – it could constitute a series of explorations. A child does not distinguish between work and play, and the longer we can put off that distinction, the better. Sorting out the washing basket with your baby can be a game of rough and tumble, peep-bo and tickles among the sheets. The task takes longer than it would if you were folding linen on your own – but it is also twice as much fun. Meanwhile, the baby has learnt something about domestic work.

One way to wean a child gently is to hand over responsibility in bite-sized chunks. Try following Jean Liedloff's golden rule: 'Never do anything for a child that he can do for himself.' You could call it minimalist mothering.

Parenting, like giving birth or dying, may be more helpfully described as a non-activity. Growing up happens anyway, whatever stimulants, proddings or encouragement we give our children. Despite our interference, many children grow up not too badly damaged. That may be the best we can say about the effect of intensive Western parenting.

We restrain and push our children at the same time. They are unwelcome in shops and restaurants, but yet they are the centre of attention wherever they go. We hate our children so much, we batter them – and we love them so much that they are spoiled by the age of two. It would be better to let them be.

'You don't have to go on being baby-centred,' Jean Liedloff told me. 'If you keep saying to a baby "what would you like to do now? Would you like this, or would you rather have that?" you drive them up the wall, and their response is anger. They can't express to you that you're not supposed to be doing this.

'By the age of four, they should actually be contributing more help in the house than they are costing, believe it or not. It sounds impossible, but that's exactly true. Not some fifteen-year-old spotty monster you have to clear up after. By the time they're eight, they should be helping you with the cooking and taking care of the next baby, and all this kind of thing.'

Maturity will emerge naturally if unhindered by parental pressure, which returns us to the question of weaning baby from the bed.

Paediatrician Dr Hugh Jolly had a lot of experience with parents who slept with their children, as he came in later years to recommend the practice. He describes the usual pattern:

Children brought up in the family bed decide to leave it at a variable age. Some are ready to take to their own bed around the age of two years but others want longer. Sometimes they decide to vary the pattern, choosing their own bed some nights and the family bed on others. Sometimes they decide to share with an older sibling who has already left the family bed. Knowing that they can come into their parents' bed in the middle of the night makes the transition easier. It is all so natural that many parents cannot remember exactly when each child decided to make the change.

(Book of Child Care)

As a baby, Frances always went to sleep on the breast, a practice warned against by experts like Dr Spock. Yet at eight months, quite suddenly, she started to find her own space to sleep in, and would turn over, away from the breast to go to sleep. She did not need to be pushed into this experience by me, but naturally altered her habit in her own good time.

At thirteen months, Frances was even more independent. On one memorable night, she actually put herself to bed. After her evening sleep, we all went upstairs together as usual, but Frances had woken up in transit to the bedroom, and started to play. Normally, she would go straight back to sleep once the lights were out, but on this occasion she was still lively. Paul and I went off to sleep on our mattress on the floor, while Frances amused herself quietly in our room. I opened my eyes about an hour later, to see that Frances had tucked herself up on her single mattress by the side of ours, without even bothering to come to me for a feed.

It is a pleasant feeling to see a baby progress, with no struggle at all, from one stage to another. It is an experience that many paediatricians and psychoanalysts have never known. Our experts, understandably, have been raised on the infant 'norms' of clinical trials in the 1950s, the only statistical evidence available to them. Their practical experience is often limited to babies who were born in hospital, who sleep apart from their mothers, and who are either bottle-fed or weaned from the breast by four months.

Lack of experience of co-sleeping also, understandably, leads parents to be frightened that it will never stop. We may imagine cuddling up to our babies at night, but the idea of sleeping with an older child just doesn't feel right. In one small study, only four per cent of parents thought a child of five years should share a bed with a parent, and no one thought a child over five should co-sleep.[7] Each society has its own, unwritten consensus, and this seems to be ours. We want to know we shall be able to set limits when the time comes.

Babies may leave the bed at any age – to suit ourselves, or them. The average seems to be around two years, or after the time when breastfeeding ends. However, independence is not something which is attained in one go. All children are prone to temporary regressions along the way – events like the birth of a sibling, illness or moving house can create a need for more night comfort. They are perfectly normal.

Perhaps it is time the 'norms' were re-evaluated, so that professionals would not express surprise or distaste when mothers say they sleep with their children, or breastfeed them beyond their first birthday. It is rare to hear a mother admit openly, and with pride:

> I breastfed my two children until they weaned themselves and it was such a lovely experience that seven years ago I became a counsellor to help others achieve it.
>
> (Mrs M. Goodall, *Parents*, April 1988)

Midwife Chloe Fisher, who advises mothers to let their babies decide the length of each feed, told me of the relief she feels to see a baby come off the breast of his own accord. It is so unusual in our society for us to allow the natural thing to happen, that we can scarcely believe it when it does. We start interfering from the moment a pregnancy is announced, and do not even trust a new-born baby to suckle according to the rules of instinct by which he is driven.

It seems almost impossible to imagine children moving into adulthood at their own pace; parents who offer comfort to their children with no strings attached. Perhaps the most we can expect of ourselves is that we should be – or try to be – 'good enough' at our almost impossible task.[8]

The next chapter considers practical aspects of co-sleeping, including weaning children from the family bed. Meanwhile, we just need to remember that we are capable of moving on. To every parent whose child is ready to move on, I would say, as I did in my letter to Leila's mother:

> I cannot give you specific advice, but I can give you permission. Permission to be the parent you need to be at all times. Permission to be good to yourself, to make the adult decisions which will help you and your family to move on to every new stage that awaits you. Permission to wean and not to wean. To make changes and do things your own way. To embrace your own fears and your child's and keep going. You'll be fine, and you'll have such fun.[2]

10 | PRACTICALLY SPEAKING

There are three rules for surviving the arrival of a new baby.
Unfortunately, nobody knows what they are.

(Leslie Moak Murray, 'Murray's Law' greetings cards)

There is no established way of sleeping with a baby. The millions of rural people who sleep with and carry their babies do not have a uniform way of going about it and why should we? They sleep on mats, they sleep in hammocks, they have male-and-female huts and extended-family sleeping chambers – they follow the expectations of their own tribe, evolved slowly over many centuries, not an idealized concept of co-sleeping.

In her review of the first edition of this book, Germaine Greer mistook the title and cover picture for a prescription: 'Deborah Jackson's argument is not that babies should not sleep alone,' she wrote, 'but that they should sleep between Mummy and Daddy, like the naked sword that lay between courting couples once upon a time.'[1] I am sorry to add another negative to this paragraph, but that is not at all what I am arguing. Despite the sub-title 'Why you should sleep with your baby', the aim has always been to offer ideas rather than recipes. It is vital that each parent carves an individual relationship with his or her own child. It must, surely, be better to put your baby in a cot happily, than to sleep with him begrudgingly.

Because the major civilizations of the world do not currently condone co-sleeping, little has been written about its practicalities. In

218

the past there has been no need for a method, just as there was no need to teach women how to breastfeed.

When we look at co-sleeping in its original context, as it is still practised by rural peoples all over the world, we find it takes as many different forms as there are families. Here, for instance, are the many ways a Maori mother in New Zealand might do it:

> Babies in a 'bassinet' would be next to a mother's bed, and she would sleep with her hand resting on the infant, or her foot rocking the bassinet. In bed, babies could be either between parents or on the outside of a bed, either being held by a parent or sleeping separately. For some mothers, the ideal was to hold the child's face into her shoulder and for both to sleep in that position. Some parents, concerned at the possibility of the infant falling out of bed, pushed the bed into a corner of the room. Some created space within the bed for the infant, using pillows to prevent the infant either rolling out, or a parent rolling on top of the infant.
>
> (M. Gantley, *Early Human Development*, 1994)

I would not wish to prescribe, but good tips are always useful. So here are some of mine – as from one parent to another.

WHAT PREPARATIONS SHOULD I MAKE?

Unless you feel your nursery looks forlorn without one, you will have no cot to buy. Some parents may find this a strangely depressing experience, because our nesting instincts are closely tied to our passion for consumer goods. Others will delight in the financial saving. In any case, babies do not sleep in a full-sized cot for the first few months, so there's no need to buy one yet. Wait until after the birth, by which time you will have got used to the idea of a baby without bars.

Small babies do not take up much space at night. Frances slept in our ordinary double bed up to the age of one with no trouble. She and I have also slept in single beds together, and it wasn't a squeeze.

You and your baby will probably cuddle up together for much of the night, and you soon get used to each other's presence.

If you have the money and the inclination, however, you may wish to invest in a king-size bed, or two singles zipped together. Some families have beds specially made to share with older children. Michel Odent, Judy Graham and their son Pascal used to sleep in a bed just six inches off the floor. Actress Jane Asher says parents may wish to construct their own bed from a simple wooden platform with two mattresses laid over it crossways. La Leche League suggests removing the legs from a standard bed. Other families simply put the mattress on the floor. Extra mattresses may then be added by the side as the children get older.

For those who intend to sleep in a bed of normal height, it is advisable to protect the edges, to stop the baby rolling out. This may be done by keeping the baby on the side next to a wall, by attaching cot sides to the bed, or simply by tucking the bedclothes under the mattress (Remember pre-duvet days?).

ISN'T BED-WETTING A PROBLEM?

When my children were tiny, I used to lay an ordinary terry nappy under them, for added protection. However, they never wet the bed, because they weren't waking up fully in the night.

The new 'ultra' brand of nappies is superb for the all-night stint. Even the Royal College of Midwives recommend *not* changing a baby during the night unless absolutely necessary. They say:

> Minimal disturbance of a baby who has wakened only to be fed may result in the baby settling more quickly after the feed. It may also help the baby to begin to appreciate that night and day are different.

> (*Successful Breastfeeding*)

Third-time mum Janine Sternberg followed the same philosophy when she slept with her daughter Sarah: 'I think I'm less disturbed by Sarah than by the other children,' she said, 'because I'm not constantly getting out of bed. Unless I can actually smell or hear that there's a dirty nappy, I don't change the nappy in the middle of the night. I reckon that if it's been changed in the late evening it can last till morning, because the whole act of changing wakes them up.'

One note of possible interest: both Alice and Joseph (my second and third children) asked to come out of nappies at night when they were eighteen months old, despite still being in nappies during the day. Cautiously I agreed, allowing them to sleep on an open terry towel instead. Each of them was completely dry at night from then on.

I concede this may have had nothing to do with our co-sleeping arrangements. However, I wonder now whether the complete security of co-sleeping added to their confidence in their own bodies. It is also strange that they did this at the same age. Frances, my first, did not have the luxury to make her own decision on the matter. I was too busy trying to potty-train her during the daytime, a struggle which was premature and counter-productive and which took more than a year to complete.

EVERY MOTHER NEEDS SUPPORT – OR DOES SHE?

Most mothering magazines advise women to wear a bra during the day and night during and after pregnancy, advice which I followed for a few weeks with my first baby until the ludicrousness of having to refix a dozen hooks and eyes by moonlight finally got to me. Frances also preferred not to have the wings of a D cup flapping in her face as she fed. I remembered the words of Barbara Henry, chairman of the National Childbirth Trust's breastfeeding promotion group, whom I had interviewed during my pregnancy: 'I think the main reason for wearing a bra is for comfort's sake. My personal view is that it's not necessary. There's no hard and fast rule about wearing a bra during pregnancy or afterwards.'

It was advice, incidentally, which the babycare magazine I was working for refused to print. It did not fit in with current thinking, I was told. Neither, presumably, did it go well with consumer features on 'choosing the right bra for you'.

So my night nursing bra was hurriedly dispatched. It was a weight off my chest. Three children later, I cannot say that discarding my bra has caused me to sag any more than anyone else of my age. At the time, it was far preferable to bags under the eyes.

HOW WILL I SEE TO FEED THE BABY?

It took me a long time to perfect this one. You need just enough light in the room to breastfeed by, but not so much that you or your partner are kept awake. Michel Odent says the baby uses his sense of smell to find the nipple in the dark, but it was some months before I let Frances find her own position on the breast. As any breastfeeding mother will know, the pain experienced when the baby misses the nipple altogether can send you screaming to the ceiling.

I tried leaving the door of the bedroom ajar (rather cold, especially in winter), or draping scarves over standard lamps (fire hazard), and settled finally on the solution of a night light. These come in a variety of fancy shapes for fancy nurseries, but the most practical are just glow-boxes that plug straight into the electric socket on the wall. Some are fitted with a fifteen-watt bulb, but mine takes ten watts, and I find that's ample to see by. After all, you only need to squint in the direction of the breast once or twice a night. The baby does the rest. By the time I was feeding Joseph, my third, I was much more relaxed and I did not need to open my eyes at all.

WHAT CAN I EXPECT ON THE FIRST NIGHT?

The first night with a first baby will probably be in hospital, where it is harder to do what you want. You must decide whether to inform the hospital of your plans to sleep with the baby, in which case, be prepared to shop around for a maternity unit which agrees to this unorthodox practice. I gave birth at the University Hospital in Cardiff, where babies were not supposed to sleep with their mothers. However, since feeding the baby in the bed *was* allowed, I just stretched the feeds into all-night sessions, and nobody was too worried.

Chairs along the side of the bed will also do the trick. Midwives with experience of mothers sleeping with their babies in hospital say it makes for a better, not a worse, night's sleep all round:

> A mother is more likely to sleep soundly in hospital if she has her baby beside her, as she will be confident that if her own baby wakes, she will hear him. She is then less likely to be disturbed by the sound of other babies in the night.
>
> *(Successful Breastfeeding)*

London's Charing Cross Hospital allowed bedsharing when Dr Hugh Jolly was consultant paediatrician there. Dr Jolly warmly advocated keeping mother and baby together. But, as the Royal College of Midwives reports, bedsharing is more common in hospitals in developing countries than it is in the West:

> In the Nair Charitable Hospital in Bombay, for example, where bedding in is, and has been, common for many years, there have been no 'accidents' as a result of babies sharing their mothers' bed.
>
> *(Successful Breastfeeding)*

At a hospital in Chiang Mai, Thailand, researchers observed mothers and babies sleeping in standard hospital beds.[2] The infants, none of whom fell out in the night, occupied the well-worn hollow in the middle of the bed. Mothers slept to one side, with their arms around the babies.

If you are planning a home delivery, there is nothing easier than cuddling straight up in bed with your new-born child – and any other member of the family who wants to join in.

WILL MY CHILD REALLY BE SAFE IN THE BED?

Many people are frightened of smothering the baby. That fear is unfounded provided you follow some common sense precautions. After a week or so, it will be obvious to you that you and your baby are well equipped to sleep through the night together, and that no harm is going to befall him while the two of you are healthy and acting sensibly. Dr Michel Odent writes in *Primal Health*:

> People warn [young mothers] that there is a risk of smothering the baby at night, but this simply does not happen, mothers always seem to be aware of their babies even while they are asleep. Believe it, and you'll see how the rest fits into place.

I would always arrange the pillows so they could not fall on top of my children in the night. Babies, of course, should not be allowed to sleep with their heads on a pillow before the age of one. After you have ensured that the pillows are straight, and that the baby cannot roll out of the bed, the only other precautions refer to the people sleeping together. Co-sleepers should observe a few important rules.

Do not sleep with your baby if you or your partner are:
SMOKERS
DRUNK OR DRUGGED
TOO ILL TO TAKE RESPONSIBILITY FOR YOUR BABY
ON A SOFA OR ON POLYSTYRENE-FILLED CUSHIONS
(these have been shown to increase the chance of smothering)
Or if your baby is:
VERY ILL (Though constant human contact and feeding may be just what your baby needs. Seek professional advice on this.)
IN A SPLINT
SWADDLED (i.e. tightly bound in sheets or other clothing so that he cannot move).

The reasons for these precautions are fairly obvious. A healthy adult body is attuned to the needs of a baby even while asleep, but this natural mechanism may not work if the mind is sedated, or if movement is otherwise impaired. Common sense will tell you what is appropriate.

Some doctors advise parents not to co-sleep if they are vastly overweight. But consider the expanse of the newly-feeding breast and the extra dimensions of the average postnatal woman. The question perhaps is whether you feel you have adequate control of your body. Can you sense your baby cuddled in to you? Observe how the infant's turned-up nose is ideally designed to breathe even when it is jammed up against the areola. If you are really worried, consult your own GP.

Another precaution concerns water beds. Some literature advises that these are not suitable for co-sleeping and yet babies absolutely adore them. They are ideal for a daytime nap, as the gentle movement simulates the curvature and sensation of being in someone's arms. However, soft mattresses are certainly implicated in incidents of smothering, so the best advice is to turn up the water pressure to its highest point when the baby is small. If you cannot do this, it would be preferable for your baby to sleep next to the bed, rather than in it.

WHAT SHOULD THE BABY WEAR?

A baby sleeping with his parents does not need to be wrapped up ready for an Arctic winter. In fact, there is no need for anything but a nappy to come between you and your child, because the benefits of skin-to-skin contact are all he needs for a cosy night's sleep. Over-heating is a factor associated with cot death and the family bed heats up much faster than the distant cot. I used to put my babies in a thin vest (or baby suit on a very cold night) because they would often kick away their side of the duvet during the night. It's lovely to leave the legs and arms free of clothing, however, for skin-to-skin contact and baby foot massages. As children get older, the less actual body contact they seek, so pyjamas are appropriate, if desired. Never cover the baby's head at night as this impairs his ability to regulate his own body temperature.

IS A BEDTIME ROUTINE IMPORTANT?

Consistency *is* important to a child: the consistency of being always with his mother or care-giver. His own patterns will evolve in whatever circumstances he finds himself, so long as she is there.

Observe a child who has been allowed to find his own rhythm of sleeping and waking. His day will have its own regularity, though it may not conform to anything in the books. Frances would sleep every hour when she was first born, then every hour and a half, and so on. The distance between sleeps lengthened until she finally took only one sleep in the day. Watching her by the clock was of no value, as her sleep shifted according to the rhythm of her waking, not according to the hour.

People often ask me whether I put Frances to bed at night with a proper routine. There was a pattern to her bedtimes, but not an imposed 'routine' as most sleep advisers understand the word. Every family is bound to have its own preference for the evening pattern, and the tea–bath–lullaby–lights-out sequence is not the only way of leading up to bedtime.

We made very few efforts to get any of our children off to sleep. They did not tend to fight sleep, because the aim was not to put them down as soon as they dropped off. This was particularly true of Alice, who was carried constantly. I never attempted to control her sleep times, which was a great weight off my mind.

Frances enjoyed some of the freedom of being a first baby, with parents determined to continue with at least some of their prenatal social life. She would play near us while we read, watched television, talked to friends or even ate out in a restaurant. As a young child, she acquired a taste for ice and lemon, as these would be served in water before the meal.

At home, the children would come to me or their father when they were ready to sleep – a quick walk in fresh air or suckle at the breast and they were off. From a very early age, Joseph learnt to ask for bed when he was tired. All of them put themselves to bed occasionally as toddlers.

By the time they started school it was important for us to make sure they had plenty of sleep, so at this stage routines came in. Like other families, we would bathe the children, read stories and give them kisses. None of them needed transitional objects. All of them started begging to sleep at friends' houses from about the age of three (and did so without any fuss). The older they became, the more likely we were to listen to their own assessment of their sleep requirements. Our aim was that bed should never be a punishment, or a trial. If one of them had difficulty getting to sleep, we would suggest that perhaps they weren't tired and that they could read a book in bed. This way, we maintained some privacy for ourselves during the evening.

When Frances went off to sleep as a baby, we held her until it was our bedtime, too. Sometimes we took it in turns to hold her all evening. At other times, she rolled out of my arms and onto the settee, and I left her there by my side. Later, she went off to sleep in the big bed upstairs, and I came back down.

In many countries, children may be observed playing on the beach or in the street at night, while their parents enjoy themselves in a taverna or bar nearby. It is a practice the British often condemn, because it does not fit in with our traditional ideas of children being seen and not heard. However, while the child of India, the Mediterranean or the Middle East causes no trouble during the evening, the British infant can be both seen and heard invading his parents' privacy because he doesn't want to go to bed. Either that, or he rises a little before dawn every morning.

CAN I GO OUT WITHOUT MY BABY?

Parents who are attracted to the idea of close-contact nurture sometimes find it hard to take any time for themselves. This is not how the system was designed. Mothers all over the world expect and receive help from friends and family in the rearing of their children. In many tribes, fathers are frequently absent, whether on hunting expeditions, or enjoying all-male sports. It often falls on women to do all the childcare and the greater proportion of other work, too. They simply could not manage alone. If you intend to embark on a programme of carrying and sleeping with your New Age baby, then you need a New Age community to match.

It is vital for the mental health of the individual and the long-term health of the couple that parents organize regular time out. At first, this might be just a half-hour trip to the pub – soon it can safely be a grown-up night at the theatre, and eventually a weekend in the country. Such events do not have to mean the end of your breastfeeding or bedsharing relationship. Teresa Wilson points out that

> Many mothers in the West aim to separate early from their babies because there are a number of separation 'ultimatums' throughout babyhood (needing a weekend away as a couple, starting day nursery/childminder), and it is accepted by many that the sooner the baby realizes that he or she is an individual and that separation is always followed by reunion, the less distressing it will be for all concerned.
>
> ('Co-sleeping', *New Generation*, June 1997)

The simple rule is to match your absences with the capabilities of your child. A newborn is fine with dad or grandma for half an hour. A six-month-old baby should be OK for two hours with a loving adult he knows well.

If you are having problems leaving with any age of child, start gently and come back soon. Be firm, be understanding and trust in your child's ability to manage without you. Our children are usually far more resilient than we imagine.

Even if you feel so happy at home that you never have the heart to go away, consider that it's our responsibility to provide children with the community to which they expect to belong. If we give our children enough close nurture, the only thing which will stop them bonding with other people is our (unstated?) reluctance to let go. Grandparents, godparents and adopted aunts can all give our children the quality of care and balance of relationships they crave.

As Jean Liedloff said, 'Babysitters, hired for an evening, can be asked to sit the baby, not just the television set. They can hold the baby on their laps as they watch the television or do their homework. The noise and light will not disturb or harm him, but being left alone will.'[3]

I started writing this book when Frances was seven months old, and she went to a child-minder for a couple of hours each weekday.

This suited all of us very well, as the minder became her extended family, and I was able to exercise my brain a little. It would, of course, be preferable if the child could join the mother at her work – but seven-month-old babies are fairly incompatible with word processors.

A mother can begin to leave her baby from birth – for a length of time appropriate to that child and his stage of development. It can be wonderful for someone else to take over for half an hour in the evenings, when many Western babies are colicky. All we need to require of our child-minders is that they should love babies, have time for them and be prepared to hold them.

WON'T THE BABY IN THE BED RUIN OUR SEX LIFE?

Where there is desire, ways will be found for partners to make love, and desire is likely to be higher if you are both getting a good night's sleep.

New parents might like to act like young lovers again: finding places to rendezvous where the baby will not be disturbed. Inventiveness is important when there are toddlers around – especially if you feel like this harassed mother:

> It is very hard to have free, open, joyous, harmonious,
> adventurous sexual relations if they are interrupted invariably
> by the patter of tiny feet.
>
> (Quoted in *Sleeping Children*)

If you take your baby into bed from the beginning, then he'll grow into a toddler who can be safely tucked up in his own room without a murmur. A tiny infant needs instant care, an adult can wait a little while, knowing he is still loved. There will be plenty of times for making love, without disturbing you or your child.

WHAT DO I NEED TO KNOW ABOUT NIGHT-FEEDING?

Feeding and sleeping happen coincidentally for the mother who shares the bed with her baby. She will soon learn to feed on her back or side, and realize that there is no need to be particularly delicate as she shifts position in the night.

In the early weeks with my first baby, I gave myself an extra pillow in the bed, not for my head, but to support my back as I fed Frances. We had a bouncy brass bed at the time, and I tended to roll away from her as I fed. Things improved when we put the mattress on the floor. Things improved even more when friends gave us their old, low, wooden queen-size bed base and we bought a giant mattress to fit. We covered this with one double and one single duvet, for flexibility of movement. While feeding the baby, I would slope my single duvet down from the top of my shoulder to below the baby's arm.

The easiest position for me was the classic 'recovery' position, taught to all students of first aid. You simply lie on your side with your upper knee raised, so leaning in towards the baby. Your lower arm either goes under your pillow, or under the baby's head, and your upper arm is free to guide the breast, or to stroke the baby. Consult a breastfeeding book for the post-Caesarian feeding position.

Dr Penny Stanway told me that it was a good idea for the baby's head to be in the crook of the arm, as this made it very unlikely that he would choke on vomit – a potential cause of death in small infants. She also suggests an ingenious way of turning over in the night:

> . . . it's easy if you leave your sleeping baby lying by the breast he was at last. When he next wants to be at the breast, roll over with him in your arms close to your chest so that he is lying by your other side by your full breast. Some mothers manage to feed their baby from the opposite breast by leaning towards him.
>
> (*Breast is Best*)

Merryl Hammond, a mother from Quebec, describes the 'leaning in' method in more detail:

I have recently discovered that there is no need to roll over or to change the baby's position in bed when we are lying down to nurse . . . when I feel it is time to change sides, I gently remove the right nipple from her mouth, shift my weight slightly by bending my left (top) leg over Karrie's legs and lifting my arm high over the top of Karrie's head. As I do this, Karrie moves her head slightly (looking for the nipple) so that she is no longer lying flat on her left ear on the bed. Her open mouth 'finds' my left breast which is now in perfect position for her. She doesn't rouse out of her sleep; Rob doesn't even know we are nursing, and I can drift back to sleep almost immediately. Despite having smaller-than-usual breasts and a history of backaches, I have found this position to be comfortable.

(*LLL GB News*, Jan–Feb 1991)

It sounds highly technical and complicated, which of course it isn't at all. Another method is to slide the baby under you as you change sides.

Babies who co-sleep tend automatically to sleep on their backs – or their sides with their heads raised on the parental arm. These are the positions which are easiest for breastfeeding. Fathers often enjoy sleeping with a baby across their chests. I am not aware of any research into the benefits or dangers of the baby sleeping prone on another person.

Do not worry too much about which breast to feed from. Co-sleeping babies suckle extensively from both sides, on and off throughout the night.[4] It is not an over-indulgence of the child to allow this, and hopefully you will learn to sleep through most feeds. Night-feeding is essential for encouraging long-term milk production. There is less danger of becoming engorged – although watch out for mastitis, often the result of a trapped milk duct. If, in the morning, you feel one side is heavier than the other, just offer that for breakfast (usually a more serious feed).

Bottle-feeding mothers can make life as simple as possible for themselves by preparing any night-feeds beforehand. One of the aims of the exercise, after all, is to avoid having to wake up too much during the night. However, bottle-feeding is likely to be more disruptive than breastfeeding, as the parent has to get out of bed to warm the feed. Mothers who have weaned their babies on to the bottle during the day may prefer to continue breastfeeding at night.

HOW CAN I DEMAND-FEED IF MY BABY IS DROWSY?

Many babies born under epidural spend their first days asleep in a hospital cot, scarcely waking to feed. Some babies (including my second, Alice, who was born at home after a drug-free labour) are simply drowsier than others.

The benefit of night-feeding is that the sleepy baby maximizes his intake, by suckling through the night. He also stimulates milk production during the crucial night period, when the release of prolactin is greatest. So even if he does not take much during the day, he is creating demand for later on.

Many mothers complain of wakeful babies, but fewer see the dangers of an excessively sleepy infant. Night-feeding ensures that all babies, sleepy or not, get the optimum amount of nourishment.

WHAT IF THE BABY WAKES UP DURING THE NIGHT?

At first, your baby may wake up at all hours wanting to play. For a new-born baby this is to be expected, and the natural response should be warm, but minimal, if you want to encourage him to go back to sleep. Change the baby's nappy if that is what he needs, smile at him if he's smiling at you, and offer him the breast. New babies are often at their happiest in the relaxed atmosphere of the bed.

Very soon however the baby gets the message that night-time is sleep time, because that is what his parents do. Close your eyes to show what's required. I would do this with my babies, and when I opened them again, they would sometimes stare up at me, then quickly close their eyes as if I hadn't seen them. This game would delight us for a few minutes until we both fell back to sleep.

The only time any of my babies cried at night was when they were ill or in pain. This happened once in twelve months with Frances, and we had to call the doctor after she had cried for ten minutes or so. I knew she was suffering, because there was simply no other reason for her to cry. New babies snuffle and make funny little noises all night long. Distracting at first, baby sounds soon become part of the auditory wallpaper. I'm sure that if a baby gets into trouble during the night, the subconscious senses that his sounds are subtly different. On one highly memorable occasion, I woke to find myself holding Frances out over the side of the bed, where she was sick. I don't know to this day how I reacted in time. As videoed co-sleeping research from California and Bristol, England has demonstrated, there may be far more to mother–baby interactions than we previously dared to imagine.

WHERE SHOULD MY BABY TAKE DAYTIME NAPS?

At first, I needed almost as much sleep as each baby, feeling quite exhausted from the birth. I would take my sleep when they did, in the big bed alongside them. Apart from that, they did a lot of their daytime sleeping in the sling.

The sling I bought for Frances was, unfortunately, not really designed for newborns, so I found it extremely difficult to get on with my normal life as my hands were tied up. I subsequently discovered the excellent Wilkinet Baby Carrier, which is suitable for all sizes of baby and does not damage the infant spine. It is available by mail order.[5]

It is a good idea to get a baby used to the sling as early as possible, because it involves a particularly tight closeness of adult and baby, which youngsters may struggle against if it's introduced later on.

Other cultures have a variety of sling arrangements that range from tying the baby to the back (Turkey), to the hip slings of the Wodaabe (central Africa), the swag straps made of pounded bark of Maori mothers (New Zealand), and the traditional Welsh shawl, which young women learn how to tie from their grandmothers. The people of South Wales have a special phrase for snuggling close to a baby:

'cutching up'. There's nothing to stop you experimenting for yourself with an old sheet and a few safety pins.

As a baby gets older, he may more easily be left to sleep by himself for a while, with the mother close at hand. When he wakes, the first thing he sees is her face, welcoming him back into the world. He does not need to scream for her attention, causing her to drop everything and come running. As far as possible, it's easier if a baby sleeps near his caretakers: in the bedroom, the lounge or the car.

WHAT HAPPENS WHEN A SECOND BABY COMES ALONG?

In some ways, this is often the natural time for the older child to graduate to his own bed. However, it may also be the natural time for an older child to come back into the family bed before moving, finally, out. This is what Frances did (she was two years, eight months old, when Alice was born). Alice, who was four by the time Joseph came along, had been out of our bed for a year or two and she did not ask to come back in again.

Older siblings have many ways of seeking out the extra comfort they need when their place is suddenly usurped by a new CAO (Centre Of Attention). Some show a renewed interest in breastfeeding. Others take to their comfort object with a vengeance. Previously settled children may refuse to go to nursery and apparently weaned three-year-olds start climbing into your bed in the middle of the night.

It depends on the size of your bed and the generosity of your heart, of course, but I think the family bed is a fantastic way of healing the potential rift created by a new baby. If your bed simply isn't big enough, you might like to consider a game of Musical Beds, a very common practice if hundreds of readers' letters are to be believed. On the other hand, if none of this is for you, then you will just need to convey your untiring love for your older children in other ways.

I should perhaps mention that when I told people I was writing a second book, they almost all replied 'What's it called – Four in a Bed?' Since we had our third child, many letters are addressed to The Jackson Five and now everyone wants to know if we are – you've guessed it . . . To answer all enquirers, yes, we occasionally (rarely) have been four in a bed. We were never five in a bed, unless you count late Sunday mornings.

MY CHILD HAS ALWAYS SLEPT ALONE, BUT RECENTLY HE IS UNSETTLED. SHOULD I TAKE HIM INTO MY BED?

While some parents may choose willingly to take their toddlers into bed, others find themselves bullied into bedsharing. When a three-year-old refuses to sleep any other way, this is often the first time parents really question the practice of keeping the child out. They are unable to deal cold-heartedly with a frightened youngster.

Despite the efforts of modern sleep advisers, there are still thousands of two-year-olds in the West who refuse to sleep alone at bedtime, or who wake in the night, begging to be with their parents. The parents are encouraged to believe that their sleepless children are either difficult or abnormal, but this is not so.[4] They are merely in tune with children the world over, who need food and the comfort of another human being at night.

Any child up to the age of three or four will benefit from a few months in the parents' bed.

To coerce a toddler into sleeping with you, patience may be required. Put him in your bed to sleep, and lie by his side. Neither withdraw, nor offer excessive affection, but let him take the lead. Reading books together in the big bed can be a great treat. Let him go to bed later than usual, if necessary, so you can all fall asleep together. Simply offering to share your bed may be all your child needs to hear.

IS THERE ANY HARM IN SLEEPING WITH THE BABY OCCASIONALLY, RATHER THAN EVERY NIGHT?

Although many British children do sleep with their parents at night, theirs is a part-time arrangement – a reaction to sickness, crying or sleeping problems. Their parents only take them into bed when they (the children) are upset or ill.

One drawback is that you are sleeping with the child at his worst.

A baby screaming in pain or a child burning up with fever, is a poor companion. After a sleepless night parents conclude that they have given co-sleeping a fair test, and it is not for them.

It is important to be consistent with the child. Ideally, a baby should sleep with his parents right through from the beginning, not just when he is ill or when he is naughty. Otherwise he will be ill or naughty in order to achieve the end result.

This is contrary to the advice of Dr Christopher Green, author of *Toddler Taming*, who suggests that illness is the *only* excuse for taking a child into bed during the night:

> A sick child on the other hand, has a rightful place in his parents' bed, although it is sometimes hard to evict him once his health has returned to normal. And all children are entitled to that enjoyable, early morning romp in their parents' bed – just as long as the cock has crowed and the tea has been made!

I am not suggesting that parents who bar the bed to their children continue the ban when the baby is sick. But they should be aware that in allowing sickness to be a ticket to their company at night, they are making an emotional statement about illness that will stay with the child. At the very least, he will grow up expecting extra emotional support when he is ill. He may even fabricate illness in order to receive that support.

Until the age of six, I used to have a nightmare almost every night, and trot along to my parents' bed to sleep with them. The nightmares were my passport to the big bed, and of course they ceased once my parents were sleeping by my side. But I remember the nightly fear of going to sleep by myself.

According to most authorities, nightmares are a 'normal' part of child development. Two paediatricians state:

> Nightmares occur almost universally in children from three to six years of age.
>
> (Snead and Bruch, *Pediatrics*, 1983)

But many parents whose children sleep with them say that the frequency and impact of nightmares are greatly reduced. Desmond Morris, for instance, tells me his son Jason does not suffer from nightmares, or any other sleep disturbance. Jason slept next to his parents until he chose to move out of their bedroom. Nightmares could be yet another product of the child's fear and lack of self-confidence when he is forced to sleep alone.

In my own experience, nightmares are extremely rare when a child is sleeping secure in the company of others. I can't remember Frances or Joe ever having a serious nightmare at all. At the age of seven, Alice once had a week of nightmares, following an upset at school. We put a Native American dreamcatcher by her bed, and this, coupled with some creative visualization and the offer of sleeping with us, helped her to deal with her anxiety.

Maternal separation has been linked to bed-wetting problems in older children.[6] Sleepwalking and night terrors[7] may also be connected with children's unspoken fears. The more security we offer our infants, the less likely they are to associate bedtime with trauma.

WHAT ABOUT TWINS?

A fascinating story about premature girl twins from Massachusetts has triggered a new kind of intensive care treatment in America. Although European hospitals often bed twins together as a matter of course, the practice in the States was always to give them separate incubators. While baby Kyrie was thriving, her smaller sister Brielle was failing rapidly. The story is told by New York columnist Liz Corcoran:

> Born 12 weeks prematurely on Oct. 17, 1995, Brielle was put on a respirator while Kyrie was able to breathe on her own.
>
> 'My husband and I came in to see the girls,' recalls mother Heidi, 'and Brielle was having a really tough day, her oxygen levels had been turned way up and she was having erratic heartbeats.' As Brielle's condition deteriorated, nurses at Massachusetts Memorial suggested the Jacksons hold their sick

daughter, telling Heidi that 'perhaps a little bit of love' would help. But, she recalls, 'If anything she was getting too stressed. I told [nurse] Gayle Kasparian that I was going to put her back in the incubator . . . and she said, "Let me see if putting her in with her sister would help." '

Kyrie was gaining weight and getting close to going home. 'We moved Kyrie way over to the other side [of her crib] and put Brielle next to her. It was really quite amazing . . . Brielle just snuggled right up against her and fell asleep.'

Almost immediately, Brielle's heart rate and breathing improved. 'My husband and I looked at each other and at Gayle and she said "I can't believe it!" We stared at her for 10 minutes to see if she was going to stay like that or whether it was just a fluke. She stayed like that. They were identical twins and they shared the same placenta and I think that was what she was used to. Brielle was used to hearing Kyrie's heart, she was used to the way she felt and smelled.'

It was kind of a miracle,' says Susan Fitzback, nurse manager at the hospital. 'But it worked and we've been doing it ever since.'

('Double Exposure', *WHO*, 17 June 1996)

Brielle's reaction was 'immediate . . . absolutely immediate'. Her blood oxygen readings stabilized for the first time since birth, she quickly began gaining weight and did not have another stressful episode.[8] Soon afterwards, studies of bedding twins together began in Oklahoma and other US hospitals started to adopt the practice.

Parents writing from all over the world have told me that brothers and sisters who sleep together are closer and tend to row less. Co-sleeping can certainly mend the stresses of a difficult day. Germaine Greer[1] recounts stories of Indian cousins sleeping together – she saw 'upon a string cot under a peepul tree in Tamil Nadu, a 12-year-old uncle fast asleep with his baby niece equally fast asleep in his arms'. Cousins and uncles, brothers and sisters, grandparents with grand-children – everyone can do this, and in some cultures, everyone does.

ARE THERE ANY PREPARATIONS TO MAKE FOR TRAVELLING AWAY FROM HOME?

A child who sleeps with his parents at home can sleep with his parents anywhere. Strange surroundings do not prevent him dozing off, because his parents are not strange, and they are the most important constant in his life.

Travelling in a plane, boat or car is easy when your baby goes to sleep in your arms. The only difficulty is reconciling the need for safety with the child's need for freedom. Small children often hate long journeys strapped into their safety seats in the back of a car, but it simply is not safe to hold a baby in your arms, even in the back. The way forward is to limit motoring trips as much as possible, choosing instead buses, trains and planes where the baby is allowed to sit on your lap.

A note on breastfeeding in hot climates: the baby needs no supplements of water or juice if he is being breastfed. On holiday in Israel with Frances at ten weeks old, I was told I should be giving her water to stop her dehydrating in the heat. In fact, all that was needed was for me to drink more water, not the baby.

On British holidays, the problem is more likely to be hypothermia than dehydration. This is the traditional wisdom: 'However cold you find the weather,' writes Kim Sullivan in *Mother* magazine (February 1988), 'remember that your baby will become colder even quicker than you when you go out of doors because you're moving around and she can't.' Ms Sullivan lists the necessary accessories for keeping a baby warm: thick blankets, hot water bottles, natural fibres, cardigan, jacket and hat, mittens, bootees and a shawl. Then put the pram hood up to keep the cold out.

On the other hand, you could put the baby on a sling, and wrap him up in your own coat and arms. A baby can and should move around as much as possible – next to your body, not on a set of four wheels.

WHAT IF MY PARTNER DOESN'T LIKE THE IDEA?

Amazing, but true: a mothers' group in Manchester discussing the pros and cons of bringing baby into bed agreed that they couldn't because their husbands wouldn't like the idea. At least, they had the idea that their husbands wouldn't like the idea.

If this is indeed the case, and not just a polite way of passing the buck, then it implies that the average man would rather risk years of disturbed nights than cuddle up with his children. Perhaps it is a matter of sexual roles: men feeling endangered by the threat to their machismo, and women reinforcing that image, with statements like this:

> Many husbands would be very unhappy at the idea of a third member of the family in the marital bed and if it is going to cause any friction then it is obviously not worth it.
>
> (Jane Asher, *Silent Nights*)

Of course, it is not only the men who object. The La Leche League recite a story of cross-cultural conflict in their book on breastfeeding . . .

> In the Zavari household, husband Hassan was born in the Middle East, where a baby sleeping with his parents is a natural part of life. Joan Zavari tells of her reaction to some of the ideas:
> 'When Hassan suggested breastfeeding, I didn't hesitate. Natural childbirth was even considered and agreed upon. However, being of a conservative nature, I had put my foot down when he suggested putting two beds together and sleeping family style. How would I make the beds? I found lots of excuses. When Stevie was born, I soon found out that some babies wake up five or six times in the night. Hassan didn't even say 'I told you so,' when I suggested putting the two beds together.'
>
> (*The Art of Breastfeeding*)

In my experience, if a mother really wants something for her child, no power on earth will prevent her from providing it. So if your partner, male or female, doesn't like the idea of bedsharing and you do, let them at least try it. It's refreshing to be woken up by a ten-month-old baby planting a kiss on your nose. Ask my husband.

DOES THE FATHER HAVE A SPECIAL ROLE TO PLAY?

I have often referred to maternal rather than paternal care, but this is for clarity rather than from any notion that only mothers can do the job. Sometimes it is impossible for the mother to feed and care for her child. Some fathers choose to look after the children while the mother goes to work.

As far as we know, the major drawback with paternal care is that dad cannot breastfeed. It may also be that the mother's biorhythms are important for her baby, in helping him to breathe regularly and develop into a healthy, well-adjusted child.[9] It is the mother who carried him in the womb, and she who may be best able to provide the sensory stimulation he needs after birth.

However, sleeping with the baby could give a new emphasis to paternal care. Some parents choose to bottle-feed their babies so that dad can get a look in. Fathers often enjoy the closeness that feeding involves.

But if a baby sleeps with you in the bed, dad gets all the closeness he wants in a full eight-hour stint. What's more, nobody has to be disturbed for the night-feeds. No one has to do shifts on the landing, warm bottles or prepare feeds.

Fathers will be able to bond with their babies as nature had intended them to – as they sleep. Even if dad is away all day, he need not become a distant figure, appearing only at bath-times and weekends.

Many mothers told me how much their partners enjoyed having the baby in the bed. Soon after the birth of her daughter, one friend wrote to say: 'She's sleeping well in our bed – half the night on Serge's chest and the rest snuggled up to me.'

It's a new way to share the care.

WHAT IF I'M AT WORK ALL DAY?

The mother who works may have problems getting to know her baby. One mother I interviewed confessed:

> You do feel you have to prove yourself. It's as though you should be performing all the time, in spite of the fact that you have children and all the extra duties they bring . . . You're juggling three things, your job, your children and your home, and something has to go.
>
> *(She* magazine, August 1988)

It's much easier to be Supermum if you're doing part of your mothering in the night.

The mother who cannot be with her baby during the day has greater need to be near him when she gets home. Otherwise, the only physical contact she gets is the brief encounter between tea and lights-out. Why take on the hassles of routine, when you could be enjoying more cuddles? And all those peaceful nights' sleep are perfect preparation for another day's work.

SHOULD SINGLE PARENTS SLEEP WITH THEIR CHILDREN?

> Many lonely mothers, whether alone because their husband is away on business or because of a marriage break-up, subtly encourage their children to come to bed with them each night as company. It is then difficult, when life returns to normal, to persuade the child to discontinue the practice.
>
> *(Toddler Taming)*

Dr Green implies that using someone for company is a negative and underhand practice. I don't see why. People *are* company, and they love to be used as such. He also takes the rather narrow view that a lone mother is an abnormal occurrence, making no mention of lone fathers, and rejects the way in which the parent 'subtly' lures the child into bed.

Germaine Greer offers a similar example, without the cynicism:

A 10-year-old Indian house-guest of mine explained to me that it was good fun sleeping with his cousins in his grandparents' room . . . If his father went away of course the little boy would have to sleep with his mother, and when his mother came to sleep with me, when I was a guest in their house, he had to sleep with his father. What was unthinkable was that anyone would choose to sleep alone.

('On Sleeping with your Baby',
Independent Magazine, 15 July 1989)

There are many thousands of single-parent families in civilized society, whether permanently or temporarily so, and each has its own reasons for living in this way. Many single parents choose to be single, and do not therefore sleep with their babies because of loneliness.

It is true that following divorce, death or separation, the adult is likely to be as much in need of company as the child. Holding someone at night is one way of expressing deep emotional need. Touch is a valuable means of communication to both adult and child. It should not be despised.

Film-maker Julian Aston told me he slept with his son after his first marriage ended in divorce. 'I used to say to him, "Why don't you sleep on your own?" He would say "You want company as much as I do," which I did.'

The single parent is not a selfish creature, using the child at a moment of crisis, and discarding him as soon as there is someone else to cling to. To many parents, single or not, the suggestion of hurriedly pushing the child out of bed when a partner comes along is incredible. The needs of the new partner and the needs of the child have to be weighed up. Why should anybody be left out of the equation?

If a parent does accept a new partner into the family bed, then initially there might be a negative reaction from the child (although even this is unlikely if the baby is secure enough). But look at it another way: sleeping with your step-mother or step-father is a quick way to get to know and accept them. I say all this in the full knowledge that suggesting intimacy between children and potentially transient parent-figures is likely to engender a hostile reaction. I tend to the optimistic view – that the vast majority of new partners are perfectly able to cuddle and nurture other people's children without abusing them. This is not, however, always the view of the courts, it is not the view of some social workers and nor is it the view of British columnist Julie Burchill: 'I cannot help but feel that adults who seek tactile gratification, however innocently, with children rather than adults are more than a little immature,' she wrote. 'Surely the lesson that Cleveland taught us is that too many parents sleep with their children already, in the most disgusting of ways.'[10]

One mother, Judith Joseph from Glasgow, slept not only with her own daughter Lisa, but also with thirty foster children over a period of fifteen years. 'A lot of the babies come to me with sleep problems,' she said, 'especially when there have been difficulties at home. I don't breastfeed them, but they love the physical contact. As soon as they feel the warmth of your body, it sends them to sleep. I always try it. Their sleep problems usually go away.'

CAN I SLEEP WITH MY SPECIAL NEEDS CHILD?

The needs of individual children will determine whether or not it is appropriate to take them into the family bed. Very poorly babies cannot be removed from their incubators, but may be hand-held or stroked if it soothes them. Premature babies who are allowed home often thrive when they sleep on their parents' skin. A blind or deaf baby will need increased parental contact at all times, not just at night. A baby with a disability will have a need to experience more of the human world for himself, in order to participate in it. Andrina McCormack writes:

> Because of neonatal problems, illness, or prematurity, many handicapped children do not begin to get to know their parents until they are days, weeks or even months old. Therefore the natural mechanisms for establishing a bond are disturbed, and have to be closely and intensively worked on. Parents of very quiet passive babies may be tempted to leave

the baby even when he or she is awake because they are relieved to have time to themselves. Parents of very grumpy babies may be only too glad to have a respite from the tension and stress that constant crying can engender. However, good parent-child bonding is essential for emotional health later on, and parents of handicapped children should recognise that they have to work a bit harder than others on this.

(Coping with your Handicapped Child)

Intensive bonding goes on at night as well as during the day. It is also a more relaxing time for the disabled child, when he does not have to cope with all the physical obstacles of daily living.

The disabled child may be more obviously needy than the able-bodied child, but we should treat all our children with special care.

Down's Syndrome children may reap great benefits from bodily contact at night, since they have poor control of their body temperature. However, night-times will not be easy for the parents. These children sleep restlessly, often kicking off bedclothes and quickly becoming cold. Chest and throat infections frequently result. Co-sleeping does provide a human thermostat for the infant, but beware:

> The practice of bedsharing is almost certainly not a good idea with these children. The habit of being in bed with a parent, not to mention the attraction of the warmth they enjoy compared to the cold when they leave it, can be very difficult to break. The director of the UK National Centre for Down's Syndrome told me of a 30-year-old man who was still sleeping with his brother and step-sister.
>
> *(Sleepless Children)*

The disabled parent, like the child, may derive great satisfaction from cuddling up to a baby during the night. It certainly makes feeding the baby much easier. But sleeping with the baby may be impossible for someone with severe physical handicap. Every situation will be different, and people should be encouraged to find their own practical solutions to our universal needs.

WHEN CAN WE EXPECT THE CHILD TO LEAVE THE BED?

Eventually, it's time for the child to move on. He may be ten months or ten years old, but it is a decision which is up to you as much as the child. You may be longing for the moment, or dreading it – but ideally, it should be just another, normal phase in the pattern of growing up.

Two to three years old is about the age when children are independent enough to sleep alone, if they started early in their parents' bed. Some toddlers join their parents for a few months, and then proclaim they have had enough.

One parent asked me 'What earthly reason has the child for wanting to leave the bed?' In primitive societies, the child sees other children move away from their parents, and he knows that this is the natural thing to do. In our families, the first child has no example to follow, and therefore may cling to the parental bed for longer.

I do not see any harm in creating a positive choice for the child to move out of the bed. When Frances was exactly a year old, we gave her her own mattress by the side of ours, and from the first night, she moved between us and her new terrain. Such a mattress can be moved slowly away from the main bed, until it represents the child's own sleeping place.

Some parents redecorate the child's nursery, and indicate that moving in there is a step towards growing up. Little friends may come to stay the night, to help initiate the new room. Simply putting up a new poster or adding a rug (magic carpet?) to a toddler's room can make it more enticing for a while. Every novelty wears off, of course, but it is surprising how children are attracted to the status implicit in suggestions like 'Big four-year-olds have their own bedrooms.'

Some children transfer to the new arrangement with the minimum of fuss. Others will need holding and reassuring before they go to sleep. One strategy is to say 'If you lie down and close your eyes, I'll stay and tidy your room.' If your child is really sleepy (and it's better to wait until they are before you try putting them to sleep by themselves), then just putting his head down will help him to drift off. Tidy up in the room, then gradually walk out of it, perhaps humming a lullaby. Eventually, you are gone. If the child calls for you, return quietly, acknowledge his need, kiss him, but insist he stays in bed. The tone should be perfect Mary Poppins: loving, but firm. The main differences between this method and traditional sleep-training, or 'controlled crying' is 1) that the child has already experienced many months of co-sleeping and is perfectly able to start sleeping alone; and 2) you are not, at any stage, expected to leave him to cry.

This is a modified version of another method known as 'kiss and retreat', as described by psychologist Olwen Wilson, head of child speciality for North Downs Community Health. Her sleep management technique bombards the insecure child with constant reassurance. She points out that 'A child left to cry is frightened, which only acts to increase the separation anxiety . . .

Of course fear is a powerful motivator, but as a child psychologist I do not recommend its use, because of the long-term emotional damage. This programme may produce a few tears of anger, but no fear . . .

The parent should be advised to follow the normal bedtime routine, then at the very end, kiss the child goodnight and promise to 'come back in a minute to give a kiss.' However, they should actually return in seconds. They should move just a little, then back to give another kiss, then a little more, then another kiss, then occupy themselves – for example, by putting away some clothes in a drawer – and give another kiss. Then out and back . . . and so on. The contract is: in bed, head on pillow, then a goodnight kiss, but no more chatter, no more cuddles, no more stories, play or drinks; just kisses until the child is asleep.

This may take 300 kisses and three hours on the first night, but it should be slightly less on the second night . . . Watch out for the fifth night; this is often the test night and may be as bad as the first. Once past the 'test night', by the sixth and seventh nights the new learning is usually secured.

(*Health Visitor*, December 1996)

This sounds terrifyingly intense, but not as harrowing as sitting outside the nursery listening to a baby scream. It's meant to be an utterly gentle way to wean, and apparently it works.[11]

These are just a few ideas to get you started. The most humane approaches are usually devised by the humans who do the caring, and I know each family is capable of devising its own ways to be kind and yet strong when it comes to weaning. I would only say one thing – if the weaning doesn't go well, and feels too much like a struggle, then perhaps this is not the time. Perhaps 300 kisses is the equivalent of 30 more nights of sharing your bed.

The way to know if a child needs comfort is to allow him to come to you. Similarly, he will indicate when he wants to move away. Ideally, parents would not offer more comfort than is required, nor reject any reasonable appeal. They can then be sure of satisfying a child's needs, and not his whims. As the psychologists put it:

> If the infant has had parents on whom he can depend, he has experienced the inevitable frustrations in gradual small doses. He develops a feeling of social trust which he demonstrates by the ease of his feeding, the depth of his sleep, the relaxation of his bowels, and by his being interested and appearing happy and comfortable during the greater part of his waking hours.
>
> (English and Pearson, *Emotional Problems of Living*)

Whatever way you choose to handle the weaning process, be aware that any attempt to hasten it unduly may end in conflict, or in the child returning to the bed for longer. The move towards independence needs to come from the child, or it will not be genuine. Independence is something we can only take for ourselves.

11 | Yes, But . . .

I don't begrudge Ferber the right to preach Ferberization or
parents who prefer sleeping sans child the right to practice it.
Live and let live. What's annoying is the refusal of Ferber and
other experts to reciprocate my magnanimity. They act as if
parents like me are derelict, as if children *need* to fall asleep in
a room alone.

(Robert Wright, *Time* magazine)

When we first told people that we slept with our baby, they gave us
that look. The 'good-grief-I-knew-she-was-mad-but-don't-say-
anything' look. Our strange nocturnal behaviour caused more
whispering among friends and acquaintances than anything we
had done before. Wear a wig, be convicted of insider dealing, but
don't take your baby into bed – not if you prefer the quiet life.

I have been challenged with just about every objection our
cotbound society could come up with, so here is a list of the strongest
– with some brief responses. Many of the topics are tackled at
greater length elsewhere in the book, but you may be glad of some
quick-fire ammunition to keep great-aunts and health visitors at
bay . . .

- I couldn't possibly sleep with my baby, I'd be far too afraid of
  smothering her in the night.

(A mother)

Julian Aston, film-maker, took a camera into his bedroom, to film himself and his wife sleeping alongside Luke, their three-month-old baby boy. 'What it showed very dramatically,' said Julian, 'was that the parents rolled about all over the place and didn't touch the baby.'

In Bristol, researchers analysing 800 hours of video material of mothers and babies reported that

> Even when asleep, mothers appeared to be aware or sense the presence of their baby in bed with them, and at no time was a mother ever observed to roll on her infant, even when sleeping very close together.
>
> (Jeanine Young, 'Bedsharing with Babies: The Facts', 1998)

Anyone who sleeps with a smaller creature will discover the same phenomenon. Fears of squashing or smothering the baby are extremely common, and based on our inevitable lack of experience. If you co-sleep negligently – when smoking, for instance, after taking drugs, or without due regard to mattress and pillow safety – then you do, of course, place the baby at all sorts of risks. Done sensibly, with foresight and sensitivity, co-sleeping is as safe as, and possibly safer than, other options.

- When the older baby gets used to attention every time he cries a little, he will soon come to want and demand it. Being rocked back to sleep, taken downstairs or into your bed can all become habits; bad because the baby's sleep is constantly interrupted and because you can never relax. The odd occasion can do no harm, but remember that it is easier to prevent a habit forming than to break it later on.

  (*The Bounty Baby Book* (23rd edition, revised), 1987)

Forming habits – what a dreadful thought. Why do professionals get so worked up about some childhood practices and not others? We put our babies in nappies, knowing they'll be toilet-trained by the time they're thirty-five. Yet babies who are given the security of being rocked to sleep, or the welcome of the parents' bed, will, we are told, be forever dependent. Please don't love them too much or they'll come to expect it.

Sometimes it's not the baby who is accused of bad habits, but the mother herself. Michel Odent says critics use this argument merely as a way of defending the rules about feeding and routine that were doled out in the first half of this century:

> Mothers of previous generations like to respect what they themselves were taught. What they call 'bad habits' are in fact normal and natural ways of meeting a baby's fundamental needs. Being accused of 'bad habits' is something which can frighten young mothers who would like to listen to their instincts.
>
> (*Primal Health*)

Let's indulge our instincts, while we can still hear them prompting us. And on the topic of demanding attention, might attention not be exactly what the human baby craves, as he makes primitive efforts to strike up a conversation with his care-givers? Anthropologist Dr Mary Ainsworth, having observed that babies in Uganda were much more advanced than their American counterparts, concluded:

> It is better for a baby to be held a lot, to be picked up when he cries, to be given what he wants, and to be given much opportunity and freedom to interact than it is for a baby to be kept for long periods in his crib apart from other people, where his signals cannot be perceived and consequently where he cannot experience a sense of predictable consequence and control.
>
> (*Infancy in Uganda*)

- All this talk of not separating mother and baby has worried me more than ever. I'm frightened to put my baby down.

  (A mother)

The trouble with childcare ideas – good or bad ones – is that they tend to get in the way of the relationship between parent and child. At best, we use them to inspire us, until the moment when we really feel we have made the idea our own. At worst, they can make us feel inept, scared, unsure of how to proceed.

Ideas are empty until put into practice. The 'idea' of carrying and sleeping with your baby is not intended to create in parents a state of nervous guilt. I've presented my research, now I am letting you off the hook. Don't be frightened to put your baby down. Don't sleep with your baby if you don't want to. The title of the book is a concept, not a prescription. If you find some ideas which appeal, use them to inform your actions, rather than to overwhelm them. Sleep with your baby because it's fun and it suits you. Carry him because it gives you pleasure, not because I tell you to. You'll learn far more from the baby than from me, and maybe some of his natural confidence will rub off.

- This led many timid parents, in avoiding overwhelming their children with the demands of habit-training, to the opposite extreme of inviting the baby to tyrannize over the family with a whim of iron. This submissive and frightened version of self-conscious parenthood ('permissiveness') was reinforced by misunderstandings of other findings as well. Many, without comprehending the inter-relationships among all the ways of behaving which make up a culture, advocated the adoption of child-rearing practices of one or another primitive society.

    (*Childhood and Adolescence*)

- We are not monkeys and we are not living in the bush . . . Tribespeople wash their clothes in the river but we're hardly likely to adopt the practice.

    (A health visitor, *Express & Echo*, Exeter, 19 June 1989)

The examples of primitive culture quoted in this book are not models of perfection for Westerners to adopt. But the study of other peoples can lead us to a greater understanding of human nature, and give us ideas for change.

If, for instance, many children in all parts of the world suffered from sleep difficulties, in the same way that they all have finger-nails, we might conclude that such problems were physiologically normal. But a brief look at other societies shows us that some are more harmonious and less aggressive than our own, and that their children do not suffer in the way ours do.

It is impossible to isolate the practice of family co-sleeping and demonstrate the effect it has on the emergent personality. Child-rearing, like cheap wine, does not travel well, as Sherri B. Shanes pointed out in chapter 4,

> My conclusion from this is that culture forms our most basic being in ways that we do not understand, and we can almost never separate ourselves from it . . . Many other elements play into the calmness of African children. One is a community consensus about the role and function of children in society . . . Also, Lobi adults are much less worried and nervous than Americans tend to be . . . I don't believe we can say that what is true in one culture will translate easily into our own, much as we might wish it.
>
> ('Do We Idolize the Tribe?',
> Sherri B. Shanes, *Mothering*, Summer 1989)

The whole point of doing things with children is that we enjoy the process. For maximum satisfaction, we would ideally learn to take pleasure from the same processes our children delight in. In many cultures, this arrangement works out just fine. The extended tribe we live in has no consensus on what parents and babies ought to be enjoying together. The fine-tuning is up to the individual.

However, it would be disingenuous to pretend that the way we handle our babies makes no difference at all. Every tribe raises children to fulfil its own expectations. For many years, anthropologists and travellers – like Ashley Montagu, Margaret Mead, Jean

Liedloff and Mary Ainsworth – have written about the obvious effects of close-contact nurture on the personality of children and adults.

Psychologists James Prescott (National Institute of Child Health and Development, Bethesda, Maryland) and Douglas Wallace (University of California Medical School) conducted a cross-cultural study of forty-nine non-literate cultures and found a 'high significant correlation' between early tactile experience and the origins of aggressive behaviour. High rates of holding, touching and carrying infants were associated with low adult aggression – and the reverse also held true.

Considering the habits of other cultures reminds us of the many connections between our infant experiences and our adult assumptions. And it stops us being so arrogant as to assume that ours are the only ways of being and behaving.

We can usefully take a practice such as co-sleeping and adapt it to our own way of life without compromising our own culture, or the history that got us here. In the words of Frances Moore Lappé, author of *Diet for a Small Planet*, we should be looking for 'lessons, not models'.[1] Lessons we can learn from other people, and not from model societies that we can copy for good or ill.

- Many philosophers extol the virtues and joys of a family
  sleeping together in one giant, bed-bound commune.
  Although this may be a terrifically enjoyable state of affairs for
  those who are deep sleepers or lucky enough not to have
  children who behave all night like soccer stars at a goal-mouth,
  the vast majority of parents I see wish their bed to be a
  private, peaceful place. They greatly resent those little intruders
  making an appearance in the wee hours of the morning.
  (Dr Christopher Green, *Toddler Taming*)

Dr Green is describing children who are normally not allowed in the big bed. In such a world, babies are often seen as intruders into the otherwise private and peaceful lives of their parents. But that does not

255

mean that bedsharing parents are philosophers who get their kicks out of being kicked in the shins by a two-year-old in pyjamas.

The toddler who began life sleeping with his parents need never play this cat-and-mouse game of imprisonment and escape from his nursery. Always welcome wherever his parents may be, he chooses instead to find his own space, first in the big bed, and later in his own room.

If, for whatever reason, he chooses to return to the parents' bed, he climbs in, already versed in night-time etiquette. Everyone else is sleeping, and he soon does, too. The child who rarely or never sleeps with his parents cannot be expected to behave in the same way. Perseverance is the only cure for his wriggling and squirming.

Parents who want to evict toddlers from their bed may wish to follow Dr Green's advice on that subject. He advocates trying this technique: 1. Put him straight back in his own bed; 2. Warn him; 3. Smack him and 'immobilize' various doors. You may, like an old-fashioned employer, wish to cut out the second stage, the doctor suggests. 'Most parents feel that this degree of civility is quite unwarranted at that time of night . . . in which case, it's a sharp smack on the bottom and back to bed.'

Dr Green admits that he spent many years smacking, immobilizing doors and dodging his own children's efforts to be with him at night. I'm not surprised.

- Apart from these rare situations [illness and Sunday mornings], I believe that children should be excluded from their parents' bed at all other times. Peace and privacy are important to people, and that includes parents.

(*Toddler Taming*)

Peace and privacy are, believe it or not, important to children, too. But one vital quality of privacy is that we take it when we choose, otherwise it's called loneliness.

In making ourselves always available to our children, we enable them to find their own independence, to move towards solitary activities when they are ready for them, and to amuse themselves for reasonable periods of time. If we are always pushing the children away, they will return, clinging, for many years to come. As new parents, it is possible to make our children a welcome part of our private world – otherwise, we should ask, why have them?

Often, it is only a question of attitude that determines whether a mother sees her baby's demands as a chore or as a delight. In the words of American doctor, Gregory White: 'If a lazy, self-indulgent, old man like me can get out in the middle of the night to help people he hardly knows, certainly a mother can do this for her own child.'[2]

- Cosleeping, the practice of parents and children sleeping together, was routine in our own culture until the 20th century . . . Concerns about potential ill effects are thoughtfully described by several prominent pediatricians and child psychotherapists and include the following: (1) cosleeping may interfere with a child's independence, (2) sleeping with parents may become a habit that is difficult to break or even an 'addiction', (3) children who sleep with parents may be more likely to witness sexual intercourse, a frightening experience for some, (4) the intimate body contact involved in cosleeping may be overstimulating to children, (5) cosleeping may reflect disturbances in the mother-child relationship or in the parents' relations with each other, and (6) children who sleep with parents may develop more sleep problems.

  (Lozoff, Wolf and Davis, *Pediatrics*, August 1984)

Many of these objections are made by scientists who worked on the premise that co-sleeping with children was undesirable. Their conclusions are coloured by this belief. To answer them point by point: (1) The more security you offer your baby, the more secure he will be. Co-sleeping can only enhance the child's eventual independence. (2) Normal, healthy children will not become addicted to the parents' bed unless this is the only good thing in their lives. Their natural inclination is to grow up and move away. (3) Children who sleep with their parents are far less likely to be frightened by sexual intercourse than children who sleep alone and stumble unexpectedly on an interlude of love-making in the night. (4) Intimate body contact enables the child to explore human touch in an uninhibited, non-sexual way, and to grow up feeling at ease with his own body. (5) Yes, some Westerners may take their children to bed as a shield for their own problems. This does not invalidate the benefits of doing so. (6) Children who sleep with their parents are likely to iron out any sleep problems they may otherwise have had – unless, of course, you count co-sleeping as a problem in itself.

- We know for a fact that people sleep better alone in bed. Studies have shown that the movements and arousals of one person during the night stimulate others in the same bed to have more frequent wakings and sleep-state changes, so they do not sleep as well.

  (Richard Ferber, *Solve Your Child's Sleep Problems*)

The assumption of many professionals is that the deeper and less interrupted the sleep, the better. But as we can observe from primitive cultures, disturbances need not ruin sleep. (Think of the Tauripan people who wake in the night, enjoy a joke and then snooze off again.[3]) The healthiest sleeper is the one who drifts lightly in and out of the state, not bothering when he is woken up, and able to close his eyes and sleep again at will.

Deep slumber is valued in our society, because we have lost the art of flexible sleeping. When we are woken in the night, we are unable to fall asleep again. We go to sleep with difficulty and we wake up unrefreshed.

Factors such as diet, exercise and fresh air can play a large part in relieving these symptoms. But we would all sleep more easily at night if we slept alongside others from birth. Then we would learn to wake and doze, to sleep and react at the same time. We would not be 'dead to the world' when we dropped off, nor would we resent the inevitable night-time intrusions that bother us all from time to time.

- I'm a very light sleeper. I couldn't take my baby into bed, because I would not get a whole night's rest.

(A mother)

Light sleepers and heavy sleepers are both likely to find life easier with the baby *in* the bed. The light sleeper is often disturbed in the night by the sounds of the baby snuffling – is he awake, or isn't he? Is that the baby crying, or the wind in the trees? With the baby next to her, the mother knows he is all right, can react instantly to his needs, and go back to sleep with minimal disturbance. By the end of a few weeks, the baby is fast alseep for much of the night anyway, and the mother finds herself quite used to his presence in bed. Breastfeeding mothers are programmed to sleep lightly, to meet their baby's demands, and breastfeeding itself sends them dozing off again.[4]

The heavy sleeper wakes up to find her tiny baby screaming in the night, because no one answered his initial whimpers five minutes earlier. With the baby sleeping by her side, the heavy sleeper will answer those cries more readily, before they become distressed.

- We're all different. Surely you don't think sleeping with the baby is going to suit every family in every situation?

(A health visitor)

If tackled with the right attitude, when the baby is new-born, I see no reason why co-sleeping shouldn't work for every family. After all, before there were separate beds and bedrooms, our ancestors simply had no choice, and would not have questioned the practice. But generations of separate sleeping have passed, and many of us have lost the art of light and easy sleep. Most of us rapidly become accustomed to someone else in our bed – otherwise we would have difficulty forming adult relationships.

If you simply don't want to try, then fair enough, but let's not discourage those who decide to manage without the cot.

- Sleeping with my baby surely isn't going to solve all my baby's problems just like that . . .

(A mother)

There are many negative factors that influence our babies' world, and we cannot control all of them – pollution, radiation and stress, poverty, diet and a sedentary lifestyle all take their toll. Under the threat of acid rain and nuclear fall-out, even the hunter-gatherer will live differently today from the way he did one hundred years ago.

But this should not stop us from giving our children the best possible start in life – and trying to improve things for the hassled mother at the same time. We can, for instance, encourage mother and baby to eat a wholefood diet. We can attempt to reduce stress, and take regular exercise. We can foster an environment where mothers may follow their own instincts.

One mother, Maggi, told me a story which illustrates how pressurized most women are when dealing with their children in a social situation. She was on holiday in France with her five-week-old baby, who was breastfeeding almost constantly. The friends she was staying with had read all the advice books, and every time the French mother fed her baby, dad was there watching the clock. They were trying to wean their four-month-old infant off the breast.

One day, the father went out and the two mothers spent the whole day together. Without saying anything, Maggi noticed that her friend took up her baby far more often to suckle, and did not wait until he cried before feeding him, as she had done before. Her manner became more relaxed, and the women were able to enjoy a day of uninterrupted mothering. The baby was far more contented.

The French mother's instincts were emerging, because no one was there to pressurize her, or to make her conform to the 'rules'.

I believe no mother would dream of putting her baby down to sleep on his own if authorities had not told her otherwise. Being left to sleep alone is not the only problem a new baby faces in the modern world, but it is one casualty of natural mothering that everybody assumes is normal. If mothers could see through this practice, they would be one more step along the way to restoring the power of parenting to their own hands.

- 'What worries me about this book is that it seems to be based on the belief that children can, and should, go through life without any suffering or conflict because it is so painful for the parents. I think the parents need to examine exactly why they fear their child's distress so much. A bit of suffering is an essential part of a child's development.'

  (Julia Vellacott, quoted by Angela Neustatter in
  New Woman, May 1989)

This criticism, from a psychotherapist, was one of the first press reactions when *Three in a Bed* was originally published. The suggestion that co-sleeping is a product of parents' neurosis is one which crops up from time to time.

Personally, I don't agree with the suggestion that children can go through life 'without any suffering'. Suffering at some level seems to be nearly inevitable. Whether or not it is essential, or somehow necessary, for children to suffer is the controversial point. I certainly don't think it is the role of the parent deliberately to create infant misery. My reaction to children's pain has always been to embrace it and – if it is in my power – alleviate it. That does not generally mean putting their needs so high above mine that I end up suffering myself.

I think most people find it upsetting to listen to an unattended baby scream. Sometimes it is possible to switch off from the sound so we do not need to respond. In the West, when we hear a baby crying in someone else's pushchair, we do not generally walk over and pick him up. Adults who belong to more open, tactile cultures might say I was neurotic not to do so. However, many people – even in our society – intervene when they hear their own baby, or a friend's baby, in distress. They feel it's the least they can do. If you find yourself psychoanalysed by someone who does not share your concept of neurosis, try turning the tables. Suggest that perhaps they examine exactly what it is they fear about people who do things differently.

- By taking the baby into bed, aren't you smothering it with affection? Won't the baby be spoiled by all this extra attention, and isn't this just an attempt to keep him a baby for longer?

  (A mother)

Babies come to us for all the love and intimacy they need. Once they've had enough, they rapidly move away. It's OK to shower a small baby with kisses all the time – tickling, cuddling, stroking and kissing are the kinds of tactile intimacy they expect. Spoiling comes with a specific range of behaviours when the child is awake, not curled up at night in your arms.

- Quite often, babies have become used to falling asleep only at the breast. They have thus no opportunity to be alone in their cot, half-awake, half-asleep, savouring the memory of a feed, and digesting the emotional experience along with the acutely physical nourishment. Emotional growth comes from digesting such an experience and, with this, the ability to start managing on one's own.

  (Dilys Daws, *Journal of Child Psychotherapy*, 1985)

- Sleeping alone is an important part of his learning to be able to separate from you without anxiety and to see himself as an independent individual. This process is important to his early psychological development.

  Ferber, *Solve Your Child's Sleep Problems*)

- It is important that the baby is put down awake, then he has the opportunity of learning to settle himself.

  (Dick and Pritchard, *Pampers First Years of Life*, 1988)

If a baby *needed* to be alone, he would not have been created such a helpless little creature. Talk of digestion and sweet dreams sounds delightful, but a baby knows nothing of this, when he is left to lie in his cot. Staring through the bars or up at a dancing mobile, he only knows that his mother is not with him. Some babies voice the wrongness of the situation by crying, others resign themselves rapidly to hours in solitary. It does not therefore follow that learning to cope alone is an essential part of child development.

Learning to separate is, of course, crucial to the forming human ego, but this needs to come from a position of strength. The child will move away when he is ready, unless he is ill or disabled. Even then, the impetus is there, it might just require a little longer.

When I hear this argument, I remember the poignant story of the grandmother under the tree, originally told by anthropologist Vidal Starr Clay in her book *The Effect of Culture*, and retold here by Ashley Montagu:

> Clay remarks that she observed a grandmother sitting under a tree next to her grandchild strapped in a plastic carrier. 'The grandmother,' reports Clay, 'told me with a degree of sadness that she wanted to pick up the baby, he wanted it, but his mother had told her he had to learn to be by himself.'
>
> (*Touching*)

There's a clash of cultures even from one generation to the next. Grandmothers all over the Western world are having to learn to be by themselves, too.

- It is a harsh life out there. All this mollycoddling won't prepare our children to face reality.

  (A father)

The stronger our base position, the better we cope with what life throws at us. By allowing the child to claim independence when he is ready for it, and to take responsibility for himself, he will not keep making U-turns to his parents to get him out of trouble. He will have a greater self-awareness and self-confidence. Strength comes from within, not from the situations into which you are forced.

- Another reaction to be taken into account is the jealousy of the siblings. It may be hard enough to take the arrival of a new baby without discovering him in the parents' bed and some tactful transferring early in the morning may be necessary to avoid discovery. Alternatively be prepared for an invasion by the other child or children and to eventually all sleeping together in a true 'family bed'.

(Jane Asher, *Silent Nights*)

Identified first by Freud, sibling rivalry is one of the great topics of the twentieth century. It is considered normal for an older child to develop feelings of jealousy about the arrival of a new baby. But as Jean Liedloff says, 'Freud had no undeprived people in his acquaintance':

If he had had the opportunity to know the Yequana, he would have found that the idea of competing and winning, as an end in itself, is quite unknown to them. It cannot therefore be considered an intrinsic part of the human personality. When a baby has had all he needs of experience in his mother's arms and parts with her of his own free will, it makes him able to welcome with no difficulty the advent of a new baby in the place he has voluntarily left.

(*The Continuum Concept*)

The suggestion that a baby should be transferred to a cot to avoid offending his older brother or sister is ludicrous. Of course the infant is going to need more physical contact than the older child. Should we not breastfeed second babies, in case we upset number one? Far healthier for the toddler to witness his parents giving cuddles and intimacy to other people than only to himself. Why not accept the bigger children into bed in the morning, and encourage them all to sleep in their own bed at night when they're old enough?

- My two-year-old is far too naughty to deal with in this way.
  He doesn't listen to a word I say, and if I took him into our
  bed, he would just fight and keep us all awake.

  (A father)

The 'naughty' toddler is an older version of the crying baby. He has
learnt that breaking the rules gets him attention and the kind of
involvement he requires from his mother. Tantrums and repeated
bad behaviour are distress signals. He is getting too much interference
from his care-givers, and not enough of what he really needs. The
child does not understand this intellectually, but he does know how
to protest.

If we expect our babies to misbehave, then they will. If we say,
'You'll get a smack if you climb up there,' then in all likelihood, the
adventuring child will test our thesis to the full. He is not being given
the chance to explore his world for himself. Instead, by disobeying,
he has the promise of perverse satisfaction from a confrontation with
his parents.

I am not suggesting we should all suddenly force our two-year-
olds to sleep with us. However, as a remedial measure, it could be just
the security the child needs. Welcoming a toddler into your bed
would be a big surprise (for both of you!). He is being treated like a
sociable being – this is his chance to act like one. He may fight at first,
but given a little patience and a wide berth, he should calm down in a
matter of weeks and you may see improvements in his daytime
behaviour.

- . . . it seems that problems encountered in sleep in child
  rearing would perhaps be best solved by bedsharing. However
  in the present climate of interest in incest in this country it
  seems ludicrous to mention it.

  (Kathryn Conder, *Midwife, HV and Community Nurse*, April 1988)

This objection was quoted earlier in chapter 8 (Not in Front of the
Children), and needs answering. Studies have shown that lack of

touch in infancy relates to an increase in violence among adults. Sexual frustrations also mount up in people who do not know the joy and release of innocent touching.

Touch your children. Give them all the cuddles they crave. Teach them not to be frightened or guilty, or hung-up about their bodies. Do not drive their needs underground. It is the touch–deprived child who is most likely to be the tormented adult, unable to distinguish between proper and improper levels of intimacy. The child who gets his fill of human contact throughout his growing years will not abuse his own children.

We urgently need to feed our ancient hunger for physical contact. Otherwise, our children will grow up to associate sensuality merely with sex, and child abuse will become even more widespread than it is today.

- For me, the most horrifying aspect was the fact that Deborah Jackson carried her baby around with her until eight or nine at night when the child would fall asleep on the sofa and stay there until the parents were ready to go to bed.

  This ties in with what the author says earlier in the book that children should be with their parents at all times. It does not, however, tie in with the fact that in order to be able to get any work done the same author sent her child to a childminder during the day. All in all I think Mrs Jackson tailors the facts in her book to fit her beliefs.

  (Anne Byrne, 'Oh baby! This is controversial', *Express & Echo*, Exeter, 19 June 1989)

To untangle each point:

1) Babies do not need to be strapped to their parents at all times. They just need some sort of fairly consistent human contact.

2) A child-minder is perfectly able to provide this sort of contact. The key is not to leave the child too young, or for too long. Anne Byrne has confused the handling of a new-born baby with the childcare of a six-month-old. (Frances was never left for longer than

she could go between breastfeeds, which was about an hour and a half, at first.)

3) Women in cultures throughout the world go to work. Some work with baby on their back. Some leave baby with grandmother, teenage aunt or father. Most return often to breastfeed, although wet-nursing by relatives and 'soul mothers' is quite common. All of these mothers sleep with their babies at night.

It all ties in perfectly.

I must add that it's not necessary to walk around until late with a baby who, having fallen asleep on the sofa, comes to bed when you do. I myself did not often do this. Sometimes I would put the baby to bed first. Sometimes I would go to bed first with my husband. Sometimes I would put children down to sleep with each other for company. The details are unimportant – we create our own patterns.

- There can be few mothers who have not at some time felt the urge to lash out at their children, despite the intense love they may feel for them at other times.

  (Brigid McConville, *Mad to be a Mother*)

The media offer many warnings about Baby Blues and maternal ambivalence. I fully expected to have mixed feelings about my baby, and to reach that 'breaking point' that many mothers had warned me about. But of all the emotions I felt for Frances, the urge to lash out was not one of them.

One study reported that sixty-eight per cent of children with sleep problems were likely to get into bed with their parents for part of the night.[5] Researchers commented that 'the mothers of children with sleep problems could best be characterized as ambivalent, i.e. positive toward their babies but expressing resentment or hurt as well'. They concluded that taking the baby into bed was valuable for the ambivalent mother:

> Sleeping with parents may occur in reaction to the child's sleep problem and/or to the mother's awareness of her partial

emotional withdrawal from the child. Such bed-sharing may be one avenue via which an ambivalent, stressed mother expresses both her positive feelings towards her child and her own needfulness.

(Lozoff, Wolf and Davis, *Pediatrics*, March 1985)

If you have someone frequently in your arms, it is very difficult to hit them, or even to feel like it. You might even find you like it.

Jerry Hall confessed last week that her 11-month-old son Gabriel shares her bed – much to the chagrin of Mick Jagger. Her admission comes only weeks after Anne Diamond said her habit of gathering her four sons around her in the night had not helped her doomed marriage to Mick Hollingsworth. Bruce Willis and Demi Moore say it's 'like a circus' in bed with their children, while both Paula Yates and Michelle Pfeiffer also make a habit of sleeping with their offspring. But they are not alone. Thousands of parents have been lured by a new fashionable diktat that says they should welcome a baby into the marital bed – at whatever cost to their relationship.

(Helen Renshaw, 'Baby makes one too many in bed'
Mail on Sunday, 15 November 1998)

Towards the end of 1998, British newspapers ran headlines on a number of famous couples who had admitted to sleeping alongside their babies and children. In the cases of supermodel Jerry Hall and television presenter Anne Diamond, this admission was swiftly followed by announcements of imminent divorce from the respective 'Mikes'. It was rather like the curse of *Hello* magazine, and perhaps the moral here is not to talk to the press about your personal arrangements. But I want to address the question that newspapers themselves were posing: is co-sleeping a recipe for marital disaster?

Mothers who breastfeed their babies for a long time and parents who co-sleep are inevitably altering the focus of their relationship. In ancient practice, this is what new parents were expected to do and society often arranged things so that they could take a break from playing husband-and-wife. Nursing a child for years rather than weeks is associated in many societies with polygamy. Men with more than one wife do not need to put pressure on new mothers to return too swiftly to an intensively sexual role.

Like breastfeeding, co-sleeping can cramp your sexual style, however imaginative you are and however understanding your partner. Some adults are more mature than others about putting babies' needs (temporarily) first. Some adults are stronger than others when it comes to reclaiming their own child-free time.

Occasionally I receive letters which indicate that while mother and child are thrilled to be co-sleeping, the other adult partner is being literally and figuratively left out – even sleeping in a separate room. Of course, if everyone is happy with such an arrangement, it is no one else's concern. However, any long-term resentment is unhealthy. As parents, we need to work out solutions which allow everyone's needs to be met in appropriate measures. We also need to be alert and adaptable to make changes as we go along.

The solution is usually one of compromise. If your think your partnership is being neglected, don't bury your concerns under the duvet. Talk. Not to the newspapers, but to each other – and make any changes you feel are humane and necessary. No family should break up over a pillow fight.

12 | A MODEST PROPOSAL

Separate sleeping is so ingrained in our culture that it is difficult even to talk about [the long-term effects] without being laughed at. To change such an apparently simple practice would in fact need very strong social support.

(Michel Odent, *Primal Health*)

I received my training as a Nursery Nurse more than 30 years ago and during that time I came into possession of a pamphlet entitled 'The Baby Who Does Not Conform to Rules'. I treasured it because there were many days when I felt that the author and myself were the only people who shared the belief that young children should be treated with respect, flexibility and love. This was especially so when I had the misfortune to work in a residential home where cleanliness, tidiness and the direction in which the cot wheels were facing was of paramount importance.

(Chloe Fisher, *Oxford Medical School Gazette*, 1982)

The management of mothering is entering a new phase at the start of a new millennium. Professionals are better equipped than ever to bring accuracy and efficiency to their work. Incubators and drips, monitors and scales combine with new operational techniques to save babies' lives and to measure their progress. There have been many genuine advances in understanding in the past twenty years.

For the parent at home, convenience baby foods and disposable nappies make looking after baby a more civilized occupation. But somehow, her job does not seem to be getting any easier. Rather than becoming more confident, the mother is losing control. From the moment she books in at the antenatal clinic, she becomes a part of the Western mothering machine. By the time she takes her new baby home to care for him, her first impressions of motherhood may be very bleak.

Seeing the same woman pushing a pram down the street two months later, she is completely overwhelmed by the 'correct' way to look after her child. She will be counting the feeds, checking off his weight against a chart, and dreading the next meal because his bite is so painful to her cracked nipples. She envies everyone she sees around her, because they probably had a good night's sleep in the last fortnight. She is wondering whether to get pregnant again at the end of the year, to get it over with – or is one enough?

It may be another eighteen months before the woman realizes that her baby really wants to sleep with her at night. Even then, she probably will not let him – or if she does, it will be a guilty encounter at midnight: 'Oh all right, get in with us.' She wants to be a good mother, but she does not know how.

Two stories – one from Thailand and one from London – illustrate the extent of the growing powerlessness of mothers in the West.

Mike Woolridge, a lactation physiologist, went to northern Thailand to study the effects of breastfeeding management on new mothers. The routine policy he observed at Suan Dok Hospital in Chiang Mai was based on American practices of fifteen years earlier. Babies were taken away from their mothers immediately after birth and not returned to them for between twenty-four and thirty-six hours.

The reasoning given for this policy was that the mothers were often in a poor state of health on arrival at the hospital. But when the mothers were finally allowed to hold their babies, no rules were enforced:

... demand feeding was universally practised, and once babies were returned to their mothers they remained with them, in their mothers' bed, at all times, both day and night.

(Woolridge et al., *Early Human Development*, 1985)

West meets East. Although the American doctors approached the arrival of the new-born with clinical caution, the Thai mothers knew what their infants really needed. As soon as they were allowed to sleep with their babies, they did so.

In July 1988, a consultant obstetrician, Pauline Bousquet, was suspended from the St Bartholomew's group of hospitals in London for refusing to use routine intervention in childbirth. Although Ms Bousquet was prepared to use drugs to induce labour, and to allow continuous foetal monitoring, she preferred to save these interventions for risky cases, rather than to prescribe them routinely. A letter to the district management describing Ms Bousquet's conduct said:

. . . there are no allegations of negligence, rather the reverse, of devoted care which is archaic and inept.

(*Sunday Times*, 10 July 1988)

Devoted care is out of date. Bring in 'the machine that goes "ping!" '[1] It is ironic that in these days of high technology, a new mother is fobbed off with a list of rules that date back to the Victorians, from whom we have received our current taboos about co-sleeping. Not one good argument for the cot has emerged in a hundred years.

Now is the time to revise our outlook. We know what babies need, and we know how to provide it. All the professionals have to do is stand back and let the mothers get on with it. It is crucial that doctors and nurses, while making the best use of the machinery at their disposal, do not put more faith in the hardware than in the woman before them − otherwise there will be a chain of authority with a computer read-out at the top, and babies at the bottom.

Every child is different, but his needs are universal. All he wants is the nurture of a mother − and given in sufficient quantity, at an early enough age, he will grow up with security, and with responsibility for himself. This is the only prescription a doctor need give to a new mother and baby.

This is my modest proposal: hospitals should give courage to a new mother, by allowing her to sleep with her baby from the first night. Maternity ward beds should be low and large, rather than tall and narrow. Fathers should be welcome at all times, and even allowed to stay in hospital when there is space. Premature babies should be carried by their mothers as soon as they can survive out of the incubator.

Parenting classes should be designed to promote maternal confidence. Advice should be given only when it is sought. Parents should be able to practise carrying and tying slings. Fashion magazines should write features on how cool it is to carry your baby on your hip.

At clinics, less emphasis should be placed on a baby's weight gain in the early weeks, and more on the baby's primary relationships. Parents should be encouraged to meet and talk without professionals on hand. Breastfeeding mothers should buy baggy jumpers and feed their babies anywhere.

If a baby has to go into hospital, a guardian should stay with him at all times. If this is not possible, he should be assigned a personal nurse to hold him and care for him. No institution should allow a baby to cry in a cot on his own.

If a parent wants to sleep with her baby at night, then no one should stop her. Taking your baby into bed may not solve all problems, but it may be the one thing that makes sense at the end of the day. At night, it is all a baby needs.

We are not the first society to separate mother and baby from the moment of birth. We are not the first to make our children unwelcome in our beds at night. We will not be the first to change our minds.

APPENDIX | BETWEEN YOU AND ME

> The bed was tilted against the wall by day, and let down at
> 6.30, when it filled nearly half the room; and all the boys
> except Michael slept on it, lying like sardines in a tin. There
> was a strict rule against turning round until one gave the
> signal, when all turned at once.
>
> (J.M. Barrie, *Peter and Wendy*, 1911)

One of the things that struck me when I interviewed parents, was
that few of them knew what others were doing. Most were surprised
to discover that thousands of families in Britain take their babies into
bed, whether on a permanent or an occasional basis. One study[1]
reported that only eighteen per cent of parents who slept with their
babies admitted the fact to their doctors. It's about time we had a
coming-out party.

So here are the experiences of some parents who have slept with
their babies, or who are sleeping with them right now. There are as
many variations of method as there are families, and a few famous
names are on the list.

I also include accounts of two women's different approaches to
breastfeeding, which have implications for maternal separation and
night-feeding. Let's begin with those:

JOY HENDERSON of Dumfries wrote this letter to the
Independent (2 August 1988) in response to an article by Isabella
Walker about the difficulties of breastfeeding. Many readers

275

wrote in with advice on preparing the nipples for the onslaught of the infant gums. Joy concentrated on the relationship between mother and baby, and how desperately they needed to be together, alone:

. . . breastfeeding is instinctive, and can be easy and pleasurable. What makes it difficult and even impossible for many mothers is the well-meant but destructive help and advice of medical professionals.

I have had considerable experience of breastfeeding, having fed each of my three children in this way until their first birthdays, and I learnt a lot during this time from my own experience and from watching other mothers. I feel that the most important factor in the difficulties mothers experience with breastfeeding is that they are emotionally very vulnerable in those vital few weeks after the birth of their baby. At this point, in sweep busy overworked nurses, midwives and doctors whose main purpose is to get one mother ticked off their list and on to the next.

I'm sure Isabella Walker has experienced as I did the student nurse, who has never had a baby herself, who grabs the baby's head in one hand, the mother's nipple in the other (this alone was an embarrassing and tension-producing invasion of privacy for me) and tries to bring the two together by brute force, in the manner of fixing a shower attachment to a tap. After two days of this humiliating and fruitless procedure six or seven times a day, it's small wonder that so many mothers give up . . .

Small wonder that at this already difficult time of hormonal upheaval and bewildering new experiences, women are coerced into a state of child-like dependence and lose all confidence in their own ability to cope.

All it needs then is for the paternalistic forces of the medical profession to pronounce that breastfeeding is difficult and complex and has to be learned, the exact angle between baby and breast must be achieved, mothers must record on paper the precise length of time spent by the baby on each 'side'. I wonder how our forebears managed without these pieces of paper and this carefully researched 'knowledge'.

What is really required for successful breastfeeding is peace, relaxation, a mother's confidence in her ability to satisfy her own child, and protection from advice and interference . . .

None of the traditional and more modern lore about angles, the correct way to hold the baby, how much of the nipple to get in his mouth, is helpful – it only serves to add to the feeling that this is a difficult thing to get right. With my first baby I religiously, for the first few weeks, pressed the breast away from the baby's nose as advised by my midwife and Penelope Leach, for fear the baby would suffocate. Finally, after a few nights of falling asleep with the baby suckling in bed beside me, and a little private experimentation, I discovered that this was unnecessary. The nature of breast tissue and the shape of the baby's nose ensure that there is always a little space for air; and even if this were not the case, it is well-known that a baby who cannot breathe will stop feeding to take a breath through his mouth. This little procedure is simply another device for complicating the mother's life and making her feel guilty and inadequate if she doesn't follow the rules.

ANGELA MORRISON, from Bristol, did her own experimenting at night, though this involved keeping the baby *out* of the bed. She followed the advice of Mabel Liddiard, whose counsel in the 1920s caused many British women to deny nightly feeds to their infants. Angela's article details the hours of crying a baby has to go through before he learns his needs will not be met. Harry was eventually educated to 'sleep through':

I have always been interested in childbirth, and somewhere along the years I acquired *The Mothercraft Manual*. When I became pregnant with Harry at 33, and with a good deal of experience with other people's babies, I turned to this book to see what Mabel Liddiard, the author, had to say about breastfeeding. The first edition of her book was published in 1923, in a climate where most working-class women bottle-fed so that they could return to work – often after only 10 days' laying-in. Her method was to instill regular feeding to enable these mothers to breastfeed without giving up their livelihood. The regime she encouraged was five four-hourly feeds a day, with an eight-hour gap during the night. In this way, the baby and the mother (and the father) have a good rest so that the baby's digestion can have a break and the mother's milk has a chance to build up again. This sounded eminently sensible to me, and I decided to try it.

I was given a good start by having a short, straightforward home delivery, a baby who was not eager to suckle, and the confidence (stubbornness!) to do my own thing. I had noticed that most families went through nights on end of baby crying when they tried to drop the night feed, so I thought: 'Why not have it now, with a tiny baby who does not know what he is missing, rather than a strong-willed one later on?' I settled on aiming for my long gap between midnight and 8 am, because this suited our usual late bedtime. As soon as my milk came in, I moved Harry into his own room and fed him at four-hourly intervals during the day. He has always been woken for the midnight feed and bedded down soon after 12.30. For the first seven weeks we would wake again around 5 am about four nights out of five. I went through a whole range of techniques to cope when he cried, but I never fed him before 7am. Mostly he could be rocked to sleep, and for the last couple of weeks before he started sleeping through he just needed turning to lie on his tummy, but there were a couple of nights when he cried for an hour in my arms, and a couple when I left him to cry himself to sleep.

If it sounds cruel, I can only say that it has been worth it. He is now six months old, and rarely wakes before 9am. He sucks his thumb for comfort, and beds down with ease. He is still fully breastfed, five feeds a day, three to four hours apart. We all appreciate our uninterrupted nights, and I have not had any problems with engorged breasts or lack of milk.

Zoologist and anthropologist DESMOND MORRIS looked beyond human example when deciding his own parenting methods in the 1960s. He observed the sleeping habits of chimpanzees and gorillas, and felt inspired to borrow their practice of keeping in touch with their offspring at night. The Morrises did not take their son, Jason, into the parental bed, but kept him in a cot by the side of them for an extended period. One or other parent would dangle an arm out of the bed during the night, for touch-comfort. It was Jason who finally made the decision to sleep in his own room, with no pleadings from his parents. This interview was conducted in 1988:

Gorillas and chimps are nomadic. They don't reoccupy the same beds – this has to do with hygiene. At the end of the day, they take a scoop of grass or straw and make a sort of nest to lie on, chimps in trees and gorillas on the ground. I noticed that the babies shared the mother's bed for the early part of their lives. At a certain point when they grow older, they will make their own bed a little way from the mother. It's the infant that makes the decision to do this. It gives the young a sense of security.

One of the things I noticed in human families, is that toddlers don't like going to bed in their own room. They object rather strongly to being isolated in this way. I started to ask basic questions about our practice of separating children at night. This was probably never done in a million years of early human nest building.

Babies during the very early stage do seem to benefit from being within reaching distance of the mother. Instead of having to cry its heart out in the next room, the baby can be comforted by a hand reaching out. It's the initial contact and intimacy that's important.

Jason made the decision to leave our room himself. I can't remember how long he slept with us. Much, much longer than the typical family arrangement.

He's 17 now, and he has never to my knowledge had any of the sleeping problems that so many children have. He is capable of sleeping everywhere – which I have witnessed, as he has travelled round the world twice with me. I have never seen him show any sense of what I would call nocturnal anxieties, or any irrational fears of the dark or place of sleep. He has no nightmares.

It's at a later stage that children are frightened of sleeping alone. I wonder to what extent this is caused by premature separation at bedtime. This might be one of the causes in later life of bad dreams, insomnia and fear of the dark.

It worries me that we always seem to know better than the child. It's like the ritual of slapping a baby to make it breathe – these things are enshrined in medical practice. If left, a baby will breathe by itself, thank you very much. What we are doing is rushing the child to the next stage, even from the moment of birth.

Child psychotherapist JANINE STERNBERG from London discovered bedsharing with her third child, Sarah. She fed all her babies in bed, but realized that the transfer to the cot afterwards was likely to wake them up. I talked to Janine when her new baby was only a few weeks old:

I slept with Sarah on her first night. Luckily she was born early after lunch, and I had a six-hour discharge from the hospital. We came home at six in the evening, and that was lovely, because Mike came in with the older children, and we all came home together. I got straight into bed with Sarah next to me.

I had this excuse, if you want, which was that the swinging crib which we'd had for the other children was broken by Daniel, who's five, while I was in hospital having Sarah. Although the cot got tied up with string, I said, 'Oh no, far too dangerous to put my baby in there.' It wasn't true – I didn't want to put her in there, and that was that!

In the night, she doesn't wake up very much. I don't want her to, this is the aim of the exercise. I can hear her snuffling and turning rather than crying. If she's clearly being restless, I plug her in and she can be back to sleep again in ten minutes. Quite often in the night she'll only take one breast. She doesn't seem to want both sides.

I could be wrong in physical terms, but it seems to me that she can't co-ordinate herself enough to get to the breast and help herself yet. But she can fall asleep, and if I'm in the right position I can go back to sleep that way too.

I wouldn't want to isolate the effects of sleeping with your baby from all other factors. After all, I suppose you could sleep with your baby at night, but neglect it during the day. Although I expect that's unlikely. It's a way of responding to your baby's emotional needs quickly.

If the baby gets enough of what he needs when he needs it, he won't look for it later on. If you don't supply those needs, he won't have the strength to go on exploring. It's from a firm base that individuality comes.

The child may grow up to like lots of cuddles. But nobody objects to that.

Childcare expert MIRIAM STOPPARD says in her *Baby Care Book* that she is in favour of bedsharing. However, like many other Western parents raised on strict ideas of bedtime etiquette, she would try many strategies before finally taking her children into bed. This meant that she and her husband Tom went through years of cot-side vigils trying to coax their babies to sleep.

I'm very sympathetic to parents with sleepless children having had two myself, one of whom was sick if he wasn't reached within a minute or two of starting to cry. I would like to give the parents of such children a hopeful message. Neither my husband nor I enjoyed an unbroken night's sleep for six years and on many days we were almost too tired to drag ourselves around; but we got through it and we've forgotten the dawn vigils . . .

We decided to do anything to ensure a full night's sleep, at least now and then. I had never believed that taking the baby into our bed could do him or us any harm . . .

We gave the child fifteen minutes to settle to any of our strategies, then we tried taking him into our bed – a sure fire success.

Perhaps the wittiest advocate for co-sleeping is American father ROBERT WRIGHT, author of *The Moral Animal: Evolutionary Psychology and Everyday Life*. This extract is from an article which first appeared in the Internet magazine *Slate* as 'Go Ahead – Sleep With Your Kids' (27 March 1997) and was later reproduced in *Time* magazine under the title 'Why Johnny Can't Sleep' (14 April 1997). Wright, who claims he 'never leaves Z-town' while his wife sleep-feeds his baby daughters, takes issue with the methods of sleep-training advocated by Dr Richard Ferber:

Many parents find his prescribed boot camp for babies agonizing, but they persist because they've been assured it's harmless . . . What sounds to the untrained ear like a baby wailing in desperate protest of abandonment is described by Ferber as a child 'learning the new associations'.

At this point I should own up to my bias: My wife and I are failed Ferberizers. When our first daughter proved capable of crying for 45 minutes without reloading, we gave up and let her sleep in our bed. When our second daughter showed up three years later, we didn't even bother to set up the crib.

She wasn't too vocal and seemed a better candidate for Ferberization, but we'd found we liked sleeping with a baby . . .

Lacking data, people like Ferber and [child-care guru T. Berry] Brazelton make creative assertions about what's going on inside the child's head. Ferber says if you let a toddler sleep between you and your spouse, 'in a sense separating the two of you, he may feel too powerful and become worried.' Well, he may, I guess. Or he may just feel cozy. Hard to say (though they certainly *look* cozy). Brazelton tells us that when a child wakes up at night and you refuse to retrieve her from the crib, 'she won't like it, but she'll understand.' Oh. According to Ferber, the trouble with letting a child who fears sleeping alone into your bed is that 'you are not really solving the problem. There must be a reason why he is so fearful.' Yes, there must. Here's one candidate. Maybe your child's brain was designed by natural selection over millions of years during which mothers slept with their babies. Maybe back then if babies found themselves completely alone at night it often meant something horrific had happened – the mother had been eaten by a beast, say. Maybe the young brain is designed to respond to this situation by screaming frantically so that any relatives within earshot will discover the child. Maybe, in short, the reason that kids left alone sound terrified is that kids left alone naturally get terrified. Just a theory.

Tears before bedtime were an everyday occurrence in the Manchester household of WENDY GOODWIN and family. Her story shows the struggle many parents have in 'training' their babies to sleep sociable hours. Wendy eventually became national co-ordinator of CRY-SIS, the support network for families with crying babies. This account of her own 'sleepless' children was given at the 1988 CRY-SIS conference, which took infant sleeping problems as its theme:

When Lucy was born 7½ years ago, things got off to a very bad start. She was a difficult breech delivery, screamed constantly from day one and slept only for half-hour snatches.

Things got gradually worse until, at six weeks, we were finally told that she had colic. More bad news – there was nothing much we could do about it, and that it would last until she was about three months old. Lucy cried for 18 out of any 24 hours for the next two months, and still only slept for very short periods.

My husband and myself took it in turns to stay up all night – it was the only way we could get any sleep. We both felt dreadful – guilty, upset, let-down, alone, unhappy and exhausted.

Lucy's colic subsided when she was four months old and from then we tried desperately to get into some sort of normal waking and sleeping routine. But Lucy did not know the difference between day and night. All life had revolved around her screaming for four long months and she still demanded a lot of attention. The only way she slept for any length of time was in bed next to us.

It took two long years finally to get her to sleep all night in her own bed . . . By the time Lucy was sleeping normally I was expecting baby number two. It had been a huge decision to have another baby – as I'm sure you'll understand. But I was determined that this time things would go according to plan.

Pregnancy and birth went extremely well and Stuart was a beautiful, healthy-looking baby. He did scream the labour ward down when 20 minutes old, but after that he was very quiet, and was the perfect new-born baby.

At two weeks, he developed evening colic. We spent four hours each night pacing the floor with him. Instead of getting gradually better, as Lucy had, he got slowly worse. I spent the next 12 months trying to find some cause of his disturbance, cutting out cows' milk, additives, colourings, eggs etc., with little result.

Stuart eventually peaked at 18 months when he whinged most of the day and cried most of the night. By this time I had tried every trick in the book. I had asked for advice at the doctor's and clinic, but was never treated seriously. I asked friends whose children slept like logs, but there was no clue why their kids slept and mine didn't.

One really bad night, I broke down and sobbed my heart out at the injustice of it all. I felt very sorry for myself – how could this happen to me twice? I was a useless mother; I shouldn't have bothered with another baby . . .

My husband ushered me into Stuart's bed and put Stuart into bed with him. He fell asleep immediately and I slept undisturbed for the rest of the night.

And so it continues. Stuart is now three and a half and still gets up each night. But at least now he only gets up once, gets into our bed and goes back to sleep. I get out and get into his – musical beds, I think it's called. I have tried from time to time to break the waking habit, but each time it has ended in tears and frustration. I have now decided that I didn't have children to fight constantly with them – and it seemed like a fight to me.

We are quite happy with the way things are now. At least everyone gets a good – if a little disturbed – night's sleep.

A prominent London journalist tells of the importance he attaches to having slept alongside his daughter when she was young. He has asked for his name to be withheld:

In the case of our first daughter, I think I was a helpful father. I was involved, and did things with the baby, but with our second daughter I played a much greater part. For one thing, I was present at the birth of our second girl, and that involved me right from the beginning.

There was just 18 months between the two girls, and my wife was very tired and rather poorly, and suffered from postnatal depression because of this. So I found myself taking over the care of the younger baby to some extent, winding her and looking after her when she cried. I was at work during the day, but I helped particularly at night, so my wife could sleep and wasn't disturbed.

I would sit over the cot and put my finger in the baby's mouth. She would fall asleep like that, but sure enough in an hour's time she would wake up again. I would be falling asleep over the cot! So I found the best way of coping with this was to take the baby into bed with me.

The baby was warmer, I could cuddle her, and often she could go through to the morning that way. From when she was really quite tiny, almost the time when she was born, I took her into bed. At the beginning I was worried about rolling over on top of her, but I found that if I put my arms round her to cuddle her, that didn't happen.

After a while, she used to call out to me in the middle of the night from her cot. It wasn't really a distressed cry, just a 'come on and get me, then,' and I would wake up and go to the cot. I didn't bother to fiddle around, I would just pick her up and put her straight in our bed.

You could say we had a system going. And then when she reached the age of one and could walk, I thought 'I'm going to train her to come to us. If she wants me, she can come and get me.' So I put the side of the cot down, and when she called me the next night, I called 'Darling, come along here!' She stopped crying, all went quiet, and pad, pad, pad along the corridor she came. It worked the very first time I tried it.

My wife and I had two separate duvets on our double bed. By now my daughter was not hungry in the night, so she would tend to come to me rather than her mother. And that pattern was established until she was round about ten or eleven.

I didn't mind her coming in to us at all. It didn't bother me. This was before we had heard so much about sex abuse, and it was all innocent cuddles. She naturally wanted to stop that when she reached puberty. My daughter is 16 now, and she is very relaxed about her body, and has a happy, steady relationship with a boy. I wish I had been that relaxed at her age.

Her sister never came into bed with us, except in the morning when we were all cuddling and shouting together. My relationship with the two girls is completely different. My wife and I were divorced, and neither she nor my elder daughter have spoken to me for two years. But I still have a very strong bond with my younger daughter, although she has been under a great deal of pressure to have nothing to do with me.

In fact, my relationship with my younger daughter couldn't be better, and it has survived this great challenge of the divorce and break-up of the family. I'm only sorry I didn't have the same relationship with the older one. Now I realise why I'm so much closer to my younger daughter. It would have been better to have treated them both in the same way.

WENDY ROSE-NEIL became Family Writer at *Woman's Realm* in 1988, and her first letter to mothers was about her own experience of bedsharing. Wendy is a founder member of The Parent Network, a national family support group.

Like most parents, I found bringing up two small children great fun and completely exhausting. I don't think I ever worked so hard in my life as I did when my daughters were under five. And, like about one third of all families, we had sleep problems with our first baby. Part of it was due to the fact that she had colic during the first two months and she spent much of her time screaming, while I felt more and more like a complete failure.

So peaceful nights were out of the question – she refused to sleep in her cot and we grew bleary-eyed walking her around the house in the small hours, trying to get her somehow –

anyhow – to fall asleep. Then one day, being incapable of sitting up with her any more, I took her into bed that night. She finished feeding and then blissfully, magically fell asleep snuggled up close to me, and we heard not a sound until the next morning.

After that we never looked back. Since then, I've been an advocate of bedsharing with babies and small children for sleeping problems, although some parents swear that taking a restless child into bed is a recipe for a disastrous night. Some parents worry they'll injure or suffocate their youngster in bed. In fact, unless you're drugged or drunk this is almost impossible – although of course, pillows should be kept away from tiny babies.

And before too long, most children do grow out of wanting to sleep in their parents' bed. Parents who want privacy find that taking their children to bed for feeding or for comfort, and then putting them back in their own bed, is a useful compromise.

So if your baby or toddler has been keeping you awake at night, you could do worse than to try this method. It might work wonders!

Actress and author JANE ASHER recommends co-sleeping in her book *Silent Nights*. But she concludes that long-term bedsharing may not be appropriate in our society, 'where one is expected to keep going for most of the day':

> . . . we expect a great deal of a new born baby when we banish him to a separate, silent room all on his own after he has spent nine months in the warmth and security of his mother's womb . . . It's a lovely feeling to have a warm snuggly baby next to you in bed to cuddle . . .
>
> There are of course some disadvantages to having the baby in bed with you. Theoretically he should space out his feeds naturally so that after a few months he is only waking once or

twice in the night, but I found with Alexander this didn't really happen. He slept in bed with us from birth, as I found it much more trouble to keep getting out of bed to feed him, and also of course it had the enormous advantage that instead of the sometimes impossible business of getting him back to sleep after a feed by rocking, singing, patting and so on, he would just drift off peacefully next to me, with no effort on my part at all. For the first few months it worked very well, and I got much more sleep than I had with Katie who had slept in a cradle.

Alexander was a large baby who needed to feed very often but as he got bigger he did indeed start to sleep longer between feeds. Then however he started gradually to return to the frequent feeds, and eventually couldn't sleep at all unless constantly at the breast. This I began to find very tiring and when I did decide to move him to his own bed it was a long and difficult process . . .

I have no doubt that having the baby next to you is the natural way and that frequent small feeds are as nature intended but in our society where one is expected to keep going for most of the day then obviously a certain amount of uninterrupted sleep at night is essential. As with so many aspects of baby care the success of sharing the bed depends on the temperaments of both mother, father and baby and must remain an individual decision.

DR DAVID HASLAM explores many ways of solving infant sleep problems in his book *Sleepless Children*, but states that he 'received more letters quoting bedsharing as a success story than any other solution'. This was his own experience:

When it came to bedtime the books were wrong too. Katy woke every single night until she was two years old, with only one glorious exception. When she wouldn't settle at bedtime and screamed, it became pointless to leave her there as the books suggested. A healthy child can scream for an incredibly long time . . .

On occasions when she woke in the night and we were both exhausted we would take her into our bed. She usually slept wonderfully, but her wriggling kept my wife awake and so was a less than perfect answer. In fact, the solitary occasion when she slept right through the night without waking was when we spent a night camping in Scotland when she was seven months old. It was bitterly cold, but she had a warm sleeping suit and did not move all night. It was so unusual that Barbara and I lay awake wondering what was wrong. Had she died? Was she still breathing? Whatever had happened?

Eventually she woke happy and bright at 8 o'clock. For a long time I assumed it was the clean Scottish air, or the novelty of camping. Could it have been the closeness to her parents that our tiny tent made inevitable?

MAGGI STRATFORD and her partner Serge, from Leeds, are unusual, in that they decided to sleep with their baby as a matter of principle. The inspiration for this came not from primates, but from accounts of primitive cultures, in particular the Yequana tribe of Venezuela. Maia Rosa had a difficult birth, but Maggi managed to keep her baby near her from the beginning:

Before the birth I was determined to sleep with my baby in hospital, but after 24 hours of labour I was exhausted and worried that this, together with the various drips I'd been given, would affect the natural alertness I knew I would otherwise have towards my baby should she wake. So I spent the first few hours of that night staring at her in her little hospital cot, holding her hand and unable to sleep with her at all.

As soon as she woke, however, in the middle of the night, I whisked her into bed with me and fed her – and couldn't put her back again! It just felt so right for us to be snuggled up together. The night staff didn't seem to notice, or assumed I was feeding her and so said nothing. As I'd arranged to leave hospital the next day I avoided what I thought might be the inevitable battle with the nursing staff.

For a few weeks our sleeping arrangements followed a pattern. When we took her to bed with us, Maia slept on my Serge's chest until she woke to be fed, then spent the rest of the night in the crook of my arm, where she could easily feed if and when she wanted to. Now at nine weeks, and having doubled her birthweight of 5lb 12oz, Maia is too heavy to sleep on us, so snuggles down either between us or on my side of the bed.

Though she does wake once or twice during the night to be fed, I wake up as soon as she does, and she has never woken up crying. Her need for food is met immediately.

I'd recommend it to anyone: a) you *won't* squash your baby; b) your baby won't have to wait to be fed, so won't cry and feeding is calm; c) you won't spend anxious moments listening out for your baby crying in another room, or rushing in every few minutes to check she's still breathing; d) most important of all – it's enjoyable, and it feels *right*.

NOTES

PREFACE TO THE FIRST EDITION

1 'One-star rating only for Dr Hugh Jolly, late Consultant Paediatrician at Charing Cross Hospital, who has now gone out of fashion, and whose Book of Child Care displays a robust common sense now decried by modern authorities. His one note of eccentricity is his passion for the family bed . . .' Jane Ellison, 'Mums brought to book', *The Guardian*, 27 October 1988.

CHAPTER 1

1 'In the actual clinical work I undertake myself I see families where there is a feeling of not being able to manage a particular state of a baby's or small child's development. The most pressing of these are often presented as sleeping problems.' Dilys Daws, *Journal of Child Psychotherapy*, 1985.

2 '. . . reduced sleep is not as harmful as is commonly believed . . . Unfortunately, however, a lifetime's upbringing that one needs eight hours' sleep a night is difficult to combat, especially since popular magazines, information supplied to the medical profession by pharmaceutical companies and many doctors actively promote this belief.' Jim Horne, *The Practitioner*, October 1985.

3 *ibid.*

4 Jim Horne, 'Quality Matters', *The Guardian*, 5 April 1988.

5 '. . . the clinical picture of the normative development of infant sleep behaviour is derived from studies of infants sleeping alone in sleep laboratories.' James McKenna, *Medical Anthropology*, 1986.

CHAPTER 2

1 e.g. 'Orphan heartbreak of girl swapped at birth', *Daily Mail*, 24 October 1995: 'The hospital mix-up happened when the babies, born within hours of each other, were returned to the wrong cots after being fed.'

2 'Ten Steps to Successful Breastfeeding' No. 7: 'Practise rooming-in – allow mothers and infants to remain together 24 hours a day.' This is one of the basic requirements for any hospital wishing to achieve a 'certificate of commitment' on the way to a Baby-Friendly Award.

3 *Successful Breastfeeding*, The Royal College of Midwives, 1988, p. 37.

4 Dr Benjamin Spock and Dr Michael B. Rothenberg, *Dr Spock's Baby and Child Care for the Nineties*, p. 259.

5 *Feel the Fear and Do It Anyway*, p. 4.

6 Quoted in *Woman's Realm*, 2 April 1988.

7 Bob Mullen, *Are Mothers Really Necessary?*

8 Ronald V. Snead and William M. Bruch, *Pediatrics*, 1983.

CHAPTER 3

1 *Letters to a Mother on the Management of Herself and Her Children in Health and Disease . . . with Remarks upon Chloroform* (new edn), Longman, London, 1848.

2 'Smiles Bull and Combe all agreed [that the mother's bosom was the baby's natural pillow] – the new baby had a low body temperature and could not generate much heat itself. After six or eight weeks, it might be moved to a cot or cradle. Chavasse originally left the baby on its "natural pillow" until it was weaned at nine months; but he changed his mind. The seventh edition of *Advice to Mothers* altered that nine to "a few", and a lengthy warning of the dangers of suffocating was added. "Careless, heavy-sleeping girls" were partly to blame – as were mothers who allowed the baby to suckle while they slept.' Christina Hardyment, *Dream Babies*.

3 'All we desire to prove is that a child *can* be brought up as well on a spoonfed dietary as the best example to be found of those reared on the breast; having more strength, indeed, from the more nutritious food on which it lives.' Mrs Isabella Beeton, *Household Management*, 1861.

4 Christina Hardyment, *Dream Babies*.

5 See chapter 4.

6 Rachel Ferster, 'The Trouble with Calpol', *Natural Parent*, January 1998.

7 *Toddler Taming*

8 Jean Robinson, 'Care of premature babies . . . learning from the kangaroo', *AIMS Journal*, vol 6 no 4, Winter 1994: 'The authors conclude "the benefit (of kangaroo mothering) does not seem to be limited to . . . heat, love and breastfeeding. They suggest there is better bonding which can affect infant health and growth even beyond the time when the baby is attached to its mother . . . It is also cheaper.'

9 *Teach Your Baby to Sleep Through the Night*, p. 53.

10 Wendy Wallace, '*A cry for help in the night*', *Daily Telegraph*, 30 November 1991.

11 'Early Childhood Co-Sleeping: Parent-Child and Parent-Infant Nighttime Interactions', Hayes, Roberts, Stowe, *Infant Mental Health Journal*, vol. 17(4), 1996, pp. 348–57.

12 '. . . in the National Childbirth Trust's experience, there's no better nappy for helping your baby's skin to stay dry.' Pampers nappies advertisement, 1993.

CHAPTER 4

1 'Dr Adamson-Macedo, from Wolverhampton University, said that why stroking from head to foot for about 20 minutes a day should be beneficial was not known. Previous work had shown that stroked babies had stronger sucking action, better hand and eye co-ordination, and vocabulary at 15 months.' 'Stroking "helps premature babies develop intelligence" ', *Independent*, 26 March 1994.

2 Ref. 'Anxiety States, A Preliminary Report on the Value of Connective Tissue Massage', *Psychosomatic Research*, vol. 27 no. 2.

3 'Kathy Sleath, neonatal sister, and Andrew Whitelaw, paediatrician at the Hammersmith Hospital, started their work on skin-to-skin contact after they travelled with UNICEF to Bogotá in Colombia, where a group of doctors were pioneering this technique . . . what struck Andrew Whitelaw and Kathy Sleath was that the mothers in Bogotá looked so happy. "There was such a contrast between their happy faces and the worried faces of the mothers in the premature baby ward back in London . . . Women feel so totally different after they have tried skin-to-skin contact . . . Some burst into tears; some say they feel their child has just been born again. One father who tried it said 'I feel pregnant now.' " ' 'Bosom buddies: how tiny babies thrive on contact', *Independent*, 27 December 1988.

4 'Scores of worried families, he says, are plagued every day by the nightmare of persistently crying and screaming babies. But the good news is that they can all be totally cured in just a matter of a few days by applying five simple rules.' 'Danger of too much cuddling', *Manchester Evening News*, 21 November 1988.

5 Kattwinkel, 1977, cited by James McKenna, *Medical Anthropology*, 1986.

6 McGinty, 1984, quoted by James McKenna.

7 'What is certain is the REM stage is essential. If for some reason – say, the use of sleeping tablets – the amount of REM sleep is reduced, when the tablets are stopped there will be a compensatory increase of REM sleep for a while. Experimental work which has deprived people – volunteers, naturally – of certain phases of sleep shows that if the sufferer is deprived of stage 4 sleep only, he will tend to be lethargic and run down the next day, but if the REM sleep is lost then more complex skills such as learning and memory will be interfered with.' Dr David Haslam, *Sleepless Children*.

8 'That both prenatal and postnatal vestibular stimuli may help develop the infant's motor skills has been documented. Masi (1979) found that the vestibular stimulation of preterm infants improved their sensorimotor functioning relative to those of unstimulated controls.' James McKenna, *Medical Anthropology*, 1986.

9 '. . . it is well known that ventilation depends on environmental (ambient) and body temperature (Lahiri and Delaney 1975); in fact, temperature is also one of the most important external modulators of sleep, especially REM sleep (McGinty 1984).' James McKenna.

10 Foundation for the Study of Infant Deaths newsletter 30, projects 53 and 66, August 1986.

11 'Studies conducted in the labs of Hofer, Reite, and Levine . . . most especially, have shown that in order to understand the form and consequences of separation

(primarily mother from infant) for the infant, we must know how the infant's body changes physiologically after separation and, thus, how through contact the mother physiologically regulates her infant's temperature, metabolic rate, hormone levels, antibody titer, sleep cycle, heart rate, and respiration so as to promote her infant's health and survival.' James McKenna.

12 T.F. Anders, *Pediatrics*, vol. 63, pp. 860–64, 1979.

13 Ref. Jim Horne, *New Scientist*, 12 December 1985.

14 Dr David Haslam, *Sleepless Children*, p. 36.

15 Michel Odent, *Primal Health*, p. 148.

CHAPTER 5

1 According to the 1996 records of the Office for National Statistics, SIDS was registered as the main cause of death of under-ones in 337 cases in England and Wales. In 424 cases, SIDS was mentioned in the registration of death as a possible cause.

2 'Rise in Irish cot deaths has British specialists worried'. *The Guardian*, 15 April 1998.

3 Gantley, Davies, Murcoff, 'Sudden infant death syndrome – links with infant care practices', British Medical Journal, 2 January 1993.

4 C. J. Bacon, 'Infant mortality in ethnic minorities in Yorkshire, UK,' *Early Human Development*, vol. 38, 1994, pp. 159–60.

5 J. K. Grether et al. 'Sudden infant death syndrome among Asians in California'. *Journal of Pediatrics*, vol. 116; 4, 1990, pp. 525–8.

6 The most recent immigrants to the UK (those resident for less than 5 years) were very unlikely to place their infants prone, the majority (47.2%) placing them supine. However, with the increasing duration of residence in the UK, this trend appears to have been reversed, with the percentage of mothers placing their infants prone increasing to 20% amongst those resident for greater than 15 years or those born in the UK. Sadaf Farooqi, 'Ethnic differences in infant care practices and in the incidence of sudden infant death syndrome in Birmingham', *Early Human Development*, vol. 38, 1994, pp. 209–13.

7 'A few SIDS deaths are also appearing among Pacific Islanders; the numbers are small, but Pacific Island health workers suggest that SIDS deaths are new to this population.' M. Gantley, 'Ethnicity and sudden infant death syndrome: anthropological perspectives', *Early Human Development*, vol. 38, 1994, pp. 203–8.

8 Gantley, Davies, Murcott, 'Sudden infant death syndrome – links with infant care practices', *British Medical Journal*, 2 January 1993.

9 Gantley, 1994, see note 7.

10 'Most interesting is that the human infant's vestibular system [touch-response] is functioning at its 'highest level of reactivity' after the first few months of life [Ornitz 1983:527], the very time period when infants are at greatest risk of dying from SIDS. In other words, at the time their respiratory [breathing] control system is the most vulnerable, infants may be most sensitive to respiratory augmentation [help with breathing] through external vestibular and auditory

stimuli [touching and noise] – cues readily available in the infant's expected microenvironment [near him] if parents and infants sleep together throughout the night.' James McKenna, *Medical Anthropology*, 1986.

11 *American Journal of Physical Anthropology* 1990 and *Sleep* journal, 1996.

12 *Bedsharing with Babies: The Facts* 1998.

13 *The English Midwife*, 1682, quoted by G. Norvenius, 'Is SIDS a new phenomenon?' in *Sudden Infant Death Syndrome. New Trends in the Nineties*, 1995.

14 'Mr J.P. Nicholl and Miss A. O'Cathain (Sheffield, Project 80) have completed a further analysis of 304 SIDS infants from the Multicentre Study of Post Neonatal Mortality . . . They also looked at evidence for some recent claims about factors associated with SIDS. They found no evidence for 'overlaying' as the cause of death in the very small number of babies who had died in their parents' beds.' FSID newsletter 34, August 1988.

15 Children and Young Persons Act 1933, part one, section 1: (2)b Prevention of Cruelty and Exposure to Moral and Physical Danger.

16 Farooqui, Perry, Beevers, 'Ethnic differences in sleeping position and in risk of cot death', *The Lancet*, 1991, vol. 338. No cot deaths reported in two years at the only hospital in Zimbabwe town, pop. 300,000

17 Analysis of CESDI results by Prof. Peter Fleming et al., University of Bristol, 1998.

CHAPTER 6

1 'Present Day Practice in Infant Feeding', 3rd report, HMSO, February 1988.

2 Chloe Fisher, *Oxford Medical School Gazette*, 1982.

3 Jane Ellen Panton, *The Way They Should Go*, London, 1896.

4 *Mother*, September 1988.

5 DTW (direct test weighing) involves putting the baby on scales after every feed. ITW, the indirect method, is a complex calculation involving measurements of urine and evaporated water-loss, but it allows mother and baby to sleep uninterrupted through the night. DTW is believed to cause a reduction in nocturnal milk intake. ITW, being non-intrusive, does not. (Ref: Stella M. Imong et al., *Journal of Pediatric Gastroenterology and Nutrition*, 1988.)

6 '. . . over 24h post-delivery, a mother . . . might be expected to give up to 8 breastfeeds, which, based on average values, may amount to a total of 3h of suckling.' M.W. Woolridge et al., *Early Human Development*, 1985.

7 *Concise Oxford Dictionary*.

8 'Breast Milk Discovery!' *Practical Parenting*, July 1990.

9 C. Lewinski, 'Nurses' knowledge of breastfeeding in a clinical setting', *Human Lactation* 8 (3); 1992, pp. 143–8. 'The study has found that this lack of knowledge, taken together with confusing advice and rigid hospital routines, acts as a barrier to successful breastfeeding.' 'Nurses Can Undermine Breastfeeding', *AIMS Journal*, vol. 5 no. 4.

10 Alisa Washington, 'How to Wreck Breastfeeding', *AIMS Journal*, Spring 1995, vol. 7 no. 2.

11 Edmund Owen, *Baby*, 1888. See page 96.

12 Comparisons of hospital management in Sweden (where mothers were only allowed contact with their babies at feeding times) and Thailand (where mothers fed their babies freely through the night), showed that mothers' milk flowed regardless of differences in policy. (Ref: Woolridge et al., *Early Human Development*.)

13 Studies from Australia (1995) and England (1988) found that when an infant does not spontaneously finish milking one breast, he might not receive the fat-rich hind milk. When professionals insist on both breasts at each meal, the baby receives only high lactose, low-fat milk, resulting in a high-volume, low-calorie feed. 'One breast at a time', *Independent*, 27 September 1995 and *LLL GB New* no. 50, Jan/Feb 1989.

14 Dr Michel Odent, 'Newborn Weight Loss', *Mothering*, Winter 1989.

15 La Leche League International have published their *Womanly Art of Breastfeeding* in many languages. The British edition is called simply *The Art of Breastfeeding* (see Bibliography).

16 e.g. Valerie Fildes, *Wet Nursing: A History from Antiquity to the Present*, 1998.

17 Norman Tindale, *Hunters and Gatherers Today.*, ed. M. G. Bicchieri, Waveland Press, 1988.

18 P.W. Howie et al., *British Medical Journal*, 1981.

19 Ref: Máire Messinger Davies, *The Breastfeeding Book*, page 13.

20 'Here in Oslo, I have seen many mothers breastfeeding their babies in cafés, on seats in shopping centres, at the station waiting for a tram, on the grass in the local park – in fact everywhere. No-one bats an eyelid and mothers do not get embarrassed.' Elizabeth Brendenfur, 'Brazen Breastfeeding', *New Generation*, June 1994.

21 'Factors adversely associated with breastfeeding in New Zealand', Ford, Mitchell et al., *J Paediatr. Child Health* 1994, vol. 30, pp. 483–9.

22 'Influences on breastfeeding in south-east England,' Clements, Mitchell et al., *Acta Paediatr.*, vol. 86, 1997, pp. 51–6.

CHAPTER 7

1 Barry and Paxson, 1971, quoted by James McKenna in *Medical Anthropology*, 1986.

2 James Prescott, *Bulletin of the Atomic Scientists*, November 1975.

3 Quoted in M. Dorothy George, *London Life in the Eighteenth Century*.

4 Quoted in Sarah Helm, 'When children were chattels', *Independent*, 5 July 1988.

5 'So what is child abuse?', Rosie Waterhouse, *Independent on Sunday*, 23 July 1998.

6 Parents from the West Country were most likely to co-sleep at some time (fifty-two per cent) and parents in the Anglia region least likely (fifty-seven per cent said they never had). The poll of 999 people was taken in spring 1998.

7 P. Blair, 'Assessing the change of risk factors associated with Sudden Infant Death Syndrome', PhD thesis, University of Bristol, 1998.

8 Analysis by Fleming et al., University of Bristol, 1998.

9 Lozoff, Wolf and Davis, *Pediatrics*, August 1984.
10 C.C. Hanks and E.G. Rebelsky, *Psychiatry*, 1977.
11 'The most suggestive feature of the relationship of mother and son is their extreme physical intimacy. Elvis slept in the same bed with Gladys until he was at the threshold of puberty.' Albert Goldman, *Elvis*.
12 Cable and Rothenberger, 'Breast-Feeding Behavioral Patterns Among La Leche League Mothers: A Descriptive Survey', *Pediatrics*, vol. 73 no. 6, June 1984.

CHAPTER 8

1 'Child sex abuse register shows twelvefold increase', Aileen Ballantyne, *The Guardian*, 5 July 1989.
2 'Experts attacked the findings because the charity's survey rated indecent exposure alongside more serious offences such as rape and indecent assault. Health minister John Bowis accused the NSPCC of 'headline-grabbing sensationalism'. David Norris, *Daily Mail*, 15 June 1995.
3 'Child abuse has an ancient history', *Independent*, 2 May 1994.
4 '. . . a staggering 60 per cent either make love for their partner's sake or because they can't tell him they don't want to.' *Mother*, October 1987.
5 The Maori, Mbuti pygmies and many other peoples expect the husband to refrain from sexual advances towards his wife for some time after the birth of a baby. Some cultures allow the man to have an affair or a second wife, where the period of abstinence is more than a few months.
6 The Andamanese, islanders from the Bay of Bengal, are typical of most non-industrial people living in primitive conditions. They 'perform the sexual act with little privacy, owing to the flimsy construction of their huts around the dance floor and to the dangers, real and imagined, of the dense jungle'. Carleton S. Coon, *The Hunting Peoples*.
7 'John used to bath with his daughters when they were younger, but had already stopped before the child abuse suspicions first surfaced. The social worker made it plain she disapproved of such "inappropriate behaviour" but now, he says, he is afraid even to show his daughters affection. At four Amy is still clingy with her mother and likes to get into her parents' bed – on her mother's side they insist. Would this be frowned on too?' Rosie Waterhouse, 'So what is child abuse?', *Independent on Sunday*, 23 July 1995.
8 Jean Liedloff, *The Continuum Concept*.

CHAPTER 9

1 In fact, iron is best absorbed from breast milk: 'Only six per cent (0.3 mg/l) of the iron in a milk formula with 6 mg/l will be absorbed. Double the iron to 12 mg/l and only four per cent (0.4 mg/l) is absorbed. It is a case of diminishing returns. In contrast, breastmilk has a 70 per cent absorption rate, so even at its lowest levels . . . the baby will get 0.4 mg/l. At higher levels the baby will get 1.1 mg/l, double the amount of iron absorbed from most follow-

on milks.' 'Any old iron', Gabrielle Palmer, *Health Visitor*, vol. 66 no. 7, July 1993.

2 This letter was also extracted in 'Having permission to wean', *Mothers Know Best*, vol. 2 no. 3, August 1996.

4 Reported by Gillian Mercer, 'Shyness is a family problem', *Independent*, 19 August 1988.

5 *Independent*, 19 August 1988.

6 Somervaille and Brightling, 'Co-sleeping within urban families in North-West London', *Maternal and Child Health*, 1993, vol. 6, pp. 102–7.

7 'Making Links with Children's Education', a pamphlet for the 2nd International Conference on the F.M. Alexander Technique, Brighton, 1988.

8 'Winnicott . . . says about the good enough mother that the infant, as he looks into her face, sees there himself – or one might say, finds there himself – because the good enough mother, because of her deep empathy with her infant, reflects in her face *his* feelings . . . The not good enough mother fails to reflect the infant's feeling in her face because she is too preoccupied with her own concerns, such as her worries over whether she is doing right by her child, her anxiety that she might fail him.' Bruno Bettelheim, *A Good Enough Parent*.

CHAPTER 10

1 'On sleeping with your baby', *Independent Magazine*, 15 July 1989.

2 Breastfeeding research by Mike Woolridge and a team from the Department of Child Health, University of Bristol. Report in *Early Human Development*, 1985.

3 Jean Liedloff, *The Continuum Concept*.

4 'Norms for sleep/waking patterns in infancy were developed in the 1950s and 1960s, decades that marked the nadir of breast-feeding in the United States . . . the norms do not apply to infants who continue to be nursed for many months.' Elias, Nicolson, Bora and Johnston, *Pediatrics*, March 1986.

A child of two, nursing and sleeping with his mother, typically sleeps for 4.8 hours at a stretch, compared with 6.9 hours for the breastfed child who sleeps alone. The child in a cot who does not nurse at night sleeps longer – an average of 9.5 hours in one go.

In other words, a child can sometimes be trained to sleep through the night alone, if he does not find the constant comfort he needs and expects. But the mother who is breastfeeding her baby can expect him to feed every two to four hours during the night (just as he does in the day).

5 The Wilkinet Baby Carrier is available from 'Wilkinet', P.O. Box 20, Cardigan SA43 1JB, Wales.

6 'J.W.B. Douglas, in a review of the problem in 1967 [*BMJ* II, pp. 233–5] found that there was a correlation between bedwetting at four-and-a-half years and the number of stressful events which occurred when the child was two or three, such as illness, operation, and separations from the family.' Dr David Haslam, *Sleepless Children*.

7 'Many parents confuse night terrors with nightmares, but they are very different.

A child with a night terror will be found screaming, sitting up, wide-eyed with dilated pupils, and very frightened and agitated. He doesn't recognise his parents during the attack and is disorientated . . . These upsetting episodes last an average of two minutes . . . Thankfully, the entire episode will not be recalled.' *ibid.*

8 'Bedding Twins/Multiples Together', Kathleen VandenBerg and Linda Lutes, *Neonatal Network*, vol. 15 No. 7, October 1996.

9 'The discovery that external rhythmic breathing cues, in this case movement, influence infants' breathing patterns implies that there is continuity in the ways that mothers' biorhythms physiologically regulate their offspring both prenatally and postnatally . . .' James McKenna, *Medical Anthropology*, 1986.

10 'Not fully in front of the children', *Mail on Sunday*, 4 June 1989.

11 'This programme has been used locally with remarkably consistent success . . . The programme is time-consuming, energetic and tiring, but well worthwhile.'

CHAPTER 11

1 Frances Moore Lappé in interview with Derek Cooper on BBC Radio Four, August 1988.

2 Quoted in La Leche League, *The Art of Breastfeeding*.

3 See chapter 2.

4 Hormones regulate our sleep patterns: pregnant and breastfeeding mothers do not enter the fourth, or deepest, stage of sleep. (Michel Odent, *Primal Health*, p. 148.)

5 Lozoff, Wolf and Davis, *Pediatrics*, August 1984.

CHAPTER 12

1 'The machine that goes "ping!" ' featured in Monty Python's film *The Meaning of Life* (UK, Terry Jones, 1988).

APPENDIX

1 Hanks and Rebelsky, *Psychiatry*, 1977.

BIBLIOGRAPHY

Mary D.S. Ainsworth, *Infancy in Uganda*. John Hopkins Press, 1967.

Barbara Aria (The Body Shop), *Mamatoto – A Celebration of Birth*. Virago Press, 1991.

Jane Asher, *Silent Nights: For You and Your Baby*. Pelham, 1984.

Norman Autton, *Pain: An Exploration*. Darton, Longman and Todd, 1986.

Bruno Bettelheim, *A Good Enough Parent: A Book on Childrearing*. Thames and Hudson, 1987.

M.G. Bicchieri (editor), *Hunters and Gatherers Today: A Socio-economic Study of Eleven Such Cultures in the Twentieth Century*. Holt, Rinehart and Winston, 1972.

Steve Biddulph, *The Secret of Happy Children*, Bay Books, 1998.

John Bowlby, *Childcare and the Growth of Love*. Pelican, 1953.

Prof. Herbert Brant and Prof. Kenneth S. Holt (consultants), *The Complete Mothercare Manual: An Illustrated Guide to Pregnancy, Birth and Childcare*. Conran Octopus, 1986.

Carleton S. Coon, *The Hunting Peoples*. Cape, 1972.

Dr Richard Ferber, *Solve Your Child's Sleep Problems: The Complete Practical Guide for Parents*. (1985) Dorling Kindersley, 1986.

Valerie Fildes, *Wet Nursing: A History from Antiquity to the Present*. Blackwell, 1988.

M. Dorothy George, *London Life in the Eighteenth Century*. (1925) Penguin, 1965.

Albert Goldman, *Elvis*. (1981) Penguin, 1982.

Dr Christopher Green, *Toddler Taming: A Parent's Guide to the First Four Years*. Century, 1984.

Christina Hardyment, *Dream Babies*. (1983) Oxford University Press, 1984.

Dr David Haslam, *Sleepless Children: A Handbook for Parents*. (1984) Futura, 1985.

Angela Henderson, *The Good Sleep Guide for You and Your Baby*. ABC Health Guides, Corsham, 1997.

Rebecca Huntley, *The Sleep Book for Tired Parents*. (Parenting Press, 1991); Souvenir Press, 1992.

Sally Inch, *Birthrights: A Parent's Guide to Modern Childbirth*. (1982) Hutchinson, 1985.

Susan Jeffers, *Feel the Fear and Do It Anyway*. (Century Hutchinson, 1987); Arrow Books, 1991.

Hugh Jolly, *Book of Child Care: The Complete Guide for Today's Parents*. Unwin, 1985.

Brigitte Jordan, *Birth in Four Cultures*. Wateland Press, 1993.

Sheila Kitzinger, *Pregnancy and Childbirth*. Dorling Kindersley, 1980.

Penelope Leach, *Babyhood*. (1974) Penguin, 1980.

Frédérick Leboyer, *Birth Without Violence*. (1974) Fontana, 1987.

La Leche League International, *The Art of Breastfeeding: The Complete Guide for the Nursing Mother*. (1958) revised edn Angus and Robertson, 1988.

Mary R. Lefkowitz and Maureen B. Fant, *Women's Life in Greece and Rome*. Duckworth, 1982.

Jean Liedloff, *The Continuum Concept*. (1975) Penguin, 1986.

Aidan Macfarlane, *The Psychology of Childbirth*. Fontana, 1977.

Leon Maidow, *Anger*. Unwin, 1972.

Brigid McConville, *Mad to be a Mother: Is There Life after Birth for Women Today?* Century Hutchinson, 1987.

Andrina E. McCormack, *Coping with Your Handicapped Child*. Chambers, 1985.

Máire Messinger Dàvies, *The Breastfeeding Book*. (1982) Century Hutchinson, 1986.

Daphne Metland, *Getting Ready for Baby*. Foulsham, 1987.

Desmond Morris, *Babywatching*. Ebury Press, 1995.

Montagu, Ashley, *Touching – The Human Significance of the Skin*. (1971) Harper & Row, 1986.

Bob Mullen, *Are Mothers Really Necessary?* Boxtree, 1987.

Michel Odent, *Entering the World: The Way to Gentle, Loving Birth*. (1976) Penguin, 1985; *Primal Health: A Blueprint for Our Survival*. Century Hutchinson, 1986.

Donald J. Olsen, *The Growth of Victorian London*. (1976) Penguin, 1976.

Gabrielle Palmer, *The Politics of Breastfeeding*. Pandora, 1988.

Maud Pember Reeves, *Round About a Pound a Week*. (1913) Virago, 1979.

Libby Purves, *How NOT to be a Perfect Mother*. Fontana, 1986.

T.O. Rognum (editor) *Sudden Infant Death Syndrome. New Trends in the Nineties*. Scandinavian University Press, 1995.

Royal College of Midwives, *Successful Breastfeeding: A Practical Guide for Midwives (and others supporting breastfeeding mothers)*. RCM, 1988.

Edith Rudinger (editor), *The Newborn Baby*. (1972) Consumers' Association, revised edn 1979.

Peter Saunders, *Birthwise: Having a Baby in the 80s*. Sidgwick and Jackson, 1985.

Dolly Scannell, *Mother Knew Best/An East End Childhood*. (1974) Pan, 1975.

Charles E. Schaefer and Michael R. Petronko, *Teach Your Baby to Sleep Through the Night*. Thorsons, 1989.

Rudolf Schaffer, *Mothering*. Fontana, 1977.

André Singer with Leslie Woodhead, *Disappearing World*. Boxtree, 1988.

Joanna Smith, *Edwardian Children*. Hutchinson, 1983.

Aletha Jauch Solter, *The Aware Baby*. Shining Star Press, 1984, 1990.

Benjamin Spock and Michael B. Rothenberg, *Dr Spock's Baby and Child Care*. (1945) W.H. Allen, 1985.

Margery Spring Rice, *Working-Class Wives*. (1939) Virago, 1981.

O. Spurgeon English and Gerald H. Pearson, *Emotional Problems of Living: Avoiding the Neurotic Pattern*. Unwin, 1963.

Drs Penny and Andrew Stanway, *Breast is Best*. Pan, 1978; *Choices in Childbirth*. Pan, 1984.

L. Joseph Stone and Joseph Church, *Childhood and Adolescence: A Psychology of the Growing Person*. Random House, 1957.

Tine Thevenin, *The Family Bed: An Age-Old Concept in Child-Rearing*. Avery, 1987.

Peter Tinniswood, *A Touch of Daniel*. Arrow, 1983.

Jane Vosper, *Good Housekeeping's Baby Book*. (1944) National Magazine Co., 1969.

Franz Wagner, *Reflex Zone Massage* (*Reflexzonen Massage*, Veritas–Verlag 1984); Thorsons, 1987.

Peter Walker, *The Book of Baby Massage: For a Happier, Healthier Child*. Bloomsbury, 1988.

Annette B. Weiner, *The Trobrianders of Papua New Guinea*. Holt, Rinehart and Winston, 1988.

William Wharton, *Tidings*. Cape, 1988.

Articles in Specialist Journals

T.F. Anders, 'Night Waking in Infants during the First Year of Life', *Pediatrics*, 1979, vol. 69, pp. 860–64.

Susan Ashmore, 'Achieving baby friendly status in a large city hospital', *Modern Midwife*, June 1997, vol. 7 no. 6.

C. J. Bacon, 'Infant mortality in ethnic minorities in Yorkshire, UK', *Early Human Development*, 1994, vol. 38, pp. 159–60.

R. W. Byard, 'Is co-sleeping in infancy a desirable or dangerous practice?', *J. Paediatr. Child Health*, 1994, vol. 30, pp. 198–9.

Clements, Mitchell et al., 'Influences on breastfeeding in southeast England', *Acta Paediatr.*, 1997, vol. 86, pp. 51–6.

Kathryn Conder, 'Sleep in Child Rearing – A Cross Cultural Perspective', *Midwife, Health Visitor and Community Nurse*, April 1988, pp. 126–7.

D.P. Davies, 'Cot Death in Hong Kong: A Rare Problem?', *The Lancet*, 14 December 1985, pp. 1346–8.

D. P. Davies and M. Gantley, 'Ethnicity and the aetiology of sudden infant death syndrome', *Archives of Disease in Childhood*, 1994, vol. 70, pp. 349–53.

Dilys Daws, 'Sleep Problems in Babies and Young Children', *Journal of Child Psychotherapy*, 1985, vol. II no. 2, pp. 87–95.

Marjorie F. Elias, Nancy A. Nicolson, Carolyn Bora and Johanna Johnston, 'Sleep/Wake Patterns of Breast-Fed Infants in the First 2 Years of Life', *Pediatrics*, March 1986, vol. 77 no. 3.

Sadaf Farooqi, 'Ethnic differences in infant care practices and in the incidence of sudden infant death syndrome in Birmingham', *Early Human Development* 1994, vol. 38, pp. 209–13.

Chloe Fisher, 'Mythology in Midwifery – or "Making Breastfeeding Scientific and Exact" ', *Oxford Medical School Gazette*, Trinity Term 1982, vol. XXXIII no. 2; 'How did we go wrong with breastfeeding?' *Midwifery*, 1985, vol. I, pp. 48–51.

Peter J. Fleming and Peter S. Blair, 'Role of Infant Sleeping Position in the

Aetiology of the Sudden Infant Death Syndrome', Chapter 2, *Current Topics in Neonatology Number 2* (eds Hansen, McIntosh), W. B. Saunders, 1997.

Ford, Mitchell et al., 'Factors adversely associated with breastfeeding in New Zealand', *J Paediatr. Child Health*, 1994, vol. 30, pp. 483–9.

M. Gantley, 'Ethnicity and the sudden infant death syndrome: anthropological perspectives', *Early Human Development*, 1994, vol. 38, pp. 203–8.

M. Hammond, 'Changing sides while nursing lying down', *LLL GB News*, Jan–Feb 1991, no. 62.

C.C. Hanks and F.G. Rebelsky, 'Mommy and the midnight visitor: A study of occasional co-sleeping', *Psychiatry*, 1977, vol. 40, pp. 277–80.

Jim Horne, 'Insomnia; some facts and fiction', *The Practitioner*, October 1985, vol. 229; 'Snoring can Damage Your Health', *New Scientist*, 12 December 1985; 'The Substance of Sleep', *New Scientist*, 7 January 1988.

P.W. Howie et al., 'Effects of supplementary food on suckling patterns and ovarian activity during lactation', *British Medical Journal*, 1981, vol. 283, pp. 757–9.

Stella M. Imong et al., 'Measuring Night Time Breast Milk Intake – Why Bother?', *Proc. 5th Asian Congress of Nutrition*, October 1987; 'Indirect Test Weighing. A New Method for Measuring Overnight Breast Milk Intakes in the Field', *Journal of Pediatric Gastroenterology and Nutrition*, 1988.

Betsy Lozoff, Abraham Wolf and Nancy S. Davis, 'Cosleeping in Urban Families with Young Children in the United States', *Pediatrics*, August 1984, vol. 74. no. 2, pp. 171–82; 'Sleep Problems Seen in Pediatric Practice', *Pediatrics*, March 1985, vol. 75 no. 3, pp. 477–83.

Penny Mansfield, 'Getting Ready for Parenthood: attitudes to and expectations of having children of a group of newly-weds', *Journal of Sociology and Social Policy*, 1982, vol. 2 no. 1, pp. 28–39.

James J. McKenna, 'An Anthropological Perspective on SIDS', *Medical Anthropology*, 1985, vol. 10 no. 1.

James J. McKenna et al., 'Sleep Arousal Patterns of Co-sleeping Human Mother/ Infant Pairs: A Preliminary Physiological Study With Implications for the Study of Infant Death Syndrome (SIDS), *American Journal of Physical Anthropology*, 1990, vol. 83, pp. 331–47.

Gabrielle Palmer, 'Any old iron', *Health Visitor*, July 1993, vol. 66 no. 7.

James Prescott, 'Body Pleasure and the Origins of Violence', *Bulletin of the Atomic Scientists*, November 1975.

J. W. Prescott and Douglas Wallace, 'Developmental Sociobiology and the Origins of Aggressive Behaviour', presented at the 21st International Congress of Psychology, July 1976, Paris.

Christopher Richard et al., 'Sleeping Position, Orientation, and Proximity in Bedsharing Infants and Mothers', *Sleep*, 1996, vol. 19;9, pp. 685–90.

Joyce Russell, 'Touch and infant massage', *Paediatric Nursing*, April 1993, vol. 5 no. 3, pp. 8–11.

A. Sawczenko et al., 'Observations of the effects of nocturnal bed-sharing upon the sleeping, micro-environment and physiology of healthy infants aged two to five months' (submitted for publication 1998).

Harriet Sergeant, 'The Japanese Way', *AIMS Journal*, Autumn 1993, vol. 5 no. 3, (précis of an article first published in the *Spectator*).

Ronald W. Snead and William M. Bruch, 'Social and Emotional Problems of Childhood', *Pediatrics*, 1983.

T. Somervaille and C. Brightling, 'Co-sleeping within urban families in North-West London', *Maternal and Child Health*, 1993, vol. 6, pp. 102–7.

A.N. Stanton and J.R. Oakley, 'Pattern of illnesses before cot deaths', *Archives of Disease in Childhood*, 1983, vol. 58, pp. 878–81.

Kathleen VandenBerg and Linda Lutes, 'Bedding Twins/Multiples Together', *Neonatal Network*, October 1996, vol. 15 no. 7.

Olwen Wilson, 'Peace at last: a model of sleep management for parents', *Health Visitor*, December 1996, vol. 69 no. 12.

M.W. Woolridge, Vivienne Greasley and Suporn Silpisornkosol, 'The initiation of lactation: the effect of early versus delay contact for suckling on milk intake in the first week post partum. A study in Chiang Mai, Northern Thailand', *Early Human Development*, 1985, vol. 12, pp. 269–78.

Jeanine Young, 'Bedsharing with Babies: The Facts', *RCM Midwives Journal*, 1998.

INDEX

649.122 JA

985836